Ref 027.626 Tuc
Tuccillo, Diane P., 1952-
Library teen advisory groups /

34028056333967
KT $29.95 ocm55765638

HARRIS COUNTY PUBLIC LIBRARY

3 4028 05633 3967

W9-CDM-503

VOYA Guides
Series Editor: Cathi Dunn MacRae

Designed for library professionals who work with teens, the VOYA Guides book series expresses the mission of the magazine, *Voice of Youth Advocates* (*VOYA*), to promote youth participation, advocacy, and access to information.

These lively, practical VOYA Guide handbooks:

- Showcase innovative approaches to the youth services field
- Cover varied topics from networking to programming to teen self-expression
- Share project ideas that really work with teens
- Reflect the real world of the library, classroom, or other spaces where teens gather
- Focus on adult mentoring and advocacy of teens
- Feature teen voices and input
- Target librarians, educators, and other professionals who work with teens

1. *Teen Volunteer Services in Libraries*, by Kellie M. Gillespie, 2004
2. *Library Teen Advisory Groups*, by Diane P. Tuccillo, 2005

Library Teen Advisory Groups

Diane P. Tuccillo

VOYA Guides, No. 2

VOYA Books
An Imprint of
The Scarecrow Press, Inc.
Lanham, Maryland, and London
2005

VOYA Books
An Imprint of The Scarecrow Press, Inc.

Published in the United States of America
by Scarecrow Press, Inc.
A wholly owned subsidiary of The Rowman & Littlefield Publishing Group, Inc.
4501 Forbes Boulevard, Suite 200, Lanham, Maryland 20706
www.scarecrowpress.com

PO Box 317
Oxford
OX2 9RU, UK

Copyright © 2005 by Diane P. Tuccillo

All rights reserved. No part of this publication may be reproduced,
stored in a retrieval system, or transmitted in any form or by any
means, electronic, mechanical, photocopying, recording, or otherwise,
without the prior permission of the publisher.

British Library Cataloguing in Publication Information Available

Library of Congress Cataloging-in-Publication Data

Tuccillo, Diane P., 1952–
    Library teen advisory groups / Diane P. Tuccillo.
        p. cm. — (VOYA guides ; no. 2)
    Includes bibliographical references and index.
    ISBN 0-8108-4982-8 (pbk. : alk. paper)
    1. Libraries and teenagers. 2. Teenage volunteer workers in libraries. 3. Young
adults' libraries—Administration. 4. Advisory boards. 5. Libraries and
teenagers—United States—Case Studies. I. Title. II. Series.
    Z718.5.T83 2005
    027.62'6—dc22

                                                          2004013873

∞™ The paper used in this publication meets the minimum requirements of
American National Standard for Information Sciences—Permanence of
Paper for Printed Library Materials, ANSI/NISO Z39.48-1992.
Manufactured in the United States of America.

CONTENTS

Contents

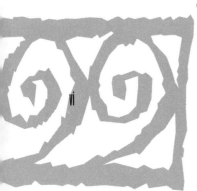

FORMS AND ILLUSTRATIONS

x

ESTABLISHING A YOUNG ADULT ADVISORY COMMITTEE or
MOB ACTION FOR FUN AND PROFIT
Christy Tyson

As a new Young Adult [YA] Librarian in a new YA area, established with an LSCA [Library Services and Construction Act] grant, the urge to panic passed quickly. After all, my professional training theoretically counterbalances panic. I've learned to research. For a successful YA program, the literature tells me, one must establish a teen board, an advisory committee, or some form of brain trust. OK. I'm game. However, advice as to how to do this successfully is not as readily forthcoming. So now, seven looooooong months later, after several misguided attempts and false starts, I have not only a functioning advisory committee but also the audacity to offer a few suggestions for those of you who might not have such a group or who might be less than satisfied with the effectiveness of your particular committee. But first, as justification for one more how-I-done-it-good tract, let me note that all those articles were right. A YA advisory committee really can increase your effectiveness. It is worth the time and effort. And it can be one helluva lot of fun!

Step 1, then, is to decide why you want this body to exist. If it's just because I (or Margaret Edwards or the Task Force on Young Adult Services or whoever) tell you it's a Good Idea, you're doomed from the start. Consider first what you want to know from these people, what you want them to produce and how much power they will have in determining policy, planning and executing programs, selecting materials, etc. In my particular case, I decided on four targets. First, being new to the community, I hoped for information about local YA concerns, issues, attitudes and problems. Second, aware that this community is more conservative than others I'd worked in, I looked for input on materials evaluation, specifically in those areas that might be offensive or embarrassing to a sizeable portion of the YA (I repeat, the YA) readership. Third, after planning one program that was less than an all-out success, I needed help in designing programs that were more appealing and/or relevant and in defining more effective publicity approaches. And fourth, to make as many groups and individuals as possible aware of our new program, I hoped to involve people from a variety of schools, ethnic groups, age levels, and social backgrounds who might serve as liaisons.

So Step 2 should be easy—just find members! I tried several different approaches. I put up a poster in the YA area with attached suggestions forms asking for ideas about materials and programs. Each form included a blank at the bottom for the name, phone and age of anyone interested in working on a "planning and book review group." (Fairly successful. Of 75 responses in 2 weeks, 20 were signed; 4 eventually became members.) I telephoned school librarians, all of whom I'd met by this time, and asked for referrals. (Almost all were receptive and wished me well; however, no potential members were referred.) I ran an ad in the school papers asking for members. (Three or four responses, one member.) But my most successful approach, if not in numbers at least in qualifications of the members, was one-on-one recruitment of regular area users (three members).

So here we have it—8 volunteers representing 5 of the city's 10 secondary schools, plus 1 who was not currently in school, and we're ready for Step 3: The First Meeting. At this stage, I was ready to be flexible as to what the group would actually do. At our first meeting, I explained what I was trying to do and suggested several areas the group might like to work on. I tried to keep things as loose as possible until they were ready to define their own priorities. By the second meeting, the group had decided to focus on outlining programs and publicity, and on reviewing books for humor, readability, and potential controversy. (With the group's approval, I sent letters to all the parents explaining our purposes in reviewing and asking them to sign an approval form if they wished their son/daughter to read potentially controversial materials. Although I'm still not too convinced of the justice of this approach, I sure feel a lot safer. About a third of the parents asked that their sons/daughters not read for controversy. Most said they appreciated being involved.) The group decided to meet once a month during the school year and every other week during the summer to work up programs for the next year.

Since then, things have really taken off. Meetings are now held every two weeks year-round. We've expanded membership to 15, largely committee recruitments. We've elected officers and established a few basic rules for membership. We've outlined eight programs for next year, including a history of rock, monthly book discussion groups, a window design contest, a science fiction festival, and a chess tournament with boards and pieces made by committee members. We have reviewed over 200 books, including many new releases, due to the cooperation of the State Library's Children's and YA Consultant who allowed us access to her collection of publishers' copies, and have published many of our reviews in the state library's newsletter. And things keep on growing. For instance, the science fiction festival planners discerned a real need for local SF and fantasy authors to have an outlet for their work. They proposed that the library sponsor an SF magazine. Barring intergalactic wars or acts of gods, *E.T.* (for Escapist Trash) will begin publication this fall.

So we're really on our way, right? Time to live happily ever after? Hardly. Sure, I've learned more about growing up in this area than I could have in any other way, short of doing it myself. And I have a much better idea of which books are likely to go. Our schedule of programs is most promising. And due to the enthusiasm of the members, word of the YA area and of the committee itself is spreading. But problems I hadn't foreseen are cropping up. As an example, my lack of training in group dynamics is becoming most obvious. Passions can run high in a group that works so closely together, and Me as Youth Counselor isn't always an unqualified success. Some members of the

group are still reluctant to disagree—with others, but especially with me—though others are quick to recognize and point out that I can be (have been, will be again) off in my judgment. As other agencies have become aware of what we're doing, we have been asked to serve as sounding boards for several new youth programs being planned. Although we have done this gladly, I can see the time when this could endanger our own work.

But that's another story. Suffice it to say that our library's committee is the most effective check we have against any tendency toward insularity and misapplication of other people's programs and principles. It has worked as I'd hoped for me, and even more has offered several unexpected but nonetheless valuable fringe benefits. And the problems? I still have faith in time, patience (my own and the committee's), and a little thoughtful research as solutions. Our greatest advantage, though, is our commitment to what we're doing. So, try it. Listen, interact, enjoy, be touched. You'll love it, too.

(Reprinted with permission from Christy Tyson. This article originally appeared in the *Young Adult Alternative Newsletter*, which ceased publication in the early 1980s.)

ACKNOWLEDGMENTS

There are many librarians and others who assisted in making this book possible. I would like to thank them all for their generosity in sharing information, ideas, suggestions, and words of wisdom that helped me to present a complete and hopefully useful portrait of the justifications for and the purpose and functions of teen library advisory councils, in many shapes and forms. All of these people are inspiring in their outstanding work with teens.

CONTRIBUTORS:
Amy Alessio, Schaumburg Township District Library, Schaumburg, Illinois
Hope Baugh, Carmel Clay Public Library, Carmel Clay, Indiana
Margaret Brown, Arlington County Public Library, Arlington, Texas
Liz Burks, Apache Junction Public Library, Apache Junction, Arizona
Jeff Edwards, Sequoyah Middle School, Edmond, Oklahoma
Terry Ehle, Lester Public Library, Two Rivers, Wisconsin
Kristi Hansen, Salina Public Library, Salina, Kansas
Michelle Hasenfratz, Sequoyah Middle School, Edmond, Oklahoma
Kay Hones, John O'Connell High School, San Francisco, California
RoseMary Honnold, Coshocton Public Library, Coshocton, Ohio
Luci Kauffman, Phoenix Public Library, Phoenix, Arizona
Jenne Laytham, Basehor Community Library, Basehor, Kansas
Mary Long, Wilson Middle School, Plano, Texas
Edee Lund, Bemidji Middle School, Bemidji, Minnesota
Lisa Matte, Jervis Public Library, Rome, New York
Connie Mitchell, Carmel High School, Carmel, Indiana
Kimberly Paone, Elizabeth Public Library, Elizabeth, New Jersey

They were not alone in their generous contributions. I would also like to thank Amy Ackerman, Anthony Bernier, Kate Brown, Mary Beth Burgoyne, Peg Burington, Dana Burton, Sarah Cofer, Nancy Collins-Warner, Patrick Delaney, Susan Dubin, Kara Falck, Kristin Fletcher-Spear, Mari Hardacre, Maureen Hartman, Rebecca Hastings, Rebecca Hine, Meghan Kennedy, Jen Maney, Jody Maples, Samantha Maskell, Carol McCrossen, Cathy Norman, Beverly Poole, Holly Priestley, Jae Trewartha, Marilyn Turner, and Kathryn Tvaruzka.

Very special thanks go to an exceptionally remarkable young adult, Teen.TAPS cofounder Katie Claussen.

Additional thanks go to Edith Cummings, Jennifer Hood, Elaine Meyers, Betty Nylen, Lyn Persson, Condra Ridley, Colleen Rortvedt, Phyllis Saunders, Linda Smith, Stephanie Squicciarini, and all the other librarians who shared insights about their work with teens.

Members of the TAGAD-L electronic mailing list also deserve recognition for giving me food for thought, quotes, concrete examples, and contacts for many of the people listed above.

Special thanks go to Christy Tyson, for her dedication to teens in establishing exemplary teen library advisory groups with strong foundations. Thanks also go to Christy for allowing me to reprint her inspiring piece reflecting on her experiences starting and running our fledgling YAAC group at the City of Mesa Library.

I would like to acknowledge all the teens who have worked on the various teen library advisory groups in the United States and other countries through the years, those contributing now, and those who will do so in the future. Your efforts are appreciated and the effect of your work on your peers is more important and widespread than you often realize. You are all truly a guiding light to me and the other librarians lucky enough to know and work with you.

Special recognition is deserving of our former City of Mesa Library YAAC members Kelly Johnson, Pamela Jean King, and Dennis Sachs, who allowed me to quote them on their thoughtful reflections regarding the importance of being part of the group.

For one of the most remarkable testimonials about the experience of advisory council membership, I am grateful to Arman Khodaei, alumnus of the Teen Advisory Board at the Allen County Public Library in Fort Wayne, Indiana. His letter appears in chapter 1.

Thanks to Kellie Gillespie, who paved the way for me by writing the first of the *VOYA Guides* series, and gave advice and guidance from her experiences as I wrote mine.

Last, but certainly not least, I would like to thank Cathi Dunn MacRae for inviting me to write this book and supporting me through its production. Also, thanks to my son, Joe, who (usually) was willing to share the computer and who serves on our current YAAC group, and to my husband, Mick, who, more times than not, slaved away at the hot stove while I slaved away on the keyboard, and often served as my much-appreciated computer technician and word processing advisor.

INTRODUCTION

I inherited a treasure. It is not an ordinary treasure, but one that has bloomed and grown under my careful care.

When I came to the Mesa Public Library—now City of Mesa Library—in 1980, I inherited the Young Adult Advisory Committee (YAAC)—now Council—that Christy Tyson established in 1977. Christy cultivated the first inklings of this treasure so well that when I began advising the group, it was a breeze. Well, almost a breeze.

It wasn't easy filling Christy's shoes. The YAAC members missed her dearly and compared everything I said and did to her. I knew something really special had happened with those teens and Christy, something real and permanent. I wanted to continue making that happen. I held on, trying my best to learn what running a successful teen council was all about. I got to know the teens. I read and reread the piece Christy wrote that is the preface to this book. In it, I found the wisdom and perspectives I needed to keep the group going.

As time passed, the teens got to know me and warmed up to me. As more time passed, new members joined and old members graduated. I realized I was continuing to build the group from Christy's foundation. The new members honed and shaped YAAC, which has been a work in progress all these years.

Running our library's YAAC group has been a delight, with its own set of ups and downs. Many librarians who are familiar with our group have asked me how I have been able to keep it going so successfully through the years. In this guide, I share the things that have made our YAAC group thrive. I will also share the stumbling blocks I have had to overcome to keep the group active, happy, satisfied, and their participation meaningful.

There are many other groups like our YAAC in public libraries, and some in school libraries, each with its own unique slant as to what a library teen council should be, right down to distinctive names. Examples of these groups from both large and small facilities will be featured. You will find mission statements, applications, sample newsletters, and other forms and information that will give you ideas to plant the seeds for a new council in your library, or to develop the one you already have.

Library teen councils have changed a great deal since their origins. Once, books were the primary focus of such groups. For our particular YAAC group, books and reading still are. With the development of improved and more widespread technologies in audiovisuals and computers, new elements have come into play. Some councils review movies along with their books. Many groups have their own Web pages and 'zines. Sponsoring programs has become a particular focus. The impact of these and other important elements is also addressed in this guide.

I have tried to include all aspects of working with teens on library advisory groups. In the examples, you will find everything from the simple to the complex. Glean what you may from my advice and information, from the wisdom of other experts (and some newbies who have quickly taken off and flown!), and from the teens themselves who are working to make their libraries and the act of reading relevant for themselves and their peers.

The best way to do this is to apply the concepts presented to how and where you would like to lead your own teen group. Whether your group is old or new, get input and buy-in from other library staff, from administrators, and most importantly, from your teens, for whatever you would like to start, expand, or improve.

I have only minimally discussed aspects of teen behavior and psychology, in the context in which it specifically relates to participation in teen library advisory groups. Other writers have covered teen behavior and psychology extensively, and I have documented books, Web sites, and articles that can provide that information. I have also mentioned many additional resources covering library services, programs, and events. In this exciting time for YA services in libraries, those resources are available to help you to learn about and develop other important aspects of your teen library service program. You'll notice teen library advisory activities often overlap and integrate those other aspects, which ultimately leads to a well-rounded YA program.

"Teen" and "young adult" are used interchangeably in this book. Teens usually prefer one term or the other, and there will be mixed preferences within groups. The majority of our YAAC group likes "young adult," but your teens might feel differently. Ask them! Although the American Library Association defines the YA service group as 12 to 18, or grades 7 to 12, you will find a few examples here that extend above or below that spectrum, just like YA services frequently do in the "real" library world.

Likewise, I have used "board," "council," "committee," and "group" interchangeably to describe teen library advisors. These are the most common choices for group names, but you will find some unique and creative ones along the way as well!

In the process of writing and researching for this book, I have learned a great deal. Some amazing things are going on in libraries that are making a special effort to serve teens well! Even more amazing is what is happening through the teens themselves in libraries that allow them a *voice* and an *opportunity for action* on teen library advisory boards.

At our library, the treasure of the YAAC group not only comes with current, active members. I am often summoned from my desk on the second floor to the YA area on the first floor to greet a surprise visitor. Former YAAC members often stop by to see me and many now bring their own children to the library. I get phone calls, e-mails,

and letters to keep me in touch. Some past members have even gone on to become librarians themselves, which is a special bonus.

I hope this book will help you to make your library teen advisory group grow and thrive like ours and many others and that soon you will see you have not simply provided a passing activity for your teens. Instead, you will realize that through providing a teen advisory group, you will be leading your teens to books and libraries—for life!

Why Teen Advisory Boards?

LEADING THEM TO BOOKS AND LIBRARIES, FOR LIFE

YAAC, TAB, TAG, YAC, LTC. The acronyms for library teen advisory councils/boards/groups go on and on. Why do such groups exist, and why are they important in libraries? Are they worth the effort? Do they really work? Do they really make a difference?

If they are done correctly, with committed advisors who really care, the answers to the last three questions are a resounding "yes!"

Before you embark on the "adventure" of starting a teen advisory group, you may be asked for evidence that this is true. In many ways, that process can be the most exciting part of establishing your group, akin to Dorothy's first step on the yellow brick road. Your proposal will be the foundation for some important and rewarding times ahead in allowing teens to make a difference in their libraries and communities.

You will discover that there are many wonderful reasons to have teen advisory boards, and a selection of those reasons is described in this chapter to assist in developing your proposal. When you tailor your justifications to your particular library setting and present them to your supervisors and administrators, you will want to help them see clearly how important teen advisors can be in making libraries operate better for everyone. You will also want to show how teens can become better, more self-assured citizens who are dedicated to their libraries through teen advisory opportunities and how that dedication can last well beyond their teen years. What better investment could a library make in time, funding, facilities, and staffing?

TEEN PARTICIPATION: THE BACKBONE OF YOUNG ADULT SERVICES

In her book on managing services to young adults in libraries, Renée Vaillancourt says,

> Establishing a youth participation group is the best Young Adult management tool I know of. It allows the librarian to get to know the local teens and to become familiar with their needs and interests. It encourages teens to get involved with the library and to meet new people. It provides library staff with a better understanding of real young adults and allows teens to have a sense of responsibility and accomplishment.[1]

We all want teens to become library users and supporters as they progress into adulthood. The best way to do that is to offer teens meaningful opportunities to become instrumental players in their libraries. Teen advisory boards show firsthand the importance of libraries by placing teens in vital roles for operational success. They also provide social connections that show teens that libraries can be fun, informational, and educational all rolled into one. Ultimately, teen advisory boards lay a foundation for lifetime library use and support.

Amelia Munson was a young adult librarian wise before her time who aspired to lofty ideals in serving teens in libraries. In 1950, she wrote:

> Young people can well understand common ownership. They are at the "gang" age and know that men must stand together and that they benefit by pooling not only their skills but their tools as well. The alert librarian will see to it that the young people in her community are given the concept of a public library that moved Benjamin Franklin to its establishment in our earliest days.
>
> Let these boys and girls help establish book collections for their own age in this spirit. Let them work out a set of rules for their use, and, if these rules deviate decidedly from those now prevailing in your library, reexamine your procedures and see if they should be liberalized. In so far as possible, let the young people share in library tasks and routines. It may seem at times that you are doubling your own duties and troubles thereby, but you are building citizenship, and that is our function. Nowhere is there a better place to learn community interest, responsibility, and understanding than in the public or school library where there are no barriers of class, race, age, sex, religion, politics or any other divisions that bedevil and beset the human race.[2]

Amelia Munson would have been impressed to see the libraries that teens have access to at the onset of the new century and would have worked even harder toward the same kinds of results she prescribed in 1950. These days, longtime teen library board advisors see the results she describes firsthand. As I mentioned in my introduction, on a regular basis, I see former YAAC members who are now parents bringing their children to the library for story times and for research. One former member completed two terms on our library board. Some former members have become librarians themselves. Others are my neighbors, and I see how important books and reading are in their families. I get letters, e-mails, and phone calls from past members who want to keep in touch, tell me what they are reading, and share with me how important being a part of YAAC was for them during their teen years.

My experience is not unique. Many librarians hear from former advisory group members about how their experience has affected them. Condra Ridley, Youth Services Specialist at Allen County Public Library in Fort Wayne, Indiana, received the following letter from a Teen Advisory Board (TAB) member who had to leave when he moved to another town.

Dear Condra Ridley,

I want you to know that the Allen County Public Library is amazing. As far as I am concerned, it is the greatest ever.

When one of your representatives came to my high school and talked about the neat prizes you offered for the library's reading program, I became somewhat interested. At first, all I really cared about was getting movie tickets, having fun, and getting books. I did not care for much beyond that, but it got me into the library's door.

Then one day Scott Mertz nagged at me to join the Teen Advisory Board, and my whole life changed. I was not entirely convinced, and for a year I procrastinated. When I finally joined, I regretted that I did not do it sooner. I did not expect it to be nearly as great as it was. Aside from allowing me and other individuals to review books and to take an active role in the improvement of the library, the Teen Advisory Board benefited me in countless other ways. As an autistic individual, it allowed me to get socially involved without feeling uncomfortable and to take an active role in the community. I really enjoyed the brainstorming sessions and the discussions dealing with the library renovation. Being involved in such a large project was exciting for someone my age.

When I left Fort Wayne, above all I did not want to leave the library. I still miss it more than anything, and wish I could have seen all the work I did for it completed.

Recently, though I am only 18, I was interviewed by ten people for a position as a standing member of the Board of Trustees for the Willoughby-Eastlake Public Libraries, a political office with a term ending in July 2009. Five of us were interviewed, and though I did not get the position, the library plans to incorporate some of my ideas. Now, I am working somewhere else as a reading tutor for elementary students. If it were not for you and the Allen County Public Library, I never would have considered running or tutoring. I owe a lot of thanks to you.

Sincerely,
Arman Khodaei

P.S. When are the Teen Advisory Board meetings? If I can, I would love to be there one last time.[3]

Positive Youth Development (PYD) and The Search Institute's "Forty Assets"

Positive Youth Development (PYD) is a current focus of several libraries and of many other agencies that serve youth. The concept stems from the Public Libraries as Partners in Youth Development initiative started in 1998 through the DeWitt Wallace-Reader's Digest Fund and coordinated by the Urban Libraries Council (www.urban-libraries.org). Nine youth participation projects in libraries nationwide have demonstrated the elements of the initiative, which encourage the following youth outcomes in after-school hours:

- Youth contribute to their community
- Feel safe in their environment
- Have meaningful relationships with adults and peers
- Achieve educational success

- Have marketable skills
- Develop personal and social skills[4]

Like the nine initiative libraries, any library can sponsor programs and activities that support these goals. The goals can additionally have a direct effect in developing The Search Institute's "Forty Youth Assets" (www.search-institute.org) among young adults. These assets are the hallmark of teens who feel a high level of contentment in life, no matter what the circumstances, and who reach a satisfying point of self-esteem. The 40 assets fall within various facets of life experiences, including support, empowerment, boundaries and expectations, constructive use of time, commitment to learning, positive values, social competencies, and positive identity. A very important way to foster PYD and the developmental assets can be through programs such as library teen councils. The assets benefit the teens themselves, of course, plus their communities at large, which naturally include libraries.

Patrick Jones, well-known teen advocate and trainer of YA librarians, stated:

We can now go to our funding institutions and say that we know through research the 40 factors that create healthy youth. We can then show them how our programs, collections, facilities, and technology build those 40 assets. If libraries build assets, we build healthy youth. If we build healthy youth, we build healthy community. This is not a theory, this is not a guess, this is a research framework about what works with kids.[5]

In support of the desired elements these assets produce, the Urban Libraries Council says about teen library *participation* programs:

Program is an organized series of challenging activities and opportunities of sufficient intensity and duration to provide significant benefits to participating youth. Libraries frequently use the term program to describe a single activity—a concert, a contest, a school visit, etc., while our definition begins with a desired outcome and works backward to provide the benefit to the youth served. Generally the longer the youth participates in a program the greater the impact.[6]

Library teen advisory boards can fit the criteria to a tee. Teens who participate on such boards work with and for one another, and also for the other teens in their communities. They are given responsibilities that positively affect the libraries they serve while gaining skills that can help them in school and in the world of work. By collaborating and sharing information with the adults in their libraries and communities, mutual respect and understanding are nurtured between younger and older generations. There is a perfect opportunity for teens to develop the "Forty Assets." Everyone benefits.

When the PYD initiative was launched, teens throughout the United States were asked what they thought about libraries. Besides definitively voicing that most libraries were "not cool," they gave advice on how to remedy the situation. One way, they said, was for libraries to accept help from teens:

> Teens were confident that they could effectively help with promotion and marketing of programs and services. They confirmed the importance of word of mouth and their knowledge of appropriate media to spread the library story. Teens who worked through the planning phase to invite their peers to participate said, "I learned that if you get people who care about something to do something, we could make a big difference. If we keep doing this then we will be able to get kids to want to go to the library more."[7]
>
> Many teens were surprised that the library offered programs for teens. They were confident that given an opportunity they could not only promote existing library services, but could create some exciting new services of their own. They wanted to showcase their talents and the talent of their peers. Teens warned, "Kids must be involved."[8]

These comments correlate well with Amelia Munson's remarks from more than 50 years ago. She advised then, as teens are advising now, that young people must be involved. When they are, some incredible things can happen not only to them as individuals, but also to their libraries.

Service-Learning

Another way that library teen advisory councils can support Positive Youth Development is by synchronizing efforts with the Service-Learning movement (www.service-learning.org). According to the National and Community Service Trust Act of 1993 (www.cnsig.gov), Service-Learning:

- Is a method whereby students learn and develop through active participation in thoughtfully organized service that is conducted in and meets the needs of communities
- Is coordinated with an elementary school, secondary school, institution of higher education, or community service program and the community
- Helps foster civic responsibility
- Is integrated into and enhances the academic curriculum of the students, or the education components of the community service program in which the participants are enrolled
- Provides structured time for students or participants to reflect on the service experience[9]

Additionally, "in community organizations, youth develop practical skills, self-esteem, and a sense of civic responsibility" (www.learnandserve.org).

Many schools nationwide now participate in Service-Learning. Young adults who serve on teen library boards in public or school libraries can receive credit toward Service-Learning participation. Local junior and senior high school guidance counselors can explain to teens how to get involved in their school district.

Most schools have a particular individual assigned as the Service-Learning liaison. If you contact that person, he or she will give you in-depth information about how Service-Learning works in your community or school. Find out how teens can qualify, what they need to accomplish to participate, and what special recognition or certification they receive when successfully completing the requirements. Tell the Service-Learning liaison what you hope to do with your group and ask if your teens can be added to the list of community agencies or school groups approved to offer credit hours. Be sure your group will be included on the invitation list and encourage their representation at any end-of-school-year celebrations for Service-Learning groups in your community.

In most cases, teens need to bring a special form to any approved Service-Learning activities so they can record their service hours and have their advisor sign as proof of involvement. At the end of our YAAC meetings, I always allow time for me to fill out and sign the Service-Learning reports for any members who have earned credits.

In addition to promoting the healthy and positive development of youth, Service-Learning participation is, in the case of public libraries, an avenue of school/public library cooperation, and in school libraries, a way to enhance the status of the library media center in the overall image of the school.

YALSA Guidelines for Youth Participation

The Young Adult Library Services Association (YALSA) of the American Library Association supports youth participation in libraries for many of the same reasons as the Urban Libraries Council, The Search Institute, and the Service-Learning movement. In addition, YALSA stresses the importance of the element of decision making to the mix:

> Youth Participation in libraries is involvement of young adults in responsible action and significant decision-making which affects the design and delivery of library and information services for their peers and the community.
>
> Youth Participation in library decision-making is important as a means of achieving more responsive and effective library and information services for this age group. It is even more important as an experience through which young adults can enhance their learning, personal development, citizenship and transition to adulthood.
>
> Youth Participation in library decision-making requires that adults recognize that young adults can make a positive contribution, and that adults respect the right of young adults to participate in decisions on matters that affect them.[10]

Further, YALSA outlines characteristics that projects involving youth should possess, characteristics that specifically match the planning, development, process, evaluation, and promotion of effective teen library advisory groups. These include focusing on issues and doable tasks of real interest and concern to youth, specifically benefiting young adults within *and* outside the youth participation group; allowing input through all stages of activities while giving evidence of youth decisions being implemented; promise of ongoing, long-term activity; and regularly recruiting new youth participants. Additionally, teens need to receive adult support and guidance, allowances by libraries for funding and administrative backing, opportunities for training and the evaluation of projects, plus the development of leadership and group work skills.[11]

Teens who are part of the decision-making process in their libraries feel a keen sense of dedication to and ownership of them. Allowing teens to be respected and represented participants in their libraries not only promotes the development of healthy youth, it extends to their peers in the community. Teens who are selecting and promoting books and other library materials, designing attractive spaces in their libraries for fellow teens, raising funds for special programs and activities, and serving in a variety of other responsible ways give a positive example and attract other teens to reading, library usage, and library support. Youth participation perpetuates youth participation.

Other Benefits

One of the greatest benefits of a teen library advisory board is social, which ties in to a number of the "Forty Assets" and which ultimately benefits the library. Teens make friends through membership and participation. Some teens are loners who find not only a place where they are respected and appreciated, but also a place where they find kindred souls. Often home-schooled teens do not have many opportunities to meet and enjoy those their own age, and teen library advisory boards can fill that gap. Football players, cheerleaders, drama club members, or computer whizzes who love to read but who have trouble finding teens who feel the same way as they do about it discover a place to nurture and expand that love. This enjoyment of reading and dedication to their library teaches teens a great deal about diversity and working together for a common goal, despite differences. I, for one, have seen through our YAAC group friendships that will last a lifetime (and even a few marriages!).

Because they have gained knowledge and experience by participating on our YAAC, our teens have the option of citing me as a reference on job applications, and I have on occasion written letters or been called on the telephone to appraise their performance. I have also been asked to write letters for teens applying or interviewing for colleges and scholarships. Other librarians find themselves in similar positions, happy to assist their teens as they mature beyond their teen library advisory groups. When teens help their libraries through effective and dedicated youth participation, librarians can in turn assist them in these ways as they move on to adulthood, as they have assisted us and the teens in our communities.

Remembering my time with YAAC always brings a smile to my face. To me, YAAC was more than an "advisory council." It was a home-away-from-home, a support group, and a social outlet. In my teenage world, which involved moving around so much I never went to the same school more than one year, YAAC was the one constant in my life that helped me keep not only my sanity, but my developing social skills.

As a teenager whose bookworm habits made me even more of a misfit than others, YAAC was an unparalleled haven for me and other "misfits" like me. YAAC blessed and encouraged us, strengthened and developed us, enabled and empowered us to recognize the special qualities we all had to share with each other, and finally the world. We ceased being misfits and became individuals.

I really wish every teenager had the chance to experience life with YAAC. It truly was the best "teaching" experience of my life.[12]

Pamela Jean King
Former YAAC member
City of Mesa Library

GETTING APPROVAL

You may have all your documentation in order, ready to get approval for your new teen library advisory board. In some cases, it may be as simple as approaching your director and asking if you may have the go-ahead to begin recruiting. In other cases, you might need to plan a bit more thoroughly and develop a proposal that outlines what you have in mind for your group and your goals for seeing it through. This proposal depends a great deal on your vision as well as the encouragement and support you already have.

If you are in a library that has never considered having a teen library advisory group and you are starting from scratch to get one approved, you might be asked to develop a written proposal to present to your administrators and possibly your city council. You will need to include your justification for starting such a group, the goals for establishing and running the group, the particulars on the recruitment and duties of members, and the role of the librarian/advisor.

STARTING FROM SCRATCH

The Moreno Valley Public Library in California (www.ci.moreno-valley.ca.us/library_main.htm) decided to start a Teen Advisory Board. First, they needed to get approval from the library board and the City of Moreno. Here is librarian Meghan Kennedy's proposal, as an example of what elements might be included when trying to establish a teen library advisory group in a community that requires an "official" stance. You may find this model helpful to emulate if you need to provide a similar proposal.

YOUTH ADVISORY BOARD PROPOSAL

The Moreno Valley Public Library currently has a Library Advisory Board that does promote the needs of the community; however, a Youth Advisory Board (YAB) would be beneficial to not only increase services to young adults within the community of Moreno Valley, but also allow young adults to become involved in the improvement of the community. By representing their peers, the members of the YAB would increase the effectiveness of our Library's services to young adults.

Participation in the YAB is a volunteer opportunity for youth; however, the City of Moreno Valley states that volunteers must be 16 or older. The Young Adult Library Services Association (YALSA), a division of the American Library Association (ALA), defines young adults as ages 12–18. Due to this, the YAB needs to be open to 12- to 18-year-olds within Moreno Valley.

Moreno Valley has 12,631 high school students and 10,299 middle school students. There are 1,619 students in private schools or home schooling (age breakdown unknown). Approximately 24,000 citizens of Moreno Valley are 12–18 years old.

GOALS

A goal of the first YAB will be to determine its bylaws. Each YAB will elect officers and revise the bylaws when needed. Overall goals will include:

- Representation of youth in Moreno Valley by their peers
- Educate youth about the Library
- Suggestions to the Library to improve youth service including program ideas
- Programs will include Teen Read Week and a Teen Summer Reading Program
- Informing peers of library events
- Book reviews for peers
- Network with YABs throughout the country via the YA-YAAC listserv provided through YALSA

SETUP

YAB members must be 12–18 years old and be residents of the City of Moreno Valley. Since there are approximately 24,000 youth who can qualify, the YAB will consist of up to two members from each high school and middle school as well as one youth in either private schools or home schooling. This would allow the board to consist of 21 members at most.

Recruitment for the YAB will be at the Library as well as through their schools, MVTV-3, and the Press-Enterprise. The first meeting will allow students to learn more about what the YAB represents, initial goals, and the requirements to be involved. Those interested will receive an application form. Some questions regarding how their peers and the Library would benefit from their membership will be included as well as parental permission. If applications from a specific school exceed the quota, selection will be made based on their answers and perhaps an interview. Applications for those who cannot join initially will be kept on file in case a member does not meet future criteria.

CRITERIA

In order for the YAB to be beneficial, meetings need to be held monthly and membership needs to remain consistent.

Upon joining, individuals will need to sign a form stating they agree to represent their peers as members of the YAB for one year—September–August. If they are unable to meet this requirement (e.g., move from Moreno Valley), the application file will be checked for others from their school. If none are available, recruitment will be done specifically at the school they represented.

As with any association, members might not be able to attend every meeting. If a member is unable to attend, it is their responsibility to inform the Library representative. If a member has two unexcused absences, they will be removed from the YAB.

OFFICERS

The YAB shall have a president, vice president, and secretary elected by YAB members. A Library representative will also be present.

The president will set up the agenda for each meeting, which will include suggestions from the Library representative as well as other YAB members. The president will preside over each meeting. The president will also represent the YAB to the Library Advisory Board or City Council if needed.

The vice-president will preside over meetings at which the president is unable to attend. The vice-president will also serve as membership coordinator, which will include informing members of upcoming meetings and events.

The secretary will be in charge of taking minutes for each meeting and making them available for the other YAB members. The secretary will also preside over the meeting in the absence of both the president and vice-president.

On the occasion that all three officers are absent, the Library representative will preside over the meeting.

If a committee is set up, a chair shall be named. The committee chair is responsible for informing the president of the committee's progress as well as updating members at the YAB meetings.

LIBRARY REPRESENTATIVE

The Library representative will be a Librarian employed by the City of Moreno Valley. Duties will include:

- Initial setup of the YAB
- Presiding over meetings when no officer is available
- Inputting suggestions for agenda items
- Receiving and considering suggestions from the YAB for improvement of service to young adults within Moreno Valley
- Assisting in programs planned by the YAB
- Reporting to the Library Advisory Board or City Council when needed
- Providing snacks/beverages for the meetings[13]

AND THE BEAT GOES ON

Providing a teen council in your library can be much more than just offering a simple program. It is a path that can guide teens to grow up positively. It can foster academic, work, and social skills, and it can lead them to become readers and library users into adulthood.

A final benefit is to the generations that follow your teen advisory council. Although there is not much documentation tracing youth library users into adulthood, one bit of research from the 1980s stands out. In New York State, Barbara Will Razzano kept track of youth who, before age 18, became library users. She found that those who began using their library before 18 predominantly became library users and supporters into adulthood. Furthermore, they in turn encouraged their own children to use libraries.[14]

I witness this benefit on a regular basis, as I watch former YAAC members bringing their children to the library today.

Teen library advisory boards hold an important place not only in our school and public libraries, but also in our communities, and especially in positively developing our teens for their futures. Although teen advisory boards in libraries are a lot of work, the advantages of starting, running, and perpetuating them are well worth it.

> YAAC was a huge part of my young adulthood. I was a shy kid who didn't have many friends that shared my love of reading. YAAC enabled me to meet people I otherwise would not have met. Maybe even more importantly, those people had new ideas and new books that affected me greatly.[15]
>
> *Dennis Sachs*
> *Former YAAC member*
> *City of Mesa Library*

NOTES

1. Renée J. Vaillancourt, *Managing Young Adult Services: A Self-Help Manual* (New York: Neal-Schuman, 2002), 34.

2. Amelia Munson, *An Ample Field* (Chicago: American Library Association, 1950), 6.

3. Arman Khodaei (former Allen County Public Library TAB member), e-mail letter to librarian Condra Ridley, 12 January 2004.

4. "Youth Development," *Urban Libraries Council* 2002, www.urbanlibraries.org/plpyd/youthdev.html (19 September 2002).

5. Patrick Jones, "Why We Are Kids' Best Assets," *School Library Journal* 47, no. 11 (November 2001): 44–47.

6. "Youth Development," *Urban Libraries Council* 2002.

7. Elaine Meyers, "The Coolness Factor: Ten Libraries Listen to Youth," *American Libraries* 30, no. 10 (November 1999): 45.

8. Meyers, "The Coolness Factor," 45.

9. "About Learn & Serve: Service-Learning," *Corporation for National and Community Service* 2002, www.learnandserve.org/about/service_learning.html (19 September 2002).

10. Youth Participation Committee of the Young Adult Library Services Association, *Youth Participation in School and Public Libraries: It Works!* comp. and ed. Carolyn A. Caywood (Chicago: American Library Association, 1995), 5.

11. Youth Participation Committee, *Youth Participation in School and Public Libraries*, 5.

12. Pamela Jean King (former City of Mesa Library YAAC member), e-mail interview with the author, 17 July 2002.

13. Meghan Kennedy, "Youth Advisory Board Proposal" (proposal presented to the Moreno Valley Library Board and City Council, Moreno Valley, California, May 2002), 1–3.

14. Barbara Will Razzano, "Creating the Library Habit," *Library Journal* (February 15, 1985): 111–14.

15. Dennis Sachs (former City of Mesa Library YAAC member), e-mail interview with the author, 17 July 2002.

2 Funding Options for Your Teen Library Advisory Program

GRANTS

You have decided to establish or expand your teen library advisory group, but realize there is another consideration: funding. How are you going to see your proposal and/or your teens' ideas through?

Luckily, there are numerous resources for monetary support of your new or established teen library advisory council. Many times libraries will offer funding as part of the regular library budget, and Friends of the Library groups will supplement such funding. There are also a number of libraries that have successfully embarked on developing their group and its programs/events through grants. These groups serve as excellent examples of how grants can produce outstanding teen library advisory programs.

Where do you find out about such grants? The American Library Association (ALA) has extensive information about numerous grant options on its Web page (www.ala.org). This is a great place to start.

Another excellent resource on the Web is "Grants for Nonprofits: Libraries" (www.lib.msu.edu/harris23/grants/2lib.htm), which includes a compilation of Web pages and books of potential interest to nonprofit organizations seeking funding opportunities related to libraries. Carefully annotated and linked descriptions will help you to discover several sources of funding for developing teen library advisory groups.

You can apply directly for a grant, go through your state library or other coordinating library agency, or work as a team in a library system or service area to submit proposals and evaluate results together. There might be a source for grants right in your hometown business community, or your Friends of the Library group might provide them.

There are so many ways to approach funding on a local, state, and national level. The important thing is to realize that the funding is out there, and if you have a worthwhile program—such as establishing a teen advisory board—you can get grant sponsorship. You just have to know where to look and who to ask.

LIBRARY SERVICES AND TECHNOLOGY ACT (LSTA) GRANTS

One of the primary grant sources for libraries, encouraging interlibrary cooperation and productive partnerships, is the Library Services and Technology Act grant program, authorized by Congress and signed by President Clinton in 1996. With its state-based approach, it sharpens the focus of two key priorities for libraries:

- Information access through technology
- Information empowerment through special services

Although government reauthorization and adequate funding are concerns with LSTA, it remains one of the best resources for developing and supporting teen services in libraries. As a matter of fact, the Young Adult section of the City of Mesa Library, complete with our YAAC, was started in 1977 with funds from the Library Services and Construction Act (LSCA), the predecessor of LSTA. Stipulated in the grant agreement was that the City of Mesa Library would commit to support and development of the YA program after the funding period concluded. This is what transpired, hence the successful YA section and services we are able to provide today.

As described earlier, Christy Tyson was the first YA librarian at the City of Mesa Library and helped its YA services to unfold. After that, she moved on to other libraries and did the same thing. When she worked at the Alabama State Library in 1989, she began the Teen Advisory Council (TAC) at the B. B. Comer Memorial Library (www.sylacauga.net/library/index.htm) in Sylacauga. This group was started with two LSCA grants of $8,159 (1989) and $6,850 (1990), and is now supported by the regular library budget.[1] TAC was the first group of its kind in Alabama and continues to be one of the most active groups in the country today.

Grants to support teen advisory groups in libraries don't stop there. The Tigard Public Library in Oregon (www.ci.tigard.or.us/library/default.asp) was awarded an LSTA grant in 2002 for its Hispanic Youth Initiative Project. The $16,200 grant was awarded by the Oregon State Library and will enhance collections and services for the area's booming Hispanic populations, with a special focus on young adults. A major component of the project is the establishment of a Hispanic Teen Advisory Group (HTAG) for the library. Local middle and high school students will meet monthly to advise the library on collection development as it expands its Spanish- and English-language learning materials, plus plan programs and events for Hispanic teens. Two computer workstations will be installed in the library with Spanish-language applications, computer tutorials, and English-language learning software.[2] Finally, the library will partner with the Tigard-Tualatin School District middle and high schools to provide after-school transportation for bilingual homework tutor volunteers.[3]

One of the most impressive examples of LSTA funds being used to develop and support teen services in libraries, and requiring the establishment of teen library advisory boards, has taken place in agreement between the Metropolitan Cooperative Library Systems (www.mcls.org/nonmembers/index.cfm) and Santiago Library Systems (MCLS/SLS) in Los Angeles and Orange Counties, California. In order to participate, libraries committed to fulfilling objectives and spending funds for YA services from October 2001 to September 2002. To be eligible, libraries had to:

- Have a Young Adult Advisory Board or Teen Council in place by October 31, 2001
- Plan at least two YA programs between October 1, 2001, and September 30, 2002, that increase library use by young adults
- Supply copies of all publicity, flyers, and handouts to be included in the MCLS/SLS YA Program Anthology
- Fill out and submit the evaluation forms provided for librarians and young adult participants for each program
- Specify a means of funding YA programs in 2002–2003[4]

Thirty-one libraries participated and each received a grant of $3,200. There were two grant goals attempting to be reached: (1) To create an environment that will encourage young adults to be engaged in public library programs and (2) to provide a series of young adult programs that meet local community needs.

Each goal had a series of objectives, which the 31 libraries came close to meeting. The second objective for the second goal was that "100% of participating libraries that do not currently have a Young Adult Advisory Board will establish one."

All the libraries used teen councils to decide upon programs. Several established new groups. Only one library lost their council, but plans to reestablish it. All the other libraries continue to have teen council meetings. Most report that one of the biggest benefits of the grant was the establishment of these groups of highly motivated and interested young adult library users.[5]

OTHER KINDS OF GRANTS AND FUNDING

It might seem as if the MCLS/SLS YA project is the first major grant project to establish a network of teen library advisory groups, but it is not. In the fall 1996, the Minneapolis Public Library (MPL) became the first public library in the country to create young adult advisory groups systemwide. This was accomplished with a $14,500 one-year start-up grant from the Minneapolis Youth Coordinating Board. The grant provided a framework for teens to meet on a monthly basis in each of the 14 community libraries of the system. Their mission was to become actively involved in developing library services and programs. The grant also funded a half-time Coordinator who implemented the program at each library.

The name of the teen advisory groups was TALK (Teen Advisors Letting us Know), and members were expected to develop book discussions, work on book reviewing and selection projects, provide programs, work on volunteer initiatives, and provide avenues for expressing creativity and energy. They were also expected to publish a quarterly newsletter with each of the 14 groups represented.[6]

Unfortunately, TALK was discontinued in June 1997 due to low attendance and the library's desire to focus staff resources differently. What started out with good intentions did not meet the needs of the teens, who showed by their lack of attendance that this was not exactly a program that worked for them despite the generous funding from the grant.

Yet Minneapolis did not let the issue of teen library advisory groups die, proceeding to develop a program that teens really wanted and to which they would respond positively. In 1999, a new initiative began at MPL with a group called Teens Meet. Teens Meet evolved into Minneapolis Public Library's Teen Advisory Group, which writes, edits, and publishes the library system's 'zine for teens and by teens called *Dreams of Ours*. The 'zine is distributed to all middle and high schools in Minneapolis and is available in the city's libraries as well as online (www.mpls.lib.mn.us/wft_zine.asp). Teens from all over Minneapolis submit creative writing, poems, reviews, or editorials to the 'zine. The Teen Advisory Group selects submissions for publication and contributes their own writing and illustrations to the publication, which comes out three times a year.

The Teen Advisory Group is now funded through Friends of the Library money and the library's Public Affairs budget. The group consists of 15 to 20 teens meeting monthly at the downtown library where Teen Specialist Maureen Hartman is based, although teen members represent many different parts of the city. Besides their work on the 'zine, the group assists in collection development. One of their projects was Stupid Paperback Day, when they helped weed the "dorky-looking" paperbacks from Hartman's recently inherited teen area.

Hartman believes the present Teen Advisory Group is successful because she considers it of the absolute highest priority, and she is pleased that her supervisors agree with her about that. However, she sees great benefit in decentralized teen library advisory groups, as the original grant was hoping to establish, so that each community library in the city would have their own little group. To make that work, a Teen Librarian was needed in each branch. A shortcoming of the original grant was that one half-time Coordinator could not take the place of branch teen specialists who would get to know the teens well and encourage them to come to meetings. Hartman believes that is why their current Teen Advisory Group is working, although not under ideal circumstances, as meetings are held at the main branch and not the community libraries. At least there the teens get specific, committed, and enthusiastic teen-oriented staff to lead them, and they are responding positively.

In addition to this group, the library is working with the Minneapolis Public Schools Middle Level (grades 6 to 8) Student Government to act as teen advisors on the new space for teens that will be part of the new central library scheduled to open in spring 2006.[7]

So you see that even if one grant project is not successful, it is important not to let the idea of implementing teen library advisory go by the wayside. Listening to the teens and channeling them a new way, and having a dedicated leader to support and cheer them on, might still achieve success, as the story from Minneapolis illustrates. This story also demonstrates how vital it is to gain teen input during the proposal and planning stages of any grant request to fund teen library advisory group efforts, and how important library administrative commitment (especially in allocating adequate staff to work with the teens) is to the cause of gaining teen library advisory contributions.

State-oriented agencies are another resource in providing specialized funding for teen advisory programs in libraries. The Nebraska Library Commission is one agency that supports such grant programs to promote library services to youth. It coordinates LSTA grants but also provides a variety of additional funding programs for all kinds of library projects. One of their award categories, which addresses projects specifically devoted to developing services for children and young adults, is Children's Grants for Excellence (www.nlc.state.ne.us/libdev/childrensgrants/aboutchildrensgrants.html). One of its 2002 awards includes a project from the Central City Public Library (www.cconline.net/library.htm) to improve teen services. The award of $2,350 was used to accomplish this goal by helping to form a teen advisory panel to give input on making the library more user-friendly for high school–age customers, improving the teen collection, and purchasing new materials.[8]

Local grants can be another approach to funding teen library advisory group programs. Often, local service organizations and agencies are anxious to find groups to benefit from their fund-raising endeavors. Be sure to contact such local organizations and agencies in your community and let them know how they can help you. Most of them probably do not even know that a group such as your teen library advisory board exists, so share that information. You might be invited to speak at one of their events, such as a luncheon, where you can explain your group's needs and gather support from their membership. Be prepared with facts, figures, and concrete ideas that warrant funding. Perhaps a teen representative would be willing to join you to present descriptions of those ideas and outline funding requirements.

The Rochester Public Library (www.rochesterpubliclibrary.org) in Minnesota received a $2,000 grant from the local Rotary Club and a $400 grant from the Optimist Club to give the Youth Advisory Board monetary support for its 2002 teen summer reading program. These grants allowed the group to expand reading incentives, provide an author visit, and schedule a martial arts demonstration. In addition, part of the money was allocated to develop a new YA books-on-CD collection.[9]

The Young Adult Library Services Association (YALSA) of ALA also provides a number of grants that support services to teens in libraries. One grant, the Book Wholesalers, Inc./YALSA Collection Development Grant is given to a YALSA member who works directly with 12- to 18-year-olds. It can directly or indirectly enhance teen library advisory board activities. For example, in 2002, one of its two $1,000 grants was given to the Val Verde County Library (www.vvcl.org) in Del Rio, Texas, which lies on the Mexican-American border and has a 75 percent Hispanic population. The grant money has been designated by the library to develop collaborative efforts with local youth groups and community service organizations in attracting more teens to the library, working through the Young Adult Advisory Board to create a plan of action and offering the first ever YA summer reading program.[10]

Another way that YALSA can benefit teen library advisors is through grant awards from the Margaret A. Edwards Trust. In 1997, the Norfolk Public Library System (www.npl.lib.va.us) in Virginia had no money for young adult librarians or materials. However, with $2,500 in grant support from the trust, plus additional funding from local businesses, teens were able to participate in summer box lunch book discussions and form a young adult advisory committee. Now the library system's branches have numerous teen advisory groups and other ongoing teen programs and participatory activities.[11]

Some grant opportunities are pleasant surprises and can be wonderful incentives for a teen library advisory council to get inspired to action—or they can be a way to start a group in the first place. It is worthwhile to keep ears and eyes open for such opportunities as they materialize. Often these kinds of grants have articles written about them in the professional journals. They are promoted through local and sometimes national media, and are included on Web sites that promote library grants.

An example is the Drew Carey Young Adult Services Program Grant awards (www.ala.org/alsc/joys/drew_carey.html), distributed by the Ohio Library Foundation after famous comedian Carey donated money that he won on two television game shows. He requested that the funds be specifically designated for young adult library services. The Cleveland Heights/University Heights Public Library (www.heightslibrary.org) received a grant award of $24,748 to develop and train a Teen Advisory Board (TAB) Critics Team to review books and other materials of interest to young adults and make recommendations for purchase.[12]

In 1999, members of the Teen Advisory Council at the San Francisco Public Library (http://sfpl.lib.ca.us) provided input that netted the library a $500,000 Carnegie Corporation grant for teen programs. The idea started when the group applied for and received a $5,000 grant from the Youth Leadership Institute under its Youth Initiated Projects funding. The idea was expanded in the Carnegie application.[13]

This money was used by the Teen Advisory Council to plan events for fellow teens as part of the High School and Beyond program, which helps teens prepare for life after graduation through programs like Financial Aid Workshops, SAT preparation classes, and more. The Teen Advisory Council members were excited about the "really cool" opportunities afforded by this grant to provide extremely valuable information to their peers.

To support the classes and workshops, the Carnegie grant funded a full-time librarian to coordinate the programs, a replenishment of the college/career materials in all 26 branches, stipends for the agencies providing the services (instructors, etc.), publicity costs, and refreshments at each program.

More recently, the Youth Leadership Institute provided an additional $3,500 to the Teen Advisory Council so they could hold two DJ skills classes at the library. The group hopes to apply for more grants to fund a talent show or some other ideas.[14]

As you can see, the Teen Advisory Council at the San Francisco Public Library has discovered the power of grants! Be sure to share this kind of information with your new or ongoing teen advisory group. Many teens do not have an inkling that there are such things as grants. Your teens may be amazed to discover they can propose ideas and get money to do special projects and activities for their peers. Part of your job is to let them know grants are an option and to teach them how to apply for and use them wisely.

Another excellent example of a large-scale library grant program coming to fruition while employing teen advisory group input is taking place at the Carver Branch of the Austin Public Library in Texas (www.wiredforyouth.com). The Wired for Youth (WFY) program was made possible with funding from the Michael and Susan Dell Foundation. It is designated for service to young people between the ages of 8 and 18. Dell offered the Austin Public Library a $500,000 challenge grant to develop the program, with a one-on-one match for every dollar the library raised. Additional funding was provided as the program proceeded successfully.

WFY centers are located in 10 libraries throughout the city. A big part of the grant project is the establishment of a Youth Advisory Committee. The group at the Carver Library has more than a dozen young men and women representing an age, race, and gender cross-section of teens and preteens who use that branch to have a say in their WFY program. The Youth Advisory Committee meets once a month to help plan and implement current programs and classes and to brainstorm for future programs and special events. They also create the *Wired at Carver! Newsletter*, which is published monthly in both print and pdf format.[15]

Says Michelle Gorman, the Wired for Youth Librarian: "[Y]our library's foundation or Friends group may be able to help you secure financial support for the development of a wired program for teens through corporate donations, grants, and other fundraising opportunities. Look for funding within your community, such as partnerships with local technology companies, computer stores, and other Internet-based businesses. Corporations, organizations, and independently owned businesses that support technology and education can be your greatest allies in locating funds for the development of a wired program for teens."

Further, says Gorman: "The most successful programs for young people are the ones that let kids take the lead in developing their own program. Ask them for help and honor and respect their opinions and expertise. Allow the teens in your library to help build a wired program, and chances are good that they will return with their friends, not only to use the technology but also to check out a book or two."[16]

Gorman's advice goes beyond establishing an WFY program. It is universal advice about developing programs for teens with their input and finding the funding to do it effectively, so that it becomes an integral part of young adult services.

On a similar note, Patrick Jones says, "Promoting healthy adolescents should not be a short-term commitment—get a grant, do a project commitment—but rather a priority that is planned and integrated into the structure of the organization, like a reference, genealogy, or children's department. Not a personal commitment, but an institutional one."[17]

As you can see, there are many ways to get funding. The important things are its ultimate effect—and library commitment. Libraries that discover appropriate funding sources and use that funding wisely to benefit teens through developing and *perpetuating* effective teen library advisory groups and their projects will find it is indeed a long-term and very worthwhile commitment. Be sure to get that buy-in and commitment before you embark on a funding proposal, and you will see success—sometimes success that spans even future generations.

TEEN LIBRARY ADVISORY GROUP FUND-RAISERS

In communities where library teen advisors are permitted to raise funds, the teens themselves often find ways to provide additional money for their projects and activities. However, there can be legal concerns and policy conflicts you need to consider. Be sure you check with your administrators and your city attorney before allowing your teens to charge money for events or services for this purpose. Many communities do not have a problem allowing their teen library advisors to raise funds when the group is part of or affiliated with the Friends of the Library or a Junior/Teens Friends group. Some libraries will allow fund-raising under any circumstances, while for others the complete opposite is true. At times, denying permission for teen fund-raising can be the philosophical base of a particular library director. At other times, it can be the policy of a complete library system or community. Be clear that you have the appropriate go-ahead when you allow your teen advisors to raise money!

The Library Teen Council (LTC) at the Phoenix Public Library (www.phoenix teencentral.org/tcwebapp/index.jsp) has fund-raising guidelines that they must follow.

MISSION STATEMENT
The Phoenix Public Library Teen Councils encourage positive relationships between teens and the Phoenix Public Library System and shall be the voice for teen issues. Each council will accomplish this by:

- Suggesting library services, materials and programs
- Enhancing awareness of library resources for teens
- Increasing the use of libraries among teens
- Promoting literacy in libraries and the community

Library Teen Councils serve as a support group for teen services at the Phoenix Public Library much like the Friends serve as a support group for the library system. Examples of legitimate fund-raisers are:

- Car washes—arrangements must be made to ensure safety of teens and the public
- Partnering with community enterprises such as Polar Ice
- Book sales—arrangements must be coordinated with the Friends Chapter at each agency
- Snack sales—must be prepackaged and bought at a commercial enterprise
- Snack sales for library staff
- Raffle and food sales at parties
- Read-a-thon
- Rummage sale

Use of funds raised by Library Teen Councils (LTC) must be in compliance with the LTC mission statement and approved by the respective agency manager. Funds raised by Library Teen Councils may be used for:

- Library or community service projects
- Educational field trips that teach library skills or resources. (Legal issues must be resolved including liability issues. Fair Labor Standards Act regulations must be followed for nonexempt staff members.)
- Educational programs that teach positive benefits of associating with the library system
- Outfitting teen spaces or other areas of libraries according to a plan developed by staff and teens
- T-shirts or other clothing that identify teens as part of the library organization

When teens *are* allowed to proceed with fund-raising, incredible ideas can be realized and teens can feel an even deeper affiliation with their libraries. Such is the case with the Teen Advisory Board members at the Camden County Public Library in Kingsland, Georgia. In 2002, they decided to hold a haunted library fund-raiser called "Library of Terror" with hopes of making it an annual event. Because they are part of the Teen Friends of the Library (www.folusa.org/html/fact19.html), they were given permission to charge for tickets and raise money for their group events and activities. The teens are extremely inspired and excited about this project to earn funds for their advisory board endeavors.[18]

Another group, affiliated with and called the Teen Friends, serves as the teen advisory group at the Ouachita Parish Public Library in Monroe, Louisiana (www.ouachita .lib.la.us). Young Adult Coordinator Holly Priestly serves as librarian advisor and works in conjunction with the Friends of the Library Coordinator. The Teen Friends, which has 35 enrolled members and averages 15 teens for each monthly meeting and project, held an "executive car wash" fund-raiser. They charged $25 to detail vehicles inside and out. Basically, it was a car wash that incorporated vacuuming, using Armor-All on interiors, and glass cleaning. Customers signed up for 30-minute slots so the teens could manage their time and quite a few cars. They did the car wash in the back parking lot of the main library branch and made $500 in six hours.

This group of Teen Friends also received grant money for a major endeavor at their library. They got an ALA grant of $1,500 from the Live @ the Library initiative plus a Louisiana Endowment for the Humanities grant for $2,500. The Ouachita Parish Public Library matched the $4,000. Then the teens planned and organized a major author visit as an Intellectual Freedom Forum for Banned Books Week. They rented a room that seats 500 at the local university's brand new library and conference center. Chris Crutcher came to Monroe and spoke to 400 junior and senior high students for a morning session, and more than 100 people attended the evening session.

The Teen Friends contributed numerous hours before the events for publicity, not only by word of mouth and "phone a friend," but also in the library copying flyers, folding posters, and stuffing envelopes. They hosted the events by acting as ushers for both sessions (thrilled to miss school!), having the memorable experience of eating lunch with Chris Crutcher, and holding an after-school informal meet-the-author gathering at the library between the morning and afternoon sessions. These activities were a major undertaking for a small community like Monroe, and everyone was excited about the turnout.[19]

Operating a teen library group under the auspices of the Friends of the Library is an option for any library. You can sign up for a group membership and budget to have the library pay the dues for the group ($40 for up to 100 members) or devise another sort of membership plan. Some libraries ask teens to pay a small dues amount (perhaps $1 per year), which could be prohibitive for a low-income teen. Other options should be available for teens unable to afford dues, however small.

Check the Friends of the Library Web page (www.folusa.org) to find out more about individual or group memberships for a Teen Friends of the Library or Friends of a School Library group.

With library approval, groups not affiliated with the Friends can provide fundraisers for their teen advisory board activities and events as well. For instance, the TAB at the Barrington Public Library in New Hampshire (www.metrocast.net/~blibrary) sponsored a dance for sixth to ninth graders. They hired a DJ and charged $3 at the door. The TAB members also baked for the event and sold refreshments. The teens took turns working the refreshment table, helped with setup and cleanup, and stamped hands at the door. More than $500 was raised for the TAB through this event and everyone had a great time.[20]

At the Waupaca Area Public Library in Wisconsin (www.owls.lib.wi.us), the Teen Board wanted to paint their YA room, The Best Cellar, as a summer project. The teens themselves did the painting. They also provided the funds to buy the paint by participating in several fund-raisers. At the local Strawberry Festival, the Teen Board sold root beer floats and made wire jewelry to sell.[21]

These are just a few examples of industrious teen library advisory groups that are able to help fund their own library programs, events, and activities. Such additional participation gives the teens an even greater sense of contributing and belonging to their library and their young adult service area. If you are able to encourage and support these kinds of fund-raising ideas, you may have a more cohesive and enthusiastic teen library advisory board.

MOVING ON

So, what are you waiting for? If you have read this far and have ambitions of either starting a new group or extending the effectiveness of an already existing one, you now know that there are numerous ways to find money to support your endeavors and those of your teens. Librarians and teens are doing it every day! The successful ones are those who propose, who ask, who commit, and then accomplish with the money they are given. The funding is out there, and there are ways to get it. Don't let funding stop you from providing the best teen services possible at *your* library!

NOTES

1. "B. B. Comer Memorial Public Library," in *Excellence in Library Services to Young Adults: The Nation's Top Programs*, ed. Mary K. Chelton (Chicago: American Library Association, 1994), 3.
2. Louise Meyers, "Tigard Public Library Receives Grant for Hispanic Youth Initiative," *City of Tigard* 2001, www.ci.tigard.or.us/news/02-04-01_hisp_youth_grant.asp (13 October 2002).
3. "Oregon LSTA Grants Funded in 2002," *Oregon State Library* 2002, www.osl.state.or.us/home/lib-dev/LSTA/2002OregonLSTAGrantsFunded.htm (13 October 2002).
4. Susan Dubin, "MCLS/SLS YA Program Grant" (memo distributed to members of MCLS/SLS, Los Angeles and Orange Counties, California, October 9, 2001).
5. Susan Dubin, "LSTA Young Adult Programming Grant Goals and Objectives: Summary and Evaluation" (report presented to the MCLS/SLS Administrative Councils, Los Angeles and Orange Counties, California, October 2002), 1, 4.
6. "Teens Have a Voice at Minneapolis Public Library," *Emergency Librarian* 23, no. 4 (March/April 1996): 65.
7. Maureen Hartman, e-mail message to author, 3 October 2002.
8. Gretchen Fowler, "$72,000 in Grants Awarded to Area Libraries," *News @ the Independent* January 3, 2002, http://theindependent.com/stories/010302/new_libraries03.html (last accessed 10 October 2002).
9. Kim Edson, "Grants for the Young Adult Summer Reading Program," *Rochester Public Library News Bulletin* 17, no. 4 (April 2002): 1–2.
10. "Winners Named for Book Wholesalers Inc./YALSA Collection Development Grants," *YALSA Awards*, www.ala.org/yalsa/awards/bkwholesalers2002.html (14 October 2002).
11. Renee Olson and Andrea Glick, "Pass the Chicken Salad: Norfolk YAs to Discuss Books Over Lunch," *School Library Journal* 43, no. 2 (February 1997): 20.
12. Cleveland Heights/University Heights Public Library Advisory Board, "Ohio Library Foundation Grant Acceptance, Resolution 35-01," *Minutes of Regular Meeting*, July 16, 2001, www.chuhpl.lib.oh.us/MINUTES/7-16-01.htm (14 October 2002).
13. Jennifer Collins, e-mail message to author, 21 October 2002.
14. Myra Grace de la Pena, "Library Teen Advisors Make a Difference," *Friends & Foundation of the San Francisco Public Library Newsletter*, January 2000, www.friendsandfoundation.org/apljan.html (last accessed 14 October 2002).

15. Michelle Gorman, "Wiring Teens to the Library," *Netconnect Supplement to School Library Journal* (Summer 2002): 18–19.
16. Gorman, "Wiring Teens to the Library," 20.
17. Patrick Jones, *Connecting Young Adults and Libraries: A How-to-Do-It Manual* (New York: Neal-Schuman, 1998), 45.
18. Victoria Miller, e-mail to TAGAD-L mailing list, 14 October 2002.
19. Holly Priestly, e-mail message to author, 30 October 2002.
20. Virginia Schonwald, e-mail to TAGAD-L mailing list, 30 September 2002.
21. Peg Burington, e-mail message to author, 26 August 2002.

Ready, Set . . . Get Started!

IF YOU LEAD THEM, THEY WILL COME

You've got your approval and your funding. Now what?

The first and most important factor in establishing a library teen council is choosing an effective advisor. The number one qualification is a person who truly, unfalteringly enjoys teenagers. Teens have a sixth sense about adults who like them. They can easily spot a person who is not sincere about working with them. The assigned staff member does not necessarily need to be a librarian, as long as the person is familiar with teen culture and young adult reading interests. However, even those things can be learned.

INTERNET LINKS AND LISTSERVS ABOUT TEEN ADVISORY GROUPS

LINKS

- "Libraries and Teen Advisory Groups": www.jervislibrary.org/yaweb/TAGs.html
- RoseMary Honnold, "The Who, What, When, Where, Why and How of Managing a Teen Advisory Board," *YAttitudes* 1, no. 2 (Winter 2002). www.ala.org/yalsa. (Young Adult Library Services Association [YALSA] member access only.)
- TAGS (Teen Advisory Group Site): www.ala.org/ala/yalsa/tags/tags.htm
- Young Adult Librarians' Help/Homepage: http://yahelp.suffolk.lib.ny.us

LISTSERVS

- CALSY-L (Canadian Library Services for Youth-List), a moderated e-mail discussion list concerned with all aspects of services to children and young adults in Canadian public libraries. To subscribe, send a message to: majordomo@hp.bccna.bc.ca, with a message "subscribe calsy-l," or go to www.gvpl.ca/calsy-l.html.
- LM_NET, a list for school librarians with general interest discussion. To subscribe, send a message to: LISTSERV@listserv.syr.edu, ignore the subject line, with the body of the message reading SUBSCRIBE LM_NET, YourFirstName YourLastName. You can also go to www.askeric.org/lm_net.
- PUBYAC, an Internet discussion list concerned with the practical aspects of Children's and Young Adult Services in public libraries. To subscribe, send a message to: listproc@prairienet.org, with a message "subscribe pubyac," or go to www.pallasinc.com/pubyac.
- TAGAD-L, a discussion forum for librarian advisors of teen library advisory groups. To subscribe, send an e-mail to: tagad-l-subscribe@topica.com.
- YA-YAAC, a discussion group that allows teen library advisory groups and the librarians who coordinate them in school and public libraries to share information and ideas. To subscribe, send a message to: listproc@ala.org. Leave the subject line blank and for the message type "Subscribe YA-YAAC first name last name."
- You can also go to www.ala.org/yalsa/professional/yalsalists.html, where you will find links to other YALSA listservs and related Internet sites.
- Online Site for YA Librarians with Information, Message Board, Chat Room: www.teenlibrarian.com.

**MUST-READ BOOKS FOR ASPIRING
TEEN LIBRARY BOARD ADVISORS**

These books will get you there! They'll give you great social/psychological background information about teens and advice for developing outstanding youth services in your library.

Braun, Linda. *Technically Involved: Technology-Based Youth Participation Activities for Your Library.* Chicago: American Library Association, 2003.

Jones, Patrick, Michelle Gorman, and Tricia Suellentrop. *Connecting Young Adults and Libraries*, 3rd ed. New York: Neal-Schuman, 2004.

Jones, Patrick, and Joel Shoemaker. *Do It Right! Best Practices for Serving Young Adults in School and Public Libraries.* New York: Neal-Schuman, 2001.

Lesko, Wendy Schaetzel. *Maximum Youth Involvement: The Complete Gameplan for Community Action,* rev. ed. Kensington, MD: Youth Activism Project, 2003. (Order at www.youthactivism.com, or by calling 800-KID-POWER.)

Vaillancourt, Renée J. *Bare Bones Young Adult Services: Tips for Public Library Generalists.* Chicago: American Library Association, 2000.

———. *Managing Young Adult Services: A Self-Help Manual,* 2nd ed. New York: Neal-Schuman, 2002.

Walter, Virginia A., and Elaine Meyers. *Teens & Libraries: Getting It Right.* Chicago: American Library Association, 2003.

Youth Participation Committee of the Young Adult Library Services Association, a Division of the American Library Association. *Youth Participation in School and Public Libraries: It Works,* ed. Caroline A. Caywood. Chicago: American Library Association, 1995.

Teaching someone to love teens is impossible. Only a person who has a natural ability to work with this age group will succeed. The advisor must be someone who has a genuine interest in teens, who can be a buddy, mentor, supervisor, and "objective adult" all in one, and who is willing to work hard to support and help the library advisory council in meeting its goals. With this kind of person at the helm, a successful and credible library teen council can result.

Find out if there is someone interested in running a teen advisory council at your library (maybe it's *you*!). If there is already an established young adult department or section, the logical person would be a library staff member who works in that area. If not, as often is the case in smaller libraries, see if anyone is interested in taking the lead. Perhaps two likely candidates would enjoy sharing the responsibility as partners. On the other hand, appointing someone who has *not expressed interest* will spell doom for your group, so you will want to avoid that route *at all costs*.

You might be pleasantly surprised to discover someone who is interested, but who needs training in dealing with teens in library settings (again, perhaps that person is *you*!). Luckily, there are many ways that aspiring teen advisory council leaders can get training and information.

There are lots of useful guidebooks available that give information about teens, books, and reading. Using them will help a prospective leader discover a wide and inspiring world of titles, authors, and genres to which teens can relate, plus information on youth participation in libraries.

There are also a number of helpful Web sites that give similar information about working with teens, books, and libraries. Training sessions are available through YALSA as well as at many state and local library and education conferences. In addition, classes in young adult literature and adolescent psychology are offered at many colleges and universities that provide teaching and library degrees. Anyone who really has a heart for working with teens in libraries can find learning opportunities to help gain important background information and philosophical bases.

HUMOR IS ALIVE AND WELL

One of the most important keys in working with teens is having a good sense of humor and knowing when to use it wisely. That means you need to be able to laugh with them as well as at yourself sometimes. Tell jokes. Read a goofy poem or wacky children's picture book out loud. Confess to a silly thing you may have done. Wear a funny hat when the situation calls for it. There is plenty of time to be serious. Enjoy your teens and have fun!

The young adults at the Twinsburg Public Library in Ohio sum it all up best when they describe their teen advisory board librarian at the end of the bio section of their Web page (www.twinsburg.lib.oh.us/teencrossing/tacbios/html):

> Oh yeah . . . the Young Adult Librarian . . . pretty much tries to get us to "follow through" with all our brilliant ideas. She tells jokes that are sometimes funny . . . and once in a while just lets us do what we do best . . . talk! She has also been known to laugh hysterically until she falls on the floor due to something one of us has said.

IF YOU LEAD THEM, WILL THEY REALLY COME?

One of the biggest issues in starting a library teen council is recruiting members. Before you start, it is important to determine exactly the age group and/or grade level your council will comprise.

Do you want to limit the membership to teens only? Will you accept anyone who is in junior or senior high school, even if they are 11 or 19? In school libraries, will membership be restricted if students do not maintain a certain grade point average? What do you envision will be the purpose of your group, and how does membership policy relate to that? Are students expected to write book reviews? Will they be making presentations to fellow students, or running programs? If so, you will need to recruit members who have the skills or can be trained to fulfill their duties.

You must also be certain that the advisor has the skills needed to train and guide the group to a particular purpose. For example, if book reviews are part of council responsibilities, the advisor must be willing and able to train them in that capacity, or have access to someone who can. If the teens will be devising a library Web page for their peers, the same holds true.

Even the most gung-ho advisor can be disappointed when a new group falls flat. How do you get loyal, dependable members who will in turn bring new members to the fold?

There are a number of ways that work:

- Talk to the teens in your library. Notice the new kid who is checking out a stack of books and invite him or her to your first/next meeting.
- Notice younger kids who like to read and tell them about your group. You will be surprised how many of them want to be like the teens and will sign up for your council as soon as they are promoted to seventh grade (or whatever grade members start in your group)!

WHAT DOES IT TAKE?

Here are just a few qualities of adults who are great at working with teens. Can you find yourself in this description?

- Easy to talk to and listens well
- Has a sense of humor
- Enthusiastic and supportive
- Smiles at teenagers
- Trusts teens
- Genuinely enjoys teens
- Encourages teens to work independently but with guidance
- Knows about teens and their culture
- Can roll with the punches
- Treats teens with respect and sincerity
- Fill in the blank _____.
  (Your teens can come up with more!)

- Design and produce an application form. (See examples at the end of this section.)
- Have promotional posters and flyers available in your library's teen section as well as in other library locations. One idea is to have your membership application on the reverse side of your flyer.
- If you work in a public library, contact your local schools. Send a letter and snappy flyer to the reading and English teachers as well as the school librarians. Send copies to each principal. Enlist their help in promoting your teen advisory council to their students by posting the flyer and including the information in their daily school announcements. Sometimes appointments by teachers, librarians, and principals do work.
- Make a display or poster for your library that advertises and promotes your teen advisory group. (See an example at the end of this section.)
- If you are a public librarian, visit the schools to do booktalks. Tell the students about the council as part of your presentation. Bring application forms, flyers, and any other pertinent information with you.
- Make sure your fledgling advisory board meeting appears in your library's calendar of events.
- If you work in a school, get information about your library advisory board in the student handbook and be sure it is covered during orientations as an extracurricular activity.
- Highlight a spot in the teen section of your library's Web page or on your school's Web page to advertise and promote your teen advisory board. Once your group is established, and you have a name and symbol, place a graphic on the Web page to attract attention.
- Send a press release to your local or school newspaper(s) with a brief description of council responsibilities, details on how to apply, plus when and where the next meeting will be held. Also try radio stations.
- Once your group is established, encourage members to invite friends or siblings. You may want to have "bring a friend" meetings for which there is no obligation on the part of the visitors except to see if the council might be for them and to have fun. Allow friends/visitors to participate even if only once or occasionally.

Libraries need to consider their own unique ways of recruiting and keeping members so that their teen advisory groups become successful. That may mean having meetings at odd times, working with preteens who may someday become future advisory board members, or recruiting through nomination or appointment.

Kara Falck, the Children's/Young Adult Librarian at Shaler North Hills Library in Glenshaw, Pennsylvania (www.einetwork.net/ein/shaler), says:

I found that having Saturday night meetings really motivated the teens to come. They are much more animated and involved. We follow an agenda where we always talk about "good books" they've read lately, discuss and plan teen programs (which is where they are the most helpful and enthused), and work on various projects. Their favorite long-term project is our "collage wall" where we collage large poster boards with magazines, photos, words, and quotes from various books, movie tickets, concert stubs, stickers, etc. They love this, and it looks great on the walls of the teen room.

I've also found that knowing the kids before they become teens is critical to recruiting them later on. I've known most of the kids on the advisory board here since they were in elementary school and so it's much easier to ask them for advice and build a rapport with them. So . . . hang in there, be patient, and look at those young grade-schoolers as your future TAG members.[1]

Your town or city publicity sources can also be excellent avenues for getting the word out to teens about your teen library advisory board. If you have cable bulletin board access, use it to post an ad about your group. If you have citywide Intranet or e-mail messaging, send posts to your fellow employees.

In Mesa, we have a little newsletter called *Open Line* that goes out with the monthly utility bills. It includes a small section that advertises upcoming activities and events in the city. If your community has a similar newsletter, ask if you can publish a blurb about your library teen council (and other teen programs) in it. When we do that in Mesa, we usually get a notable response from citizens who discovered our teen library offerings in this manner.

Big promotional campaigns extending citywide or countywide are another great way to recruit members to your teen library advisory board. The Fort Vancouver Regional Library District in Washington (http://66.96.75.5) designed a campaign to raise teen awareness and library usage. It was launched to coincide with the American Library Association (ALA)-sponsored Library Card Sign-Up Month in September and YALSA's Teen Read Week in October. The ads appeared on and inside buses, in movie theaters, as high school video announcements, and as posters and banners throughout the three-county library district.

The message? "Not Just for Geeks Anymore! It's *Your* Library." It comes complete with a Web address that leads interested and curious teens to the Young Adult Advisory Board Web site: yaab.org.[2]

DESIGN A CATCHY TEEN LIBRARY ADVISORY BOARD PROMOTIONAL FOR YOUR LIBRARY WEB PAGE
Bay County Library System
Teen Advisory Board

Talk about books
Evaluate and select teen material
Encourage new ideas
New and improved teen services

Author visits
Design a teen library Web page
Volunteer at the library
Increase library awareness
Students, grades 6-12
Offer your ideas to librarians
Review and discuss books
Young Adult Summer Reading Program

Become involved in your community
Opportunity to express ideas
Assist with teen programs
Read new books
Develop new teen library programs

The Bay County Library System is looking for area teens, ages 12 to 18, to serve on the Teen Advisory Board. The board helps the library staff in creating teen programs and services, helps in selecting and evaluating teen materials, and helps in updating the Bay County Library Teen Web Page. Meetings are held once a month. If you are interested in becoming a board member, fill out an application and bring it into any of the area branches, or call 894-2837. From Bay County Library System, Bay County, Michigan (www.baycountylibrary.org/TeenPage/teenboard.htm).

Application for Membership

Reasons to join the Lester Public Library Teen Advisory Board
- Free Food!
- Volunteer and become involved in your community.
- Earn special library privileges.
- Meet new friends.
- Help choose books, CDs, movies, and magazines for the library.
- Plan programs for you and your friends.
- 'Cuz it's fun!

Responsibilities of a TAB member
- Attend all meetings and be an active participant.
- Attend as many programs as possible and help with setup and cleanup.
- Be a responsible library user.
- Help to promote participation in the Teen Advisory Board.

To become a member, fill in the following information and bring it to the Youth Desk.

Name: _____ Grade: _____

Address: _____ Phone: _____

_____

Why do you want to be a member of the Teen Advisory Board?

_____
_____
_____
_____
_____
_____
_____
_____

To be used by staff only

☐ 1st Meeting_____
☐ 2nd Meeting_____
☐ Info sent _____
☐ Membership card_____

City of Mesa Library
Young Adult Advisory Council
Application for Membership

Date of application _____

Name _____

Address _____ Phone _____

City, State _____ Zip_____ Grade_____ Age _____

School _____ Birthdate _____

E-mail Address _____

Name of Parent(s)/Guardian(s)_____

In case of emergency, contact _____ Phone_____

Please answer the following questions as completely as possible.
We are looking for members who are willing to read a variety of types of books, although it is fine if you prefer a certain kind (like science fiction, romances, historical novels, etc.).

1. What kind of books do you enjoy reading?_____

_____

2. What kind of books do you dislike?_____

_____

3. Are you willing to review books both orally at our meetings, and in written form for our **Open Shelf** newsletter?   Yes ☐   No ☐

4. Are you willing to participate in YAAC special programs and activities?   Yes ☐   No ☐

5. List five books you have read in the last few months.

Title   Author

_____

_____

_____

_____

_____

Your goal is to read and share 20 books every six-month period of time as a member.
Meetings are usually held every two weeks and take place on Saturday mornings from 10 to 11:30 in the Youth Activity Room. When membership is approved at the end of your second meeting, you will receive membership card, T-shirt, and become an official library volunteer on YAAC.

We want YOU for Y.A.A.C.!

What's Y.A.A.C.?

The Young Adult Advisory Council (YAAC) is a group of teenage volunteers representing many of Mesa's junior and senior high schools. They hold meetings twice monthly to review books for their **Open Shelf** newsletter and to plan special activities. They also help the librarians in the City of Mesa Library's Young Adult section at the Main Library as volunteers and assist with programs.

You may qualify if you are:

- Between the ages of 12 to 18 (in junior or senior high school)
- Male or female
- Tall enough to reach standard book shelves
- Of undetermined weight, but generally considered to be a "heavy reader"
- Known to frequent libraries, bookstores, and paperback racks of local emporiums
- Suffering from a reading addiction, and usually have one or two books with you at all times
- Guilty of ever reading by flashlight under the covers at night when you are supposed to be asleep

Apply for membership at:

City of Mesa Main Library
Youth Services
64 E. 1st St.
(480) 644-2734

CITY OF **MESA**
Great People, Quality Service!
PUBLIC LIBRARY

Application form on other side

IF YOU FEED THEM, THEY WILL COME

Most YA librarians assume food is the big draw to their teen advisory board meetings. That might be true in many cases. Edible treats are a nice incentive to get teens to participate in anything. For some teens, however, food is simply a matter of necessity for them to be content during your group activities.

Because of several scheduling factors, our Young Adult Advisory Council (YAAC) group meets at 10 A.M. on Saturday mornings. Many of the members do not eat breakfast before coming to meetings, preferring to enjoy the legendary teen late sleep before tumbling out of bed and heading to the library. Often, the treats we provide are actually breakfast.

For groups that meet after school, food is important for a similar reason. School is out, dinner is still at a distance, and the teens are hungry for a snack after a busy day.

Whatever the reason (and most growing teens do just enjoy snacking!), your group will have more energy and be more focused and in better spirits when you feed them. It is a matter of providing not only special treats they enjoy, but actual fuel for your members to participate efficiently at your meetings.

Obviously, feeding a group of teens on a regular basis can be expensive. You might be able to budget for such refreshments in your programming budget line. Maybe the teens themselves would be willing to rotate bringing refreshments. Sometimes we have "goody potlucks" when everyone brings a favorite treat to share, or one of our members feels like baking and surprises us with brownies. However, whenever possible, it is better for you to provide treats. For example, what if you ask the teens to bring treats, and the person who signs up forgets? What if everyone cannot afford to take a turn? The bottom line is that your teens are at meetings providing the library with a service, and they deserve to be treated with snacks.

You do not have to give them gourmet meals. Cookies, muffins, chips, juice, and soda make good basic snack choices. So do fruit slices and an occasional celebratory cake or pizza. The key is variety, finding out what your teens enjoy, and determining what you can afford.

If you do not have a refreshment budget, you might try asking your Friends or other local groups for support. Maybe stores or restaurants would be willing to donate to the cause. Although they do not provide food for our YAAC meetings, our local Old Country Buffet restaurant is a reliable source for donated cookies at programs sponsored by YAAC for teen participants. The trade-off is we put out little promotional brochures for their restaurant with the cookies. Remember, funding is almost always available if you look for it! It is worth checking out what might be a resource and asking! Just remember to write or have your teens write thank-you notes, and keep any promotional agreements you make.

You might investigate purchasing refreshments in advance for a number of meetings. By doing so, you may be able to get a quantity discount. Your library may also have a discount purchasing agreement with a store that can provide refreshment items. Be sure to find out! Besides saving money and staying within your budget, buying in advance in bulk can also save you time. Some stores that provide city discounts will even deliver! Check with local pizza establishments as well, to see if they will give you a discount for ongoing purchases. A bonus with pizza is they will, in most cases, also deliver.

A great investment is a popcorn machine. After the initial purchase, you will have a good, wholesome, fun-to-make snack that teens love. They are affordable too, as bags of popping corn are inexpensive. These machines are easy to operate and can be used for other library programs and activities. Another option is buying microwave popcorn packets in large quantities and popping it up in your staff lounge in time for teen library advisory board meetings.

Whatever works! Ask your teens what kind of snacks they enjoy, find out how to provide them, and go for it!

NOMINATING, APPOINTING, AND INVITING MEMBERS

It may seem that the ideal way to begin recruiting start-up teen library advisory board members would be through the teens themselves volunteering to apply. Despite the fact that this method is successful in most cases, in others it may not work. What does?

Some libraries have found that nominating or appointing teens can be another great way to get members. Others have extended invitations to particular teens who have shown interest in some previous events or activities.

At the Waupaca Area Public Library in Wisconsin (www.owls.lib.wi.us), the Young Adult Coordinator found it always a struggle to get teens to attend any YA programs or activities. In order to reach out to teens, she decided to form a Teen Board at her library. Letters were sent to all high school club advisors, all middle school directors, and the youth directors at local churches. The letters requested nominations for the Teen Board and explained what such a board would do. Teachers were asked for teens in grades 8–12 but several nominations for seventh graders were also accepted.

The response was tremendous! Over 40 nominations were received. Peg Burington, the Assistant Director/Young Adult Coordinator, and now Teen Board advisor, drafted a letter of congratulations and invited the nominated teens to a pizza party. Before the party was scheduled, Burington called the high school secretary to determine a good night to avoid conflicts with other activities. The letter asked the teens to respond as to whether they would be able to attend, and invited them to bring a friend. Half of the teens invited showed up and others who were not able to attend e-mailed or called to let her know.

The first meeting was a big success! Everyone ate pizza and listened to music, and the teens filled out a questionnaire and shared their responses. Several programs were planned on the spot and future program ideas were discussed.

Burington reports that the group continues to evolve from this promising start. Members have been gained and lost, as is normal for any advisory group, but the important thing is that these teens are now a part of an active, viable group that has brought YA services at the Waupaca Area Public Library to life.[3]

The recently designed letterhead for the YA department reads, "The Best Cellar: Designed for Teens by Teens." (See two letters at the end of this section: a recruitment letter to teachers and youth advisors, and a nominee welcoming letter.) To truly bring this slogan to fruition, the Teen Board painted The Best Cellar teen area this summer (see chapter 2), now helps with collection development, plans to develop an online newsletter, and has input on teen library programs.

Many experienced librarians have described successful ways they have given fledgling teen library advisory groups their wings:

Start with a group of sixth going into seventh graders. The best recruitment other than through summer programs is having members bring a friend.[4]

If you know any of the teachers, ask them to approach specific teens. They usually know the kids better than we ever will, and will know which ones to try. Ask each English teacher to recommend two kids if you don't know specific teachers yet, but teachers of any subject work great.[5]

I found that going to the popular clubs at school and doing a short presentation on what you are hoping to do is a great way to get the word out. I presented to the Key Club, the Community Service Club, and the Student Council.[6]

When looking for new TAB members, I decided to have the teens who had attended my really neat summer reading program fill out applications. They had a great time over the summer and were ready to transition summer reading into a chance to be on TAB. I now have 13 teens on the board who range in age from sixth grade to a junior in high school.[7]

When I was starting up an advisory group and was new to town, I got suggestions from the middle, high, and parochial school librarians. I asked for a boy and girl from each school and got a terrific nucleus that's still active three years later, although I have added new kids each year and now have 12 members. My group is by invitation, and I contact each person personally ahead of time to make sure they're interested.[8]

I issue personal invitations by talking to the kids and that seems to work well. They do feel special, and I have an opportunity to get a good mix of social groups and boys versus girls.[9]

As you can see, there are a variety of ways to approach and get teen library advisory group members. You might decide to focus on one, or try a combination of methods, depending on your current teen clientele, how well you know them, and how they have responded to other programs and activities in the past.

The
Best Cellar
Designed for teens by teens

Waupaca Area Public Library
107 South Main Street
Waupaca, Wisconsin 54981
Phone 715-258-4414
Fax 715-258-4418

November 11, 2003

[Click **here** and type recipient's address]

The Young Adult Department at the Waupaca Library is seeking enthusiastic, motivated teens to form a Young Adult Advisory Board. This group will help plan events, make collection decisions and redefine the Young Adult Room. I am asking your help in generating a list of teens who would be positive representatives of the Waupaca Teen Community. Please nominate one or two students (from eighth through twelfth grade) who you feel would make a positive contribution and would benefit from being a part of such an organization.

Teens benefit from serving the community by gaining confidence and feeling needed. By being directly involved in programming for young adults the advisory committee will provide opportunities for teens to socialize in a safe setting. The benefits to the community are long reaching, as the young adults of today are the citizens, parents and civic leaders of tomorrow.

Once formed, the Young Adult Advisory Board will assist in making decisions directly affecting young adult materials and services at the library and they will be involved in the long-term planning process necessary to meet the growing needs of youth in our community. It is my hope that the process will be fun and exciting and will bring together many differing viewpoints. Please send any nominations, including the address and/or phone of the nominee, to Peg Burington at the Waupaca Area Public Library.

Sincerely,

Peg Burington
Assistant Director/Young Adult Coordinator
Waupaca Area Public Library

I nominate _____

and/or_____

for membership in the Waupaca Library Teen Advisory Board.

_____
(your signature)

The
Best Cellar
Designed for teens by teens

Waupaca Area Public Library
107 South Main Street
Waupaca, Wisconsin 54981
Phone 715-258-4414
Fax 715-258-4418

Dear

Congratulations! You have been nominated to be a part of the newly formed Young Adult Advisory Committee at the Waupaca Area Public Library. This group will help plan events, make collection decisions and redefine the Young Adult Room. It is my hope that this group will be fun and exciting and will bring together many differing viewpoints.

The first meeting has been tentatively scheduled for February 19 at 4:30 pm. During this first get together we will decide on a name for our group, talk about goals, share conversation and eat pizza. I have to know how much pizza to buy, so please let me, Peg Burington, or the staff in the Young Adult Room, know whether you are able to attend. You are encouraged to bring a friend.

I look forward to spending time with you. If you have any questions, please don't hesitate to call the Best Cellar or email me. <pvuringt@mail.owls.lib.wi.us>

Sincerely,

Peg Burington
Waupaca Area Public Library
Assistant Director/Young Adult Coordinator

YOUR FIRST MEETING

You have recruited a group of teens and are now ready to hold your first meeting. Here are some simple steps to a successful start.

- **Schedule a comfortable meeting place.** Be sure there is ample room for the number of teens you expect. Choose a place you can use on a regular basis. Make sure there is a place to store supplies as needed.
- **Contact members beforehand to remind them about the meeting**, the closer to the meeting date the better. Telephone calls are most effective but time consuming. You might have a teen volunteer willing to call your prospective members for you. E-mail might work, if you are sure the addresses are correct (teens are notorious for revising their addresses) and that your teens regularly read their e-mail. Mailed notices can also work if the teens actually read them (sometimes mailed items get tossed by other family members). Ditto for leaving telephone messages. Your best bet is to do a combination of two of these things.
- **Set an agenda.** You can e-mail the agenda ahead of time, or you may want to wait until the actual meeting to distribute copies. (Teens will not remember to bring the agenda.) Another option is to write the agenda on a white board or chalkboard instead of printing it out if such equipment is available. That may be much easier for the teens to follow, and it saves paper, too.
- **Be sure to have refreshments!** Remember, if you feed them . . .
- **If you want them to discuss books, ask them to come prepared** to talk about one they have recently read. You will need to do some training on how to do oral and written book reviews, but you can save that for a subsequent meeting. Just let them know you are planning to do that in the future, and in the meantime hand out some samples and simple book review instructions.
- **At the meeting, introduce and share something about yourself.** You are going to serve as one of the objective adults in their lives who will be guiding them in a new and valuable experience. Be open and friendly, and they will love you!
- **Make them feel welcome and important.** Give them an idea of what your library needs from them and how special their function will be.
- **Have some ground rules and explain them.** Teens want guidance and strong but flexible leadership. Let them know up front that in order for your group to function effectively, you need to set some ground rules. You may also want to have your teens help to set their own ground rules.
- **Do some icebreakers.** A simple one is having people tell their names, what school they attend, and a unique fact about themselves. A variation is Two Truths and a Lie, where two facts are correct and the group must guess the lie. You can also try something silly and fun, like a game of Telephone. Try to connect the icebreaker to a message. For example, you might tell them how important good

communication will be to the functioning of your group. Telephone might be a perfect tie-in for that. The World Union of Jewish Students posts an outstanding section for icebreakers on its Web page (www.wujs.org.il/activist/activities/games/index.shtml). Try it for more great ideas!

- **Let them help you develop a plan for the group's operation.** Although you will have some needs and expectations, give the group a chance to create a mission statement and objectives that will encompass those as well as new ones the group decides upon. This may take a few meetings or more—do not rush into it!
- **Allow the group to select a name** that fits their mission and purpose.
- **Discuss officers and possible roles.** If they want to have them, let the group decide what officers there will be and how they will be chosen. Elections can be one approach, or they might decide to have you appoint officers. Have the teens work with you to determine what the duties of each office will be.
- **Decide how often the group will meet** and when is the best time for everyone. Set a time for the next meeting.
- **Follow up with written information they can keep**—meeting minutes, guidelines, meeting schedule, mission statement, list of officers, duties, and so on. Some groups post this information on their library's teen Web page.
- **Post additional details and membership criteria** about your established group on the school or library Web page.
- **Consider setting up a group message board on the Internet or establishing a listserv** for members on e-mail.

WHAT TO INCLUDE IN YOUR MEETING AGENDA

Are you wondering what to do at your library teen council meetings? Is planning the agendas puzzling? Here are some tips for establishing your agendas.[10] Most meetings range from one to two hours, so work with your teens to choose about three to four topics and activities per meeting according to the time you have allocated:

- Devote a short period, perhaps 20 minutes at most, to learning something new about the library, books, and reading. You may demonstrate how to do more in-depth computer searches, teach your group to shelf-read, explain how a story time for young children is planned, or show them how to booktalk.
- Do a collection development/management advisory activity, through which your teens recommend new materials, deselect old ones, or plan special promotional and marketing strategies for your YA collection.
- Get input on making the teen section a more attractive and inviting place for them and their peers.
- Discuss books they have recently read, and encourage members to write reviews for your Web page or newsletter if you have that forum in place for sharing reading reactions. Don't forget to share what *you* have been reading, and to bring

some new books and/or galley copies for them to take and read in preparation for the next meeting.

- Develop and work on a plan for upcoming programs, events, and activities to be offered for teens and children by your group at your library. Ask for volunteers to assist with other special library events, such as a Friends of the Library book sale, as needed.
- Invite a guest to demonstrate a skill or technique, like scary storytelling or face painting, that your teens can learn just for fun or to employ at a future program.
- Talk, plan group social activities, listen to music, or play a game.
- Enjoy refreshments, but give a break or two to refill snacks so teens will stay settled while various discussions/activities are taking place.

NAME THAT GROUP!

Help your teens to choose a name that suits them and your library. You will need to guide and moderate, as selecting a "cool" name might be difficult for consensus. Share the examples listed here to give them some ideas, as well as presenting the pros and cons for choosing "common" versus "unique" names. Give them the option of revising or changing the group name in the future when they feel it is appropriate.

Here are some examples of unique names or creative usages of common names:

HABIT is the very individualistic title of the Hoover Public Library's Teen Advisory Board in Alabama (www.hoover.lib.al.us). It stands for "Hoover Advisory Board of Interactive Teens." Their motto is "Make Reading a Habit!" (By the way, they did think of and use it *before* the 2001 Teen Read Week motto.)

POPULAR OR UNUSUAL TEEN ADVISORY BOARD NAMES

ACT—Advisory Council of/by/for Teens
CTA—Council of Teen Advisors
LTC—Library Teen Council
TAB—Teen Advisory Board
TAC—Teen Advisory Council
T-MAD—Teens Making a Difference
YAAC—Young Adult Advisory Council or Committee
YAB—Young Adult Board
YAAG—Young Adult Advisory Group
YAG—Young Adult Group
WRAP—Writers and Readers Advisory Panel

Other creative names come from the Carnegie Library of Pittsburgh (www.clpgh.org/about/web.html). Their teen advisory board was once called SCALE, which stood for Society of Carnegie Adolescents for Library Enrichment. Recently, the group changed its name to C-TAB, for Carnegie Teen Advisory Board. The revision demonstrates the need to allow not only creativity but also flexibility in naming your group, which might change as dynamics evolve.

The teens at the North Liberty Community Library in Iowa (www.north libertylibrary.org) named themselves TAG (Teen Advocate Group) and use the game of Tag as the basis of their catch phrase, "TAG: We're It." They use TAG on everything from T-shirts to posters, and love it when people ask what it means so they can do a spiel for the group!

Likewise, a simple YAC is dubbed "YAC 'n Snack" by the members of that group at Colorado's Pikes Peak Library District (http://library.ppld.org). It also helps to have the teens develop a mascot or symbol to go along with the name. At City of Mesa Library (www.mesalibrary.org), the YAAC symbol is the yak (complete with horns) and our talkative teens pride themselves on loving to "yak."

Allow your teens to be creative, and if you have an artist in your group, he or she might even be willing to make a matching design for your publicity and membership T-shirts. The idea is to give your group a sense of cohesion through a name, symbol, and/or mascot.

This step is more important than it might seem. Think of schools and team names, mascots and uniforms. Your teens will be trying to achieve the same sense of spirit and unity as any other group, so help them meet that goal.

WHAT IF THINGS GO WRONG?

Scene One: The big day has arrived. You have a room all set for the teenagers who will come to your first teen library advisory board meeting. There are snacks and drinks for the participants, and you have ideas for introductions and icebreakers. One lone teenager walks into the room, and even though you wait 20 minutes while chatting with this teen, you realize she is the only one coming. Now what do you do?

Scene Two: You have a fledgling teen advisory council, and they have already started planning some activities for fellow teens. One member in particular seems interested and excited about being part of the group, but a few meetings later he just stops showing up. You can't imagine what is wrong, and decide to find out why he has stopped coming to the meetings. You call him, and he says he is just too busy with school and has to leave. Later, you see his dad in the library, and he confides that the real reason his son left was that a girl he liked from your group jilted him.

Scene Three: Your new group is large and active, but there are a couple of teens who lack respect for the others' opinions and disrupt the meetings. You have talked to them in private about the problem behavior, but it continues. You can't even imagine why these teens want to be part of the group if they cause so much trouble! They do though, and something has got to give.

SOME SOLUTIONS

Even the most enthusiastic advisor can be disappointed when a new group falls flat. Despite your best efforts to get a new teen library advisory group going, or to keep one in action, you might sometimes find yourself facing similar scenarios to the preceding ones. There are many factors to consider in working with teens and establishing a teen library advisory group. Being aware of potential problem situations, and determining solutions, will help you to get your group on its way and/or keep it on track.

No One Showed Up!

If you think you have done everything right in preparing for the start of a new teen library advisory council, and no one shows up, you will want to try a few things:

First, examine your advertising and recruitment process. Did you reach enough teens with information about your group? You might need to expand the scope of your advertising. If you had an open membership process, you might want to try contacting the schools and pursue the route of appointments/nominations, and vice versa.

Did you forego having a formal application? Try developing an application form and distribute copies in the library, the schools, and at youth agencies. Get your application on the library Web page. The nice thing about having teens apply ahead of time is that you then have contact information and can better coordinate and confirm meetings with them.

Evaluate your meeting time and place. Is the timing convenient? Is the place difficult to access? If you have set your meeting for Saturday morning or Tuesday after school, and most of your prospective members have extracurricular team activities on the appointed day, you might need to set your meeting for an evening or another day, when there are fewer conflicts. Likewise, if bus schedules prohibit teens from getting to your library at a particular time, or nights are inconvenient for parents to drive them there, you will need to adjust the meeting times to get a better match.

I Only Got One or Two Teens!

That is a start! Ask the teen(s) who did show up why they think others could not make it that day. Those teens might have some insights that can help you plan better for the next meeting. Spend your regular meeting time with them. Find out their expectations for a teen library advisory group and share yours. See if they can bring a friend or friends next time. Try to engage them in a fun activity and take note of their comments and suggestions to help your group grow and to improve your YA services. Remember, beautiful, blooming flowers start with little seeds; take *your* little seeds and use them to help your new group grow and bloom.

She Was Such a Great Member—and Disappeared!

Teens are busy, busy, busy. Often, they bite off more than they can chew and find themselves needing to give up one or more activities. Some teens have no problem turning in a resignation if they are feeling overwhelmed. Others have a more difficult time. If they like you and have enjoyed participating in your group, they might feel sad at having to leave. Their parents may have dictated they make a choice between, say, band participation and your group, and they are uncomfortable making that choice. They may also worry about your feelings, and would rather just disappear than face you with a resignation. They know you like them and it hurts to break away.

You might call or e-mail to see "what's up." They will probably tell you then that they need to resign. Let them know you understand and it is fine. Assure them that if they find time and would like to participate again, they are more than welcome to rejoin the group.

It is okay for you to feel sad or disappointed at losing a wonderful teen member of your group, and to sincerely say you will miss working with them. Just remember how hard it is for them to leave, and keep it positive and upbeat.

One girl came in to our library, walked up to me, and told me to *sit down*. She was going to give me some bad news. I was afraid she was very ill or something else terrible had happened. Then she resigned from YAAC due to joining the swim team at school. I felt relief, then encouraged her to come back if she wanted when swim team was over. It was evident she felt better after telling me and was satisfied with my response.

As in any teen group, romances and friendships will develop. You will find some teens continue the relationships that start in your teen library advisory group well after their memberships end. Others face interpersonal conflicts in the midst of being active board members. When breakups or arguments happen, it can mean one or both parties decide to resign. It is usually not a reflection on you or your group. Teens (adults, too) have a hard time being around a person with whom they are angry or unhappy, or being in the place where they met, and they are more at ease if they make a clean break. Be patient and understanding when these things occur if you become aware of the circumstances, and remain neutral as you would in any conflict situations brought to your attention by members. Intervene only in the case of outbursts during meetings; most of the time teens part ways *outside* of meeting time. It is okay to let the teens know you will miss their participation as you would in any case of departure from the group.

Why Can't They Get Along?

Frustrations arise when librarians who advise teen library boards find that some of the teen members just can't seem to get along. Perhaps there is a personality conflict between two members and they bicker. One teen might talk incessantly and disturb the group. Cliques can form—yes, even in your group!—and pit themselves against each other. It is important to address these situations as they occur.

One of your jobs as advisor is to guide and keep harmony in the group. Sometimes that means you must sit down individually with disruptive members and explain how their behavior is unacceptable. Ask them how they think the problem can be resolved. Give them a chance to try again. Remind them of the consequences if they choose to continue the negative behavior. Unfortunately, sometimes that means revoking membership as a last recourse. You might try asking such members to leave temporarily and give them a chance to participate again at some point in the future, similar to what you might do with disruptive teen customers in the public areas of the library.

Be sure to talk to troublemakers in private. Calling them on their behavior in front of the group will embarrass them and make them angry. Remember, though, that you are not a counselor or trained therapist, and that you need to remain objective and enforce library policies at all times.

One way to keep problems from happening in the first place is for teen library advisory councils to plan and develop bylaws or guidelines. These standards help to keep the group on track and address behavior expectations at the same time. You can refer to them when you need to reinforce the fact that certain behaviors by members are not acceptable.

BYLAWS AND MEMBERSHIP AGREEMENTS

Groups that have bylaws and membership agreements are one step ahead of the game. These documents give the teens a focus and rules to follow. They know up front what expectations will be, and if they do not keep their commitment to adhere to the bylaws or agreements, they risk losing membership. Documents can be as simple or complex as your teens, library staff, and administrators desire. The important thing is that they work for your group and have the flexibility to be adjusted whenever necessary.

The following example of bylaws comes from L. E. Phillips Memorial Public Library in Eau Claire, Wisconsin (www.eauclaire.lib.wi.us), whose Young Adult Advisory Board (YAAB) is an active group started in 1999. They sponsor several big programs a year that draw at least 250 teens and offer workshops and other activities. YAAB was instrumental in getting a $25,000 remodel of the teen area approved and completed in November 2002.[11]

BYLAWS FOR YOUNG ADULT ADVISORY BOARD (YAAB)

L. E. Phillips Memorial Public Library, Eau Claire, Wisconsin www.eauclaire.lib.wi.us/youth/teens/yaab/yaab_bylawsprocess_bylaws.htm

Article I: Name

This organization shall be called "The Young Adult Advisory Board of the L. E. Phillips Memorial Library" and abbreviated as "YAAB."

Article II: Mission

The mission of YAAB is to promote L. E. Phillips Memorial Public Library to young adults by:

- Advising library staff about young adult programs
- Creating an inviting atmosphere at the library by maintaining a safe, attractive young adult area
- Promoting ideas in the young adult collection
- Promoting and encouraging reading by young adults
- Advocating the rights of young adults

Article III: Membership

Section 1

YAAB shall be coordinated by an adult volunteer or library staff member who will supervise all YAAB meetings, activities, and special programs.

Section 2

YAAB shall consist of no more than 15 members. Members will be accepted to the board based on the following criteria:

- Availability of a seat on YAAB
- Quality of responses on YAAB application

Section 3

YAAB membership is open to young adults in grades 6 through 12. Members must have a valid L. E. Phillips Memorial Public Library card that is in good standing (no excessive fines as described by the library's policy). YAAB members with fines must make an effort to rectify the matter.

Section 4

YAAB members must have parental permission to join the board. Members will be given specific permission slips for specific YAAB activities (field trips, special projects) that will need to be turned in before a member can participate.

Section 5

Membership shall commence at the next YAAB meeting after being accepted on the board and will continue until the member graduates from high school.

Section 6

A member shall become "inactive" after three unexcused absences. Active members will have unexcused absences pardoned after six months. Inactive members will not be informed of meetings or provided minutes from meetings. An absence shall be considered unexcused when a member is absent from an official YAAB meeting and makes no effort to inform the YAAB Coordinator. It is solely up to the YAAB Coordinator to decide if an absence is excused or unexcused.

Section 7

When membership is available, the YAAB Coordinator and current members will actively recruit new members.

Article IV: Officers

Section 1

The officers shall be a president, a vice-president, and a secretary elected from the members of YAAB. All officers should make a special effort to attend all meetings, programs, and special events sponsored by YAAB.

Section 2

The president of YAAB will work closely with the YAAB Coordinator to organize YAAB meetings. The president will assist the YAAB Coordinator in creating the meeting agenda and will preside over the YAAB meetings. The president will act as a contact person for other YAAB members who want items added to the meeting agenda.

Section 3

The vice-president will serve as the president in his or her absence.

Section 4

The secretary will keep minutes of YAAB meetings, providing a copy to the YAAB Coordinator in a timely fashion for distribution. The secretary will inform the YAAB Coordinator of absent members at meetings. The secretary will keep track of all votes taken at each meeting. The secretary will serve as the president in the absence of the presiding president and vice-president.

Section 5

Officers will serve a one-year term, from September to the following August, based on the school-year calendar.

Section 6

Each August, a new election will be held. Officers may not serve in the same office two years in a row, although they may run for and be elected to a different office. A member may run for and be elected to a previously held office after one year of not holding that office.

Section 7

In order for an election to be final, ballots must be turned in by at least two-thirds of members.

Article V: Meetings

Section 1

The regular meetings will be held once a month, the date and hour to be decided by the YAAB Coordinator or at the previous meeting.

Section 2

Special meetings may be called by the YAAB Coordinator to complete tasks as needed.

Section 3

Minutes of the previous meeting shall be mailed to all active members within one week of the meeting. Members will be provided with a folder to store their meeting minutes and are required to bring copies of the minutes to each meeting. A master copy from all meetings will be kept by the YAAB Coordinator in case any member loses any copies of the minutes.

Section 4

Proceedings of meetings should be governed by *Roberts Rules of Order*.

Article VI: Code of Ethics

Section 1

YAAB members will keep the YAAB Mission at the forefront of all YAAB activities.

Section 2

YAAB members will show respect for other YAAB members, library staff, and library customers. Members will demonstrate respect for others by listening attentively when someone else is speaking, asking questions when clarification is needed, and by refraining from negative comments when responding to other people's ideas.

Section 3

During all YAAB meetings, activities, and library functions, YAAB members will act in a way that reflects positively on the L. E. Phillips Memorial Public Library.

Section 4
YAAB members will show respect for library materials and property by taking care to leave meeting spaces neat and orderly.

Section 5
YAAB members will strive to make use of their time during meetings and while working on projects by staying on task.

Section 6
YAAB members will respect the privacy of other YAAB members.

Article VII: Removal of Members from YAAB
In the extremely rare case that a member of YAAB is consistently disruptive to the mission of YAAB, it is the responsibility of the YAAB Coordinator to remove that person from membership. The YAAB Coordinator will make every attempt to resolve the situation without removing a member from the Board.

The Ashtabula Library Teen Advisory Group (ALTAG) of the Ashtabula County District Library (www.ashtabula.lib.oh.us) in Ashtabula, Ohio, has clear and helpful bylaws (www.ashtabula.lib.oh.us/teen/altag/bylaws.htm) posted on their Web site that include mission, membership, officers, meetings, committees, a code of ethics, removal of members, raising and disbursing funds, and programs and activities. The teens state at the beginning of their bylaws:

"Note to Members: These are the 'rules' of ALTAG. All of our activities must relate to our mission, and we must conduct ourselves and our meetings according to these bylaws. The bylaws may be changed as our group changes. Any member may propose a change to the bylaws." The ALTAG teens themselves have a direct say in what is contained in their bylaws, which creates a better buy-in to what the group is trying to accomplish.

The Xtreme Teen Council at the Lawrenceburg Public Library District in Indiana (www.lpld.lib.in.us) also publishes their bylaws on the Web (www.geocities.com/lplteencouncil/XTCBy-laws.htm). Jody Maples, Youth Services Manager, says: "To provide structure and standards of behavior for our meetings, we felt it important to establish a set of bylaws for our council. The format we used as our guide came from the Louisville Public Library. We are a fairly new council, so we may have revisions as we continue to grow in membership."[12] This is an important concept to remember. Bylaws need to be evaluated on a regular basis, as teen advisory boards grow and change. Being open to revisions is the name of the game.

The Samuel L. Bossard Memorial Library (www.bossard.lib.oh.us/index.html) of Gallia County in Ohio also has an active teen library advisory group called StarBoard. There is an extensive constitution and bylaws for the entire young adult program at their library, including a section specifically addressing StarBoard.

StarBoard members worked very hard on writing their constitution and bylaws. They met for that purpose during after-hours parties at the library. The teens thought it was really cool that they were allowed to hang at the library after it was closed! During these meetings, the teens played games, watched movies, ate, and worked on the constitution and bylaws. Some areas of the bylaws they did not write, such as the teen coordinator job description, and the collection development and Internet Web site policies, but they did make recommendations as to what should be added to the definitions. Everything else was their call. They came up with the rules to follow when in programs, in developing programs, and in selecting the teen advisory group members. Teens on StarBoard were very active and played a viable role in forming the teen division of their library.[13] Although StarBoard's advisor, Jae Trewartha, moved on to a position in another library, teens continue to be active at Bossard Library, doing monthly movie nights, game nights, producing a newsletter, having a teen "lock-in," and looking forward to the renovation of the library's young adult area.[14]

The YAAC group at the City of Mesa Library has rules and guidelines for membership rather than bylaws (see the box with guidelines for membership). Teens receive the rules and guidelines before attending their first meeting and sign an official library volunteer acceptance agreement that all library volunteers must complete. Signatures of parents, teens, and library staff are kept on file in the volunteer office. This is required proof of volunteer service so that teens are covered for insurance purposes. You might want to check into your library's volunteer policies to see if you also need to require such proof in the event that a teen gets injured while serving during a library advisory board activity.

RULES AND GUIDELINES FOR THE YOUNG ADULT ADVISORY COUNCIL
CITY OF MESA LIBRARY, ARIZONA, WWW.MESALIBRARY.ORG

1. Members who cannot attend a particular meeting are responsible for informing the YAAC Advisors of that fact and the reason for absence. Missing an excessive number of meetings and activities without good excuse will result in a loss of membership.

2. Members are expected to behave appropriately at meetings.

3. Each member of YAAC should read and review a minimum of 20 books per six months at Main and 1 book plus review at Dobson Ranch per month. Both oral reviews at meetings and written reviews (either short-format or extensive) are expected. Selected reviews will be published in the newsletter.

4. Members are automatically considered official library "volunteers" and are given credit for meeting and project time on official library statistics. Members may use this volunteer experience on job or other applications as a work reference, or for Mesa Public Schools Service Learning credit. As official library volunteers, members are exempt from fines and may use library in-house Internet three hours per day.

5. All members are expected to participate in any of YAAC's special projects, as needed.

6. All members are responsible for books checked out on their library card and must make sure that no other member takes a book before it has been checked back in to the library. Books that are to be reviewed for YAAC may be checked out for a 45-day period. For 45-day checkout, YAAC membership card must be presented at the Circulation Desk.

7. YAAC meetings will take place two Saturday mornings each month from 10 A.M. until 11:30 A.M. at Main. Schedules will be sent to all members. Dobson meetings are held once a month from 10 A.M. to 11 A.M., usually on the first Saturday, and only during the school year.

8. Membership cards will be issued after attendance at and participation in two meetings, with approval of the advisor. Official members also receive a YAAC T-shirt.

9. Members will occasionally be asked to help set up/take down tables and chairs in the Youth Activity Room for meetings and programs, as needed.

Teen library advisory boards can develop simple codes of conduct that can serve as good reminders for behavior at each meeting. Teen members need to have input in the development and revision of codes of conduct while advisors serve as guides for teens as they develop the codes.

Policies on behavior can be as simple as finding a method to determine who has the floor, with everyone else promising to keep quiet while that person speaks. At the Fairport Harbor Public Library in Ohio, the TAG teens agreed that a silver spoon would be the key to what person has the floor at meetings, and Cathy Norman, their advisor, says it works for them.[15] Other library groups have used such items as a rubber chicken or a Nerf ball. Allow the teens to choose what they prefer, no matter how wacky it might seem!

At their September 20, 2002, meeting, the Teen Library Advisors at O'Connell High School in San Francisco decided upon rules (in their own words) that were recorded in the minutes:

- You have to be here every Friday but if absent (school readmit).
- If not here Fridays, after three times unexcused they are out.
- You have to participate at least once a month.
- You can't be here just for the food and field trips.
- You can't be playing games and wandering around. You have to be here to help the library.
- Pay attention to all ideas.
- If playing games or talking during meetings you will be kicked out for that Friday.
- Have fun!

49

The Teen Advisory Committee of the Cumberland Public Library in Rhode Island (www.cumberlandlibrary.org/TAC.htm) has their Code of Conduct posted right on the teen Web page. The code is based on the Cranston Public Library, Cranston, Rhode Island (http://138.16.137.60/index.htm), teen advisory committee's code.[16] It states:

- Members will need to keep the goal of the committee as a priority for their activities.
- During meetings, committee members will act in a way that reflects positively on the Cumberland Public Library.
- Members will show respect for other committee members, library staff, and library patrons.
- Committee members will leave their meeting space neat and orderly.
- Members should be open to ideas from any member or staff person and talk about these suggestions in a constructive way.
- No teasing, bullying, or insulting of another person will be tolerated in the meetings.

Talk to your teens and find out what is a reasonable code of conduct for them to follow. Post the code in a prominent place where they meet, include it on the library's teen Web page, or simply include it as a printed handout of information for new members. Ask the teens how they can best remember to follow the code, and go with their recommendations.

IF YOU ARE LEAVING OR REPLACING A DEPARTING ADVISOR

You have established a teen library advisory group and it is going great guns. It has been your responsibility, and you have not had the benefit of sharing the group with a coadvisor. You have gotten to know your teens and they like and admire you. They have developed programs, helped you revamp your YA collection, promoted reading to teens in your community, and learned to use the library Web page to communicate with other teens, all under your guidance. Parents have told you what a wonderful activity your advisory group is and how their sons and daughters have grown through the experience of participating in it.

Now you have to tell them all you are leaving!

If you have taken on a new job, or you are retiring or moving away, you will need to make a clean break with your teens. You need to leave them happy, comfortable, and confident that they can move on without you. This process may be more difficult than you anticipate, so be prepared!

First of all, teens take many things to heart. They may take the fact you are leaving very personally, even though that is not reality. They will miss you dearly, and their feelings might be hurt. It is important that you level with them. Tell them why you are leaving and that you will miss working with them. Let them know that they did not do anything wrong and they have nothing to do with your decision to go. Help them to understand that people move on to other phases in their lives, but that does not mean you do not treasure the experiences you have had with them.

If you know that a replacement will be following you shortly, explain that to the teens and introduce them to that person if possible. Let them know that the new advisor will give them the same caring and careful attention that you did, but at the same time help them to understand they will be working with a unique individual who may have some new ideas and perspectives. Encourage them to be open-minded. Try to guide the transition so it will go smoothly. If the new advisor can attend some of the group's meetings and participate in some of their activities before you leave, it will greatly help the teens to adjust.

If you do not know your successor, you do not know how soon someone can take over for you, or there is concern no one will be available to take your place, explain that to the teens. Find out what library staff member will temporarily be their contact, and learn the library's plans for the group. Depending upon the scenario, you need to do whatever you can to help your teens keep their group going. It is essential to share as much information as you can in a timely manner and to be honest with your teens.

There might be some teens who really want to keep in touch with you when you leave. Those of us who have long-time active groups and have watched teens "graduate" from us have seen this process in reverse. Some former members keep in touch, some go their own way and we never hear from them again, some have sporadic contact. The same will hold true when you leave. You will have some teens who want to contact you after you leave, and it is up to you to decide if you would like to have them do that. In the case that you don't mind, one of the best ways to keep in touch is through e-mail, or even snail mail.

Because you are the kind of person who enjoys working with teens, you will find yourself missing them as well. Even though you might be in touch with some, as time goes by you will drift farther away from them. They will have a new advisor and be moving on beyond your sphere of influence. Tune in to their Web page, get on the mailing list for their newsletter, and send a card during the holidays. Just because you have left doesn't mean you don't care any more. Acknowledge your own feelings and be kind to yourself in this regard! Keeping in touch might be more important to you than you realize.

Now for the opposite scenario! If you are the new kid on the block who is taking over for a beloved teen library board advisor, keep in mind the behavior of teens (or anyone) in the position of dealing with a new leader. You might feel you have to prove yourself (you probably do!) and that it will take time for the teens to adjust to you and your individual ways (most of them will!). Prepare to be patient and to hang in there.

I remember what it was like when I first came to Mesa, as I described in my introduction to this book. It took a long time for the teens to make the adjustment to me.

At first, it felt as if I was not quite cutting it, but then I realized if I was just myself with them, and showed them that I really cared, they would come around. The majority of them did, a few of them didn't.

I tried not to feel badly about the members I lost. That was bound to happen. They really felt close to Christy. However, I found the ones who remained were the more difficult challenge! They frequently compared what I said and did to her. She was a great advisor, and I understood how the teens could get so attached. I worked hard to keep my attitude upbeat and positive, but sometimes their attitudes did bother me even though I never let on to the teens. (Remember, when an *advisor* leaves, teens might take it personally. Well, the *reverse* can happen for the new advisor who takes over a group of teens! It is important to remember *not* to take it personally!)

As time went by, new members joined the group who never knew my predecessor. The group began to become cohesive again. Eventually, I was the only leader the current members knew. Things looked up from then on. It took about two years for the complete transition. The same thing will happen for you if you find yourself in the same position. Be yourself and show you care, and the teens will come around!

JUST KEEP LEADING THEM, AND THEY WILL FOLLOW

Starting a group and getting it well established is challenging, and the best is yet to come. There will be more challenges and many rewards as you take your new group forward or lead your older group on to new things. Build a strong foundation for your group in whatever ways are successful for you, them, your library, and your community. You will be greatly surprised at what they will accomplish.

Remember, commitment, flexibility, and good leadership will take your group a long way. Oh, and don't forget the food . . . and fun!

NOTES

1. Kara Falck, e-mail to TAGAD-L mailing list, 29 August 2002.
2. "Not for Nerds Anymore," *American Libraries* 33, no. 10 (November 2002): 8.
3. Peg Burington, e-mail to PUBYAC mailing list, 9 April 2002.
4. Linda Rogers, e-mail to TAGAD-L mailing list, 22 October 2001.
5. Joyce Maltby, e-mail to TAGAD-L mailing list, 23 October 2001.
6. Rita Peterson, e-mail to TAGAD-L mailing list, 18 December 2001.
7. Sara Schieman, e-mail to TAGAD-L mailing list, 22 October 2001.
8. Sally Leahey, e-mail to TAGAD-L mailing list, 22 October 2001.
9. Virginia Schonwald, e-mail to TAGAD-L mailing list, 15 August 2002.
10. Linda Rogers, e-mail to TAGAD-L mailing list, 24 December 2001.
11. Kati Tvaruzka, e-mail messages to author, 19 and 21 May 2003.
12. Jody Maples, e-mail message to author, 22 May 2003.
13. Jae Trewartha, e-mail message to author, 15 October 2002.
14. Betty Clarkson, e-mail message to author, 4 September 2003.
15. Cathy Norman, e-mail to TAGAD-L mailing list, 20 March 2001.
16. Jennifer Hood, e-mail message to author, 19 September 2002.

4 Libraries Are NOT Boring: Activities, Events, and Projects That Make a Difference with Teens

DEVELOPING A MISSION STATEMENT

For a library teen advisory group to really focus on their purpose and goals, it helps to establish a mission statement. It is important to include the input of the teens themselves. Your group might be ready to develop a mission statement soon after forming, or they might feel the need to wait a while to observe how the purpose of the group appears to be unfolding. This is another instance when your guidance as their advisor comes into play. You will want to make sure that whatever the mission your teens set out to fulfill, it meshes well with the mission of the library as a whole and follows official library policies and procedures. For example, as discussed in chapter 2, if the teens want fund-raising to be part of their mission, but your library prohibits or restricts fund-raising, then you will need to inform them of the rules.

Some mission statements are short and to the point. As Joyce Maltby, YA Librarian, states, the teen advisory group mission at the Findlay-Hancock County Public Library (www.findlay.lib.oh.us) in Ohio is: "To make the library a better, more appealing place for young adults who want and/or need to study, meet and recreate!"[1]

Your group must decide how long and/or complex their mission statement will be. This process will take time and thoughtful discussion.

Cathy Norman, the Youth Services Librarian at the Fairport Harbor Public Library in Ohio, shares her recommendations regarding establishing a teen library advisory group mission statement:

Let your kids find their footing first. We functioned for almost two years with no written mission, goals, etc. The kids needed to get to know each other and to get to know the library from a different direction—that is as active, working members of the library hierarchy. Those years of hanging out benefited them in a number of ways. The kids got to know each other, they got to think about the purpose of the group besides eating pizza once a month, and they got to see their ideas come to fruition. They determined what worked and what didn't, so when they sat down to establish structure they recognized the need for it and provided all the input themselves. It was a great process and I think those two years of "getting to know you" really made the difference.[2]

If this process works for your group, that is great. You might decide to try this "wait-and-see" format, and find perhaps that a wish list of activities to help the teen section

MISSION STATEMENT FOR THE TEEN ADVISORY GROUP

Fairport Harbor Public Library, Ohio

www.ncweb.com/org/fhslibrary

VISION

The Teen Advisory Group of Fairport Harbor Public Library strives to be an integral part of the Fairport Harbor community by showing teens how to be better people, encourage individuality, and develop latent interests through the promotion of library use and reading in Fairport Harbor.

MISSION

Our mission is to increase awareness of Fairport Harbor Public Library's collection and to promote use of that collection throughout the community. We also aim to develop awareness among Fairport Harbor youth that Fairport Harbor Public Library provides a safe and constructive atmosphere of mutual respect and acceptance regardless of who you are or what you believe.

OBJECTIVES

The Teen Advisory Group will volunteer in and out of the library. We will promote library use in the community. We understand that young adults can be active participants in the community's perception of the library.

STRATEGIES

We will:

- Promote literacy
- Recruit Teen Advisory Group members
- Plan and implement programming
- Read, review, and/or recommend materials
- Attend Teen Advisory Group meetings

of the library, plus some basic guidelines, can direct your teen advisory group members until they are ready to write their mission statement.

TEEN LIBRARY ADVISORY BOARD OFFICERS

Like any other official young adult group, teen advisory boards in libraries often operate best with peer leadership in addition to the leadership of their adult advisor. Depending on the mission and the organization of individual teen advisory boards, members will want to consider what officers to have as leaders of their group, or whether to not have officers at all.

Smaller groups might wish to keep officers to a minimum, for instance, simply having a President and Secretary. Larger groups might need a wider number of officers. Group members and their advisors will need to decide the numbers and kinds of officers that will best suit their needs. They will also need to decide whether to hold official elections or simply to appoint officers. Other considerations will be how long offices will be held, when installations will take place, and specific duties and responsibilities.

Specific information about offices, term lengths, and duties can be reflected in the teen library advisory committee's bylaws (see chapter 3). You will find more information about officers (or opting not to have officers) in the featured library descriptions in chapters 7 and 8.

Some groups do decide to forego officers altogether. In these cases, teens may take turns being in charge of running meetings or being the chair of a special committee. Other duties may rotate between teens, so that everyone has a chance to take minutes or plan the agenda.

Talk with your teens to find out how they think their group will function most effectively. Your newly established group might decide that officers are a good idea for the future, waiting a while before electing them. Then everyone would have a chance to get to know one another first, a similar situation to Fairport Harbor Public Library waiting to develop a mission statement.

TEEN ADVISORY GROUP PROJECTS

Projects for teen advisory board members come in all shapes and sizes. Some projects are particular to their own library, such as helping to plan and run a program, assisting with preparing materials for library events, developing a forum for peer readers' advisory, or assisting with a teen library Web page. Others are projects that extend beyond the teens' own library, sometimes even projects with a national scope. For example, teens might be invited to be panelists at a program for youth librarians at a professional library conference, they might participate in special pilot projects for YALSA, or serve as teen partner book reviewers for *Voice of Youth Advocates* magazine.

Teen Book Reviews and Other Newsletters

What better way to encourage reading among fellow teens than to provide outlets for peer readers' advisory through a teen advisory council? Sometimes teachers, librarians, parents, and other adults will, despite their best intentions, promote reading to young adults unsuccessfully. Granted, there are many teens who respond positively to the booktalks, reading lists, and "best book" suggestions we provide. However, many skeptical teens either find it hard to connect with just the right book for their particular interests and tastes, or depend on their friends and acquaintances to recommend reading—when and if they *do* read. These teens are more comfortable relying on those their own age than the adults around them. That's where peer readers' advisory comes into play.

There are many ways that library advisory board teens can serve as peer reader advisors, such as doing booktalks, making book displays, and writing book reviews. The most important functions of teen advisory boards are to make libraries a welcome and exciting place for fellow teens, to promote books, and to foster literacy. Peer readers' advisory accomplishes all these things. One of the most effective ways is through newsletters, which can reach a large audience in and beyond the library itself.

The concept of employing newsletters to encourage teens to read is not new. Years ago, the New York Public Library published a mimeographed sheet called *Back Talk*, which contained the frank opinions of teens about the books they had read. Later, the Enoch Pratt Free Library in Baltimore adapted the idea to a multilithed pamphlet called *You're the Critic*, which was published monthly during the school year. The publication was in high demand and copies were distributed through the school libraries and all of the Pratt Library branches.

The board of *You're the Critic* was composed of one representative from each public, private, and parochial high school in the city. The Young Adult Department head at the Central Library served as the advisor. Besides the book reviews, *You're the Critic* included an editorial, plus some original poetry, announcements, and movie reviews. A library display of titles reviewed in the newsletter was popular.

With *You're the Critic* as an example, other cities began similar newsletters. Margaret Edwards, Pratt Library's famous pioneer for young adult librarians, said: "A book-reviewing publication is good promotion for reading since the recommendations teen-agers make to each other are often more effective than those the librarian makes. Also, although books of all levels of difficulty are included, the teen-agers often review books so complex that the librarian would hesitate to suggest them himself for fear of dismaying readers."[3]

At the City of Mesa Library, the Young Adult Advisory Council (YAAC) follows suit by writing and publishing a newsletter called *Open Shelf*. This newsletter has existed since 1977, when the group was formed. At first it appeared as a column in the *Mesa Tribune*.

Becoming a member of YAAC was a wonderful point in my life. Not only was it an acceptance into a peer group I truly related to, but it also helped me find my voice—something that was not always welcome in other places in my world. I was *allowed* to have an opinion, something rather lacking in the life of many teens. It certainly was lacking in mine. My opinions were not always agreed with—just as I was comfortable enough to disagree with others—but they were accepted, or at least tolerated! I especially loved writing for and being editor of the review sheet that we put out. I was "published," and that was great for my self-esteem. It made the library not only a place to get books or meet friends, it made it a place of acceptance, where I mattered. Very little can match that feeling and I'll always treasure that time. Not to mention the great parties!

Kelly Johnson, former YAAC member and Open Shelf *editor, City of Mesa Library; wife, mother of book lovers; office manager of the Ketchikan Public Library, Alaska*

In 1979, through a cooperative effort with Mesa Public Schools, *Open Shelf* began to be published as a book review newsletter and continues today. Each month, from September through May, a two-sided, single-page issue of *Open Shelf* is published by the City of Mesa Library. Copies are picked up by Mesa Public Schools Media Services, which in turn distributes the issues to all junior and senior high school media centers along with their audiovisual deliveries. This process saves postage and assures that the issues will be delivered quickly and efficiently.

Issues are displayed in the media centers, and some teachers post and use them in their classrooms. Librarians promote the newsletter to teens when visits are made to schools for booktalks. In the summer, YAAC publishes its popular 16-page issue of *Open Shelf*, which offers a large selection of summer reading suggestions for teens.

In addition to distribution in the schools, *Open Shelf* is available at all three City of Mesa Library branches. It also appears on the "Teens" page (www.mesalibrary.org/teens/readinglists/openshelf.htm) of the library's Web site, with archival copies going back three years. The newsletter receives the most hits of any postings on the "Teens" Web page. (See YAAC Book Review Tips for the *Open Shelf* newsletter at the end of this section.)

In addition to YAAC's *Open Shelf* newsletter, which is produced at the main library branch, the Dobson Branch Library's YAAC publishes a quarterly book review newsletter called *Branches*.

Other teen library advisory groups also publish newsletters. Teen GAB (Guidance and Action Board) of the Northwest Library of the Worthington Library System in Columbus, Ohio (www.worthingtonlibraries.org/index_flash2.cfm), decided they wanted to do a newsletter when they began meeting two years ago. They started off publishing *The Gabble*, which came out every three months and consisted of book reviews, poetry, and cartoons, all original work by the teens. *The Gabble* went out of print when the group decided to launch a new teen newsletter, called *Etc. Etc.*, a cooperative effort between Teen GAB and the teen advisory board of another library in their system. The newsletters are produced in print format as the teens do not have a Web site.[4]

At the Welles-Turner Memorial Library in Glastonbury, Connecticut (www.wtmlib.com), the Teen Advisory Board (TAB) produces an online newsletter that features book reviews. Called *Teens Tell It Like It Is: Book Reviews* (www.wtmlib.com/ya/teen_reviews.htm), it allows teens from the community to contribute their reactions to books and share them with other teens. TAB includes a 1 to 5 rating system for readers to use in evaluating titles:

* I'm gonna be sick
** Better than rotten eggs

*** Better than algebra
**** Pretty cool!
***** Blew me away! Wow!

Review rating systems work well with teens. Teen reviewers enjoy allocating ratings, and readers of the reviews appreciate their ability to get quick and concise impressions of the books, magazines, and other media. Besides, rating systems are just plain fun!

Another library with online young adult reviews—and more—is the Public Library of Mt. Vernon and Knox County in Ohio (www.knox.net). Teen members of their Young Adult Advisory Board produce *IMPACT: The Young Adult Newsletter* (www.knox.net/knox/library/youth/ya.htm), which includes "books, movies, music, computers, techno/video game reviews written by teens" and ". . . the rants and raves of the Young Adult Advisory Board." Topics covered in the newsletter are poetry and stories by teens; opposing viewpoints by male and female Young Adult Advisory Board (YAAB) members; fun local weekend activities; movie news and links; music news, reviews and links; technological updates; easy and fun recipes; and the latest "tasteful yet quirky" humor.

The Teen Library Council (TLC) at the University Place Library (www.pcl.lib.wa.us/teen_council/TLCArchiveTOC.htm), which is part of the Pierce County Library System in Washington state (www.pcl.lib.wa.us), also has an online newsletter. TLC members review and recommend books and movies and feature an "Author Spotlight."

The Ouachita Parish Public Library in Monroe, Louisiana (www.pcl.lib.wa.us), publishes its Teen Friends group's *Vaguely . a newsletter*. It is different from other teen advisory group newsletters in that it consists mainly of short columns written by the teens. The columns include such topics as young adults having a voice through their library, adopting a pet monkey, pondering colors and what they mean to us, and defining censorship. Of course, the teens also provide information about library events for young adults and how to join their group message board on Yahoo.

As many teen newsletters do, the Teen Friends provide a disclaimer that says, "This newsletter was written BY teens FOR teens. The views expressed in the newsletter are not necessarily those of Ouachita Parish Public Library or Friends of the Ouachita Public Library." (See sample issue of *Vaguely . a newsletter* at the end of this section.)

Other teens might be a bit more creative with their disclaimers. The Young Adult Advisory Board at the Boulder Public Library in Colorado (www.bplyaab.org/main.html), which has an extensive selection of original teen work on its Web pages, states, "Warning: This site created and maintained exclusively by middle and high school students. May contain creativity, originality and wit, as well as in-depth discussions of books, music, movies, poetry, creative writing, and catapults as a possible alternative to modern plumbing."

If your teens choose to produce a newsletter, you might want to consider including a straightforward or creative variation of those statements. Check with your library administrators to see if they require some kind of a disclaimer.

Teens usually love to see their opinions and ideas published, and to have a place to share the reactions and ideas of other teens. Newsletters give them that opportunity, also allowing them to promote the library and its young adult services in print, online, or both. Ask your teens if they are interested in producing a newsletter of some kind. Not every group will be excited about the idea. One TAGAD-L librarian, Rebecca Van Dan, of the Middleton Public Library in Wisconsin (www.scls.lib.wi.us/middleton/midhpf.html), posted, "I've seen some TAC groups put out newsletters, but ours is adamantly against anything that smacks of homework." If yours buys in, you will want to help and encourage them to bring their newsletter to life.

YAAC Book Review Tips for Open Shelf and Other Publications

1. After reading the book, tell briefly what happens without making your comments too short, giving a good overview of the story. A couple of paragraphs or so is fine.
2. Comment on your main characters. They make the story live! Tell a bit about them and how they affect the plot.
3. Setting is important. Tell where and when the story takes place. Is the setting in the United States, a foreign country or on another planet? Is the story taking place now, sometime in the past, or in the future?
4. Give your opinion! This is a major part of any review. You need to tell what you thought about a book and also why you felt that way. Without your opinion, stated clearly and completely, readers will not know the value you have placed on a book and why you have (or haven't) recommended it.
5. Longer, more complex reviews of a book or even a whole series are always welcome. They help to balance out the shorter reviews.
6. Write carefully! It is hard to understand scribbled handwriting. It takes valuable time to look up details that might be right there in the review but are written unclearly. Typed reviews are easiest to read and are appreciated.
7. Remember to use complete sentences, and watch your spelling and grammar!
8. You may take book review forms home and prepare them before YAAC meetings. You may also type or write reviews on regular paper, or submit *Open Shelf* reviews electronically to the Editor through e-mail if you wish. Just be sure to include all the information requested on the official book review form.
9. If you need help with a review, just ask. A librarian or a fellow YAAC member will be glad to help you make your review the best it can be. You will also want to read other people's published reviews for examples on how to do them.
10. Reviews on nonfiction books are needed as well. These are nice for a change of pace. Be sure to tell what each book is about, your opinion of it, and whether or not it is accurate in its information. You will also want to comment on any illustrations or photos included.
11. Thanks for all the work you do on book reviews, and remember the important job you are doing helping other teens to find good books to read!

Youth Services - City of Mesa Library
64 E. 1st Street • (480) 644-2734

open shelf

February 2004

mesa public library young adult advisory council book review newsletter

---

letter from the editor

Here at YAAC, we're too cool to have dates on Valentine's Day...at least that's what we tell ourselves. If your love life's not very exciting, we have eight action-packed books to fill up those empty Friday nights. We even have – gasp! – a comic book (oh, excuse me, a "graphic novel") review for all you manga fans out there. Happy Valentine's Day and (more importantly) happy reading!

teens_info@ci.mesa.az.us

Erin Hutchinson
open shelf Editor

rating system

bad	★
so-so	★ ★
good	★ ★ ★
excellent	★ ★ ★ ★

Visit the Library's Web Site:
www.mesalibrary.org
and see the Teens page!

The Caine Mutiny
By Herman Wouk

So...excruciatingly...long. And yet, so good. Willie Keith, the main character, is a WWII sailor. He goes through all the trials and tribulations of Navy life before getting onto the minesweeper *Caine*. Then, he experiences the Navy.

Wake up, wake up. Sounds boring, but it's not! Yes! Shocking. It's actually funny. Honestly, I read this book for school and chose it only because I linked mutiny to pirates to action. The mutiny (which happens about 100 pages from the end – everything else just "leads up" to it) isn't like that at all. Oh well. Still, surprisingly good, for a WWII novel. If you must read one, read this.

—Alyssa Ratledge ★ ★ ★

Trickster's Choice
By Tamora Pierce

16-year-old Aly doesn't know what to do with her life. Never mind that most noblewomen her age are either betrothed or married already. All Aly likes doing is spying. During Tortall's war with Scanra, Aly's been breaking coded messages from her father's agents. All she wants to do is be a spy, but her mother, the king's champion and first female knight in a century, and her father, the king's spymaster, are not about to let their only girl become a spy and die in some god-forsaken place. When Aly is captured by pirates and made

a slave on the Copper Isles, the trickster god makes her a wager: "Keep these noble children alive until mid-summer and I'll talk your father into letting you be a spy." How can she refuse? *Trickster's Choice* combines the political struggles of Tudor England and Indonesia, giving this thrilling story a taste of the exotic that makes it a wonderful book.

—Patricia Langevin ★ ★ ★ ★

Marmalade Boy series
By Yoshizumi Wataru

I have come to realize that there are far, far too few reviews concerning manga out there. So, I set out on my mission to change that! (Well, at the least, I'm reviewing these because they are incredibly good. More on that in a minute.)

One day, Miki Koishikawa's parents come home and tell her with bright, happy faces that they're getting a divorce. Well, needless to say, Miki is a little shocked and demands an explanation. It turns out that while on a vacation cruise in Hawaii, her parents had met up with another couple and decided to switch partners. Both families would move into one big house and live together, so that "nothing will change." Right, Mom. The other couple, the Matsuuras, also have a son, and that's when things get interesting...

Yuu Matsuura is apparently sweet as a strawberry, but underneath this kind exterior he is not quite ripe. Miki discovers this one day during breakfast and decides to give him the nickname, "Marmalade Boy." But Miki still falls in love with him. (All sigh—ready: "Aw...")

Things take off from there in this Brady-bunch family, going everywhere from teacher/student romances to illegitimate children. But despite the rather soap op-era-ish quality, these eight books kept my interest and my laughter going. Guys out there may not enjoy the series as much as girls, but hey, they'll never know until they try... So, do just that! Pick up a copy of *Marmalade Boy* and enjoy!

—*Jenny Knatz* ★ ★ ★ ★

The Lord of the Rings Trilogy

By J. R. R. Tolkien

In honor of the premiere of the *Return of the King* movie, I went on a mission to read the entire trilogy in one week. I lost sleep, I failed a final exam, but the books just kept getting better. For those sorry folks out there who have not read the books or seen the movie, the basic plot is that there is a hobbit, a really short person with hairy feet, named Frodo, along with three other hobbits, an elf, a dwarf, two men, and a wizard, who go on a journey to destroy the One Ring of Power to keep evil from taking over Middle Earth. Ah, beautiful!

—*Lora Eubanks* ★ ★ ★ ★

The Wolves of Calla

By Stephen King

As the fifth installment in Stephen King's *Dark Tower* series, *The Wolves of Calla* is the continuing story of Roland of Gilead and his journey to find the Dark Tower. In this story, Roland and his companions, Eddie, Susannah, Jake, and Oy, find themselves in a small town plagued by a huge problem. Roughly once a generation, creatures called the Wolves ride through the town and steal children. The gunslingers are asked by the townspeople to help stop this event.

The Wolves of Calla is an excellent book, but to fully understand it, the other four novels in the series need to be read. There are frequent references to the previous books, and it would be generally confusing if *The Gunslinger*, *The Drawing of the Three*, *The Wastelands*, and *Wizard and Glass* were not in the back of a reader's mind. These stories are more adventure/science fiction than horror, but of course being by Stephen King, there are some violent and frightening scenes. This series is rumored to be the last of King's books.

—*Elizabeth Dormady* ★ ★ ★ ★

Martyn Pig

By Kevin Brooks

Martyn Pig has a horrible name, a horrible house, a horrible father, and what seems like a horrible life. His dad is a drunk. He spends all the money he gets from his former wife for Martyn's support on drinks. Generally, he is aggressive and tries to hit Martyn. When a freak accident occurs, and Martyn tries to push away his father's violence, his father hits his head on the mantle and dies.

Traumatized, and by some means insane, Martyn decides not to call the police for fear that they would accuse him of murder. He finds himself, hours later, with the body still on the floor, afraid of a "crime" that was really an accident. When he tells his beautiful neighbor, Alex about what happened, she agrees to help him to conceal the body.

In a strange series of complicated events, the world turns upside down and there is no straight ending. As Martyn states himself: "Most mysteries are a ball of wool. You pull one end and you know that eventually you'll get to the end. But this story is like a bunch of chaotic knots. You pull one end and it all moves at the same time."

Apart from a compelling mystery and great storyline, the book contains a lot of theories. These include theories about life, and thoughts on random subjects. These things make you consider the storyline, and within it Martyn's own thoughts which are some of the most interesting and mystifying things you can read. The descriptions of life and the theories are almost as good as the plotline. I recommend it for all readers, as I think this is one of the greatest books in YA fiction.

—*Rosalinda Albrecht* ★ ★ ★ ★

The DaVinci Code

By Dan Brown

This book has everything you could possibly want. From swords to planes to conspiracies, this is your book. *The DaVinci Code* is about a two millennia Vatican cover-up of Jesus' and Mary Magdalene's "relationship." The two main characters go on a quest to find the truth, and on the way find the Holy Grail.

Read this book! Not only will you want to sleep on it, there are so many plot twists you can't put it down.

—*Matt Stone* ★ ★ ★ ★

"Harrison Bergeson"

by Kurt Vonnegut, Jr.
A short story from *The Flying Sorcerers* collection, edited by Peter Haining

Wouldn't you like to live in a world where everybody is equal? If you're in Harrison's world, you probably wouldn't.

Harrison's world is not different from ours (in that it's called planet Earth). But time wise...it's a lot different. The year: 2081. He lives in this time where beautiful ballerinas wear masks to conceal their beauty; where hot guys are a walking junkyard with scrap metals hanging all over them to hide their perfect bodies; where the smart ones wear earplugs that send hard, annoying beeps to prevent them from using their intelligence (they're not supposed to think at all). All of these are for just one thing: to make everybody equal. Everybody's equal, nice and even. You're not smarter than your little sibling, and you're not prettier than anybody.

I had to read this story for my English literature class and it was very interesting. Read it!

—*Geralden DelRosario* ★ ★ ★ ★

mesalibrary.org
City of Mesa Library on the Web

CITY OF MESA
Great People, Quality Service!

OUACHITA PARISH PUBLIC LIBRARY TEEN FRIENDS

Vaguely. a newsletter

VOLUME 1, ISSUE 1

OCTOBER 2002

Intellectual Freedom Symposium Chris Crutcher Comes to Town

Amanda Teague

Chris Crutcher is coming here to speak at an Intellectual Freedom Symposium on September 26, 2002.

9:30-11:00 am : ULM library's 7th floor conference room. Majority seating for Middle and High school students.

3:30-4:30 pm: After school pass – meet the author hosted by the teen friends and open to the public in the OPPL main branch.

5:00- 7:30 pm: ULM library's 7th floor conference room. All seats open to the public.

All sections free of charge and there is a limit of 500 seats per section at each event held in the ULM library.

Sponsor: OPPL Young Adult Dept.

Funding by: American Library Association: Live @ the Library initiative, Louisiana Endowment for the Humanities, Ouachita Parish Public Library, and the University of Louisiana at Monroe English Department Hosted by: Teen Friends of the Ouachita Public Library.

About Chris Crutcher: Crutcher writes from a realistic perspective on the issues that teens face every day. He was trained as a psychologist and taught at an inner city school system in Oakland, California for ten

Crutcher at home in Spokane, Washington

years. He has won the National Intellectual Freedom Award and The Margaret A. Edwards Lifetime Achievement Award.

" I have one thing to say to the censors. Shut up." - Chris Crutcher

OCTOBER IS:

- *Alternate History Month*
- *Auto Battery Safety Month*
- *National Animal Safety and Protection Month*
- *National Apple Jack Month*
- *National Cookie Month*
- *National Stamp Collection Month*
- *National Toilet Tank Repair Month*
- *Vegetarian Month*
- *Right-Brainers Rule Month*
- *National Breast Cancer Awareness Month*

Unheard Thoughts

Jon Tillman

What do young adults think about? Well, mostly "why -Why can't we do this or that,. Young adults are starting to speak out about the world around them and now they have someone to listen... now

we have the library. At OPPL, the young adults have there own place to hang out. We can also come and join in an organization known as the Teen friends group. This is only one part of

the YA department. During the summer there is a reading program that has so Much more than reading.
Come by and check it out. We'll be here.
'Till next time ciao.

Are you ready to have a monkey?
Amanda Teague

Do you think you want a pet monkey? Awww! How cute, how sweet.

Yeah, when they're babies but when they're grown watch out they bite HARD!! Did you consider the cost of raising a monkey? Fifty dollars per monkey per week. Are you ready to pay that every week? Most of us aren't.

Did you know that most vets would not even take monkeys as patients?

Are you prepared to drive for hours to get to a vet? And what if the monkey has an emergency and needs medical help NOW?

Oh yeah, did you know that having a monkey in some states is illegal.

Do you have the time and space for a monkey? If you get a monkey you have to spend the next 30 to 40 years with that monkey and no vacations because it's nearly impossible to find a monkey sitter. All monkeys need lots of space inside and out so

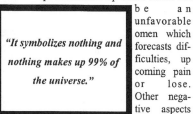

This is George. George is neurotic. Is your monkey neurotic?

be prepared to give whole rooms of your home to your new life long house guest. You know the kind that show up then just hang around not even picking up after they trash your house. If a monkey, any monkey is not physically, emotionally, and intellectually stimulated they can become neurotic like my sister's old dog– which is not a good thing.

Colors: Black
Amanda Teague

Black is the negative or your shadow; it often represents depression. Black is used to absorb negative energy but it does absorb magical energy and other positive energies as well. Black can represent night or darkness. Some, but not all, believe it represents evil. It symbolizes nothing and nothing makes up 99% of

> *"It symbolizes nothing and nothing makes up 99% of the universe."*

the universe. All colors of the color spectrum make up black. Black can be an unfavorable omen which forecasts difficulties, up coming pain or lose. Other negative aspects

are grieving, hopelessness, and despair. Some positive aspects of black are rest, sleep, patience, attraction, and a hope for a new beginning.

This is the beginning in a series of columns that will ponder different colors and what they mean to us.

A Note from Holly
Holly Priestley, YA Coordinator

I know a lot of you have seen me or Patricia running around our parties and workshops with the digital camera snapping shots of you with food in your mouth or in a strange Twister position. However, most of you never see the pictures after the workshops. Where do they go? Do they fly off to picture-neverland? What fun is it to pose for all those pics if you never get to see them? Never fear! Holly has

come to your rescue! (Or at least, I like to think I have…)

I have set up a group on the web where you can go to see the pictures. Also, you can chat with other teen friends, read and post to a message board, vote in YA department polls, and do so much more! First you need to get a Yahoo account. (They are FREE!)

Then go to the website listed here and click on "join this group." You will be asked for your Yahoo name and password. After you join, don't forget to post a message telling us who you are! And, remember to check the site every few days. I will be looking for you!

Join the group @ Yahoo! Groups
http://groups.yahoo.com/group/opplteens

Newdow Wants New Dough
Darryl Smith

A lot of things have been happening since the dreaded day, September 11, 2001. Some things have been reasonable, yet overused. Some things have been just plain stupid. However, a new case has arisen that is not exactly stupid, but unreasonable. In California, a man has protested about his child saying "Under God" in the Pledge of Allegiance. Many "true blue" Americans were outraged.

However, some were calm and realized that the thing would "blow over" sooner or later. However, calm soon went to panicky as the California court ruled in favor for the man. His name is Michael A. Newdow. Mr. Newdow is a Sacramento atheist. An atheist is a person who doesn't believe in God or Jesus. He has a eight year old daughter. He became seriously offended when she was "forced" to say the Pledge of Allegiance. He took this matter to court and won. In some states, it is now illegal to tell children to say the Pledge of Allegiance. However, it may take months to activate this law. Mr. Newdow also filed lawsuits against the government for putting "In God We Trust" on U.S. coins.

He is not unfamiliar with harsh treatment from Christians. "I'll bet you there is something thrown through my window in the next few days," he told the Chronicle Sacramento Bureau.

Will lawsuits change US money?

The issue has many Americans up in arms. Some say that the Pledge of Allegiance should be thrown out. Others think it should remain. My deacon read the book of Psalm and the ninth chapter. In it, it states that everyone should have one God. However, are atheists wrong? This issue hasn't gotten out of hand...yet "Under God???" Does it really link the state and the public???

Maybe, maybe not. This battle is not over. As Jay Leno said, "Yesterday, a California court ruled the Pledge of Allegiance unconstitutional. Boy, I bet a lot of people said "Amen!" to that."

Those Three Little Words
Staci Adams

When you were younger, about 8 or 9, I'm sure you said, "You're my girlfriend or you're my boyfriend." And, you assumed that meant 'let's play chase at recess.' But that is not the case these days. When you become a young adult you begin to develop a relationship with your man or woman.

Have your parents ever told you that it all beings with kissing? Well, whether or not they have- it's true. On a girl's first date (or any date for that matter) a girl will spend hours getting ready. Normally you are nervous while you are getting ready because you are scared that you will mess up. Then, the door bell rings just as you are finishing putting on your lipstick. Your date tells you that he's taking you to dinner and a movie. The movie you can handle, but you aren't so sure about the dinner part, because you (like most girls) still have that fear of eating in front of guys. But you can handle the conversations of getting to know each other better. You finally finish with dinner and you are anxious about getting to the movies. When you get to the ticket booth he asks you what you want to see. Of course, you chose that sappy love story. The movie will, no doubt about it, get you what you really want - that first kiss of the night. But the next thing you know, you're making out! Weeks go by and he begins to get bored of just making out and wants

> *"You start to cry and then you ask him about those three little words that started it all."*

to take it to the next level. You hear that he has told all of his friends that he's going to go all the way with you at Friday night's big party. But the thing is you aren't ready to go all the way! You are just happy with making out! About three days before the party, he tells you –for the first time– that he loves you. You're so surprised that you say it

(Continued on page 4)

Ouachita Parish Public Library Teen Friends

OPPL
ya dept

1800 Stubbs Ave.
Monroe, LA 71201

Phone: 318/327-1490
Fax: 318/327-1373
Email: ya@ouachita.lib.la.us

Vaguely. a newsletter

Supervisors	Holly Priestley
	Ronnie Donn
	Patricia Lee
Editor	Amanda Teague
Columnists	Darryl Smith
	Nelita Bailey, Pres
	Jon Tillman, VP
Contributing	Staci Adams

www.ouachita.lib.la.us

Ouachita Parish
PUBLIC LIBRARY

Friends of
Ouachita Public
LIBRARY SYSTEM

This newsletter was written BY teens FOR teens. The views expressed in the newsletter are not necessarily those of Ouachita Parish Public Library or Friends of the Ouachita Public Library.

What is censorship?
Nelita Bailey, Teen Friends President

What is censorship? That's the question everyone has asked since we started publicizing the Intellectual Freedom Symposium featuring Chris Crutcher (to be held on September 26th 2002.)

Censorship is the restriction of any material that is deemed "unfit" for certain groups of people. Anything and everything can be censored. All it takes is a group of likeminded and "narrow" minded adults who have decided FOR US AND OUR PARENTS that something of specific content is too graphically violent, sexual, racist, or vulgar for OUR maturity level. However censorship itself is not the

problem. The problem is when a small group of people tries to decide what material is best for an entire community. This is nothing like the government— where the smaller group is comprised of officials elected by the larger community; it's more like a dictatorship, where the community has almost no power over their destiny. Think of it this way. . . your parents decided to let you, a minor, catch the new R rated action movie with them, no big deal right? What if someone you've never met and doesn't know the first thing about you or your parents decided it was against the law for your parents to allow you and

them to view such inappropriate material. Is that fair?

Censorship Fast Fact of the Day: Nothing is sacred.

I could use many examples of extreme censorship, but there's one example in particular that I think everyone can relate to. After all, our country was supposedly founded on its very morals. Tyndale's Bible was first banned in 1525. Why? Because the Church didn't want "common" people interpreting it for themselves.

Information is power.

Those Three Little Words: Cont'd

(Continued from page 3)
back. He then asks you to go to the party and you decide it will be fun.

It's finally Friday night and your boyfriend picks you up, half wasted. You get into the car anyway. As the night moves on he gets more and more wasted. Finally, he asks you if you want to go upstairs. You tell him no, but he won't listen. So, he uses his backup plan. He tells you that he loves you for the second time. Oh! How you love to hear that! You believe him and you decide to experiment for the first time. You think to yourself, "Everyone's doing it, so why can't I ? Plus, he

loves me!"

Afterwards, you go back down stairs, and you realize it's time for you to go home. So you take his keys and give them to his brother because he's totally wasted.

The next day he calls you and says it's over. You start to cry. You ask him about those three little

words that started it all. He then tells you, " I only said 'I love you' to get you to sleep with me." So you cry until you can cry no more. How could this happen? You thought you could trust him...

So before you go off and start to go to far with a guy (or girl if you are a guy), ask yourself, "Is it really love or is it a trap?" Don't make a mistake and have to start a family early. As anyone can see you can be in love with him (or her) and the feelings aren't mutual...
But you believe they are .

How to Produce Newsletters

Newsletters published by teen advisory boards provide an opportunity for members and other teens to share all sorts of ideas and information, including their reactions to books, music, magazines, movies, video games, and other media. Where teens are concerned, communication is the name of the game, and positive channels for that communication are magnetic.

There are a number of options for acquiring contributions. Teens can submit reviews independently and plan and prepare the newsletters as a group, or the group can appoint a leader or editor (and possibly coeditor) to collect reviews and put the newsletters together. Reviews can be submitted in longhand (if they promise to write neatly and legibly!) or as word-processed documents printed out and submitted, or sent in through e-mail attachments. The more flexibility teens have for turning in their work the better response you will get from them.

The teen advisory board members can decide on format, deadlines, and what goes into their newsletter and also be in charge of the editing. Then the librarian advisor can assist with final editing and assuring that the newsletter gets published according to the teens' wishes. The teens themselves can be responsible for the typing and layout, or if the school or library has access to a graphics specialist, that person may make finishing preparations. Newsletter issues can be published via the library's copy machine, or if many issues are needed, resorting to a city or school print shop might be in order. The newsletter can be distributed in the library, the junior and senior high schools, local youth agencies such as the Boys and Girls Clubs, and other locations as the teens decide.

It is up to you as the librarian advisor to help the teens figure out how many copies are needed per year and to make sure funds are available to cover paper and printing costs. Requests for funds need to be submitted each year with printing or programming budgets. If outside funding is required, you must allow time to seek out that funding, apply for it, and get it approved and underway. If you are planning to help your teens publish a newsletter, the key is to plan ahead! You don't want to discourage your teens by not having set the stage for the final steps of publishing.

Likewise, if you and your teens decide to publish or include your newsletter or reviews in the teen section of your library's Web page, you will need to meet with the library's Web master in ample time to make arrangements to have the information included. Again, plan ahead and work out how you would like the newsletter or reviews to appear on the Web page and the process you must follow to get it started and have it continued. Each school or library has its own policies for setting up and submitting information to the Web page, and you will need to make sure that your group follows those instructions.

When you publish teen work, you might want to consider whether or not to include the contributors' names. The Chicago Ridge Public Library in Illinois has a Teen Advisory Board that produces its Teen Café Read pages (http://chicagoridge.lib.il.us/teen_cafe_read/teen_cafe_read.html). Within those sections it states: "The Chicago Ridge Public Library is very concerned about the privacy and safety of the Teen

Advisory Board members. Therefore, only the first initial of each member's name is being displayed on this page."

If you decide to include teen reviewer biographies in your newsletter, whether in print or on your Web page, you might want your teens to think of pseudonyms or just give their first names or initials. For security and safety, do not allow them to include their own e-mail addresses or telephone numbers in the text. If you do want to include an e-mail address for questions or comments from readers, obtain an address for contact directly to you or another library staff member, not a teen. I have an additional "teen info" e-mail address posted on our Teen Web page that delivers messages directly to me, allowing me to field any unscrupulous messages.

You will also want to find out what your library's policies are about publishing work by minors and how much information about them can be permitted in newsletters or on your Web pages. If written parental permission is required, you will need to get the proper forms and obtain signatures before publishing teens' work. Unfortunately, in these times it is better to be more cautious than not when dealing with minors.

An excellent online resource for learning about all aspects of producing newsletters, especially if you are working with teens, is *Hot Off the Press! Newsletter Publishing Made Easy* (www.cplrmh.com/newsletter.html). It is edited by RoseMary Honnold from the Coshocton Public Library in Ohio, who also provides the *See YA Around: Library Programming for Teens* Web page (www.cplrmh.com).

HOW WE STARTED OUR TEEN NEWSLETTER

I can't even remember where the idea for a teen newsletter came from. I think it might have come up as a suggestion during one of our meetings regarding ways to promote all our teen events. Advertising for our programs has always been a problem. We were hoping a newsletter that teens wrote themselves would be more appealing to a teen rather than the library's normal monthly events handout. We talked about the newsletter for months.

Everyone liked the concept, but they were hesitant about volunteering. I got names and contact information for about one person per meeting who really wanted to help. After about four or five months, we had enough people who had volunteered. During the initial months, I was somewhat leery that we would have enough volunteers. While I wouldn't mind writing the articles myself, that would defeat the purpose. We were looking for articles about our teen events written from a teen perspective. I can laud our programs as much as I want, but let's face it, I ain't no teen!

To attract teens to our programs, we need to show that teens find the programs interesting. To start the newsletter (and because the teens weren't quite sure what to write about), I gave out "assignments," based on which teens visited which branch and who had attended recent programs. Our three main stories were a recent teen lock-in, construction at one of the branches, and a summation of exactly what we did at our TAB meetings. I also added sidebars with new books and CDs. Frequently, all the new stuff is checked out and the teens never realize what great materials we have. I wanted to make sure that they knew we were ordering fun stuff. We plan on adding book reviews in the future.

The initial newsletter, *YA Today*, was prepared on Microsoft Publisher. While Publisher is exceedingly easy to use and has a quality professional look to it, the sheer size of the document took up three discs to save it. And that's only a one-page document! Also, Publisher was available at only one staff computer. Every time I wanted to use it, someone else was sitting there. So, while Publisher is easy, it's quite possible our next newsletter will just be on Word. (See *YA Today* on the next page.)

Amy Ackerman, Blake Library of the Martin County Library System, Stuart, Florida (www.library.martin.fl.us)

Martin County Library System Teen Advisory Board

Volume 1, Issue 1

November 2002

YA Today

Brand new YA Books!

- You Know You Love Me! : A Gossip Girl Novel by Cecily von Ziegesar

- 9-11 Emergency Relief : A Comic Book To Benefit the American Red Cross by various authors/artists

- Hanging on to Max by Margaret Bechard

- Daughters of the Moon series by Lynne Ewing

- Wonder Woman : The Hiketei by Greg Rucka and others

- Big Mouth & Ugly Girl by Joyce Carol Oates

- The Haunted Shop by Lois Gladys Leppard

- Knocked Out By My Nunga-Nungas by Louise Rennison

- Muses on the Move series by Clea Hantman

RESULTS FROM THE LAST FEW TEEN ADVISORY BOARD MEETINGS

By Hilary P.

A Teen Creative Writing Workshop was suggested but it is unlikely that will be held this year, but the beginning stages are already underway for next year's possibility. Other programs suggested were performing a play, holding a talent contest, and redoing our Teen Career Series during the year on Saturdays. [If more interest is shown in these sorts of programs, we will be more diligent about pursuing them.] The library also has a volunteer program that includes story-time assisting, computer coaching and shelving books, or anything else that needs to be done. [For more information on volunteering, contact Terry Dick at 219-4906.]

Some new CD suggestions were : Nelly, Kelly, System of a Down, U2, Backstreet Boys, Steven Curtis Chapman, IMX, Dave Matthews Band, Bruce Springsteen and the E Street Band, Ben Folds and Trick Daddy. Soundtracks suggested were : Mortal Kombat, Queen of the Damned, Blade, Donnie Darko, Charlie's Angels, Gone in 60 Seconds and Like Mike.

DVD/VHS suggestions were : All About the Benjamins, We Were Soldiers, Black Hawk Down, Speed 2, The Fast and the Furious, Super Troopers, American Outlaws, Resident Evil, Donnie Darko, Rocky Horror Picture Show, The Blob, Juwanna Man, Dragonfly, Life as a House, Interview With a Vampire, XXX, Fight Club, The New

The TeenZone at the Blake Library

Adventures of Pippi Longstocking, Devil's Arithmetic, and the Nuremberg Trials.

Book suggestions were more craft books, RL Stine and more of the Chicken Soup series.

We have a new comic book selection! More comics suggested were DragonballZ, Adventures of Tin Tin, Garfield, Dennis the Menace, Peanuts, Nancy and Shoe.

No food or drinks are allowed in any of the Martin County libraries and we are sorry to say there is nothing we can do about this. [There were plenty of valid suggestions for alternate solutions, but none of these are financially feasible at this time. The Blake Library Friends of the Library will be starting an

outside coffee cart sometime in the future.]

Later hours were mentioned again, but nothing can be done to fix that as well, unless more staff is hired.

If you have any suggestions or questions, please contact Amy Ackerman at 221-1401 or at aackerma@martin.fl.us.

[Items in brackets were added to this article by Amy Ackerman, YA Library Lady.]

**Teen Advisory Board
Meeting Schedule:**
November 21 (Stuart)
6:00 to 7:30 pm
December 12 (Morgade)
6:00 to 7:30 pm
All teens are welcome to attend! (psst....free pizza!)

TEEN LOCK-IN AT THE BLAKE
BY LAUREN B.

On August 2002, there was a teen lock-in at the Blake Library. About 20-30 teens showed up. The lock-in was a hit! It started at 8:00 pm and ended at 8:00 am the next morning. There was one very important rule—NO SLEEPING!

During the lock-in, we all got to know each other and made new friends. We played games such as Toss the CDs, Pass the Book Between Your Knees, and the most favorite by far was Race the Rolling Library Carts Between the Chairs! These games were all part of the Library Olympics.

After the fun and games, we had ice cream at 1:30 am! Some people got chocolate happy and decided to play Flashlight Tag and Capture the Book—a library version of Capture the Flag.

I had a chance during the lock-in to ask some people what they thought of it. Some responses were, "It's so cool!", "I can't believe they're doing this! The library people ROCK!" and the most popular answer was, "This is better than a slumber party at my friend's house!" (Now, now, let's not get carried away here.)

Many people would enjoy having another lock-in. Everyone enjoyed the games, food, and movies. Every person that I asked, "Do you want to have another lock-in?" said, "Yeah! This is a great idea!"

If we have another lock-in, you'll come too, right?

MAJOR CONSTRUCTION!
BY NICOLE L. AND BRITTANY L.

With their screw guns, saws, and grinders, something new is being built at the Indiantown Branch.

From the official blueprints, the workmen go inch by inch building the new 5,000 sq. foot addition to the existing 5,000 sq. feet of an excellent library.

This extension includes 10 excellent construction workers, some heavy duty hand tools (including their sledge hammer which actually weighs 10 pounds, down to that little screwdriver that weighs a couple of ounces), the blue prints, and of course, the big cheese, Jerry Hennis.

Included in this new section will be a larger conference room and a smaller conference room, which will share a little kitchen area. The children's room will be twice as big as it is currently. There will also be an abundance of stoarage space and a large workroom/

lunchroom for staff and volunteers.

In remodeling the existing section, the area that is now the children's room is going to be in the YA section, which will include a variety of books and several computers.

"I'm excited that the young adults will have their own section, " says Renita Presler, the Branch Manager.

"It will be wonderful!" "It's going to be bigger, prettier and cooler!" say Sabrina Zirkle and Janet Rosado, library staff commenting on the new building.

The library closed October 19th and will reopen hopefully by Christmas.

"I want to see what it is like when it is finished!" said the Big Cheese, Jerry Hennis.

Indiantown Branch Renovation

New cds!

- "Read and Burn" by Wire
- "Sea Change" by Beck
- "Sheryl Crow" by Sheryl Crow
- "The Spirit Room" by Michelle Branch
- "Back In Black" by AC/DC
- "The Joshua Tree" by U2
- "Queen + Greatest Hits III" by Queen
- "So Much Shouting, So Much Laughter" by Ani DiFranco
- "Music From Vanilla Sky"
- "All That You Can't Leave Behind You" by U2
- "Under Rug Swept" by Alanis Morissette
- "Incredible" by Mary Mary
- "Rule 3:36" by Ja Rule
- "Untouchables" by Korn
- "Let Go" by Avril Lavigne
- "Yankee Hotel Foxtrot" by Wilco
- "Full Moon" by Brandy
- "Become You" by Indigo Girls
- "Cocky" by Kid Rock

[These items are undoubtedly checked out. If you don't see them on the shelves, don't become discouraged! You can always have an item reserved for you. Ask a staff member for details.]

Teen 'Zines

Although there are sometimes overlaps and combinations with other publishing projects in print and on teen Web pages, some teen library advisory groups concentrate specifically on developing forums for teen creative writing and displays of artwork. Production of these 'zines is one of the latest teen trends. Many teens have hopped on the bandwagon, finding support for 'zines through their libraries.

For the last two years at the Eden Prairie Library (www.hclib.org/AgenciesAction .cfm?agency=ep) in Eden Prairie, Minnesota, part of the Hennepin County Library system, a Teen Editorial Board has been compiling writing from teens around the community into a 'zine called *Through Our Eyes*. They print a run of 2,000 and distribute them locally throughout the community.[5] This is only one example of a teen library advisory group successfully producing a 'zine.

As described in chapter 2, the Teen Advisory Group at the Minneapolis Public Library produces a "by teens, for teens" 'zine called *Dreams of Ours* (www.mpls.lib .mn.us/wft_zine.asp). *Dreams of Ours* is distributed to all middle and high schools in Minneapolis and is available in all city library branches as well as online. Teens from all over the city submit creative writing, reviews, or editorials, and the Teen Advisory Group evaluates submissions for publication. The Teen Advisory Group also contributes their personal writing and illustrations to the 'zine, which comes out three times each year.[6] In July 2002, the Teen Specialist promoted the project by showing a videotape of the Teen Advisory Group and *Dreams of Ours* as a feature on a local television program, *Whatever*, a teen-produced news-magazine airing on Saturday mornings.[7]

Phoenix Public Library's Library Teen Council (LTC) produces a 'zine called *Create!* (www.phoenixteencentral.org/teenzineframe.html). In 2000, members of the LTC who were interested in writing and the arts pursued the 'zine as a group project. In order to help the project take off, they held an art and writing contest at the library for teens in four categories: art, writing, poetry, and photography. Hundreds of entries were received and the contest was very successful in launching the first issue of *Create!* Now, teens can find submission guidelines on the Teen Central Web page and pick up a pen, brush, or camera to enter work for the next issue.

Often, a minority of teen library board members will be interested in working on a 'zine. It is usually the writing- and art-oriented teens who enjoy this kind of participation. One way to allow interested teens to become involved in this kind of activity is to have a subgroup or separate committee to work on the 'zine itself, and perhaps have other members agree to work on the promotional aspects.

At the City of Mesa Library, we have a separate editorial board for our teen literary magazine *FRANK* (www.mesalibrary.org/teens/pdf/frankbrochure.pdf). Some members participate in YAAC as well as *FRANK*, while others prefer to spend their time concentrating solely on one group or the other.

Again, it is the same story. Ask your teens what they want, find out their interests and abilities, and tailor your teen advisory board program to what the *teens* would like to accomplish. If that includes a 'zine or literary magazine, help them to meet that goal.

If you are not a particularly literary or art-oriented person, you might feel unable to guide a project like a teen 'zine. However, there are usually a number of resources in most communities to assist you. Start by asking for help in the local schools. A teacher or librarian may be knowledgeable and interested in partnering with you. If you have a college or university in your town, find out if there is an instructor or student who might be willing to assist in your 'zine project. You might even discover an older teen who has worked on a school newspaper or literary magazine, and recruit him or her to help you.

VOYA Librarian/Teen Partner Reviews

The young adult library journal *Voice of Youth Advocates* (*VOYA*) gives librarians an opportunity to share teen reactions to new books for young adults through its book review section. To get started, you must get yourself on board as a *VOYA* reviewer, if you are not already. Find out how to become a reviewer through the *VOYA* Web site (www.voya.com) or by contacting the book review editor at 4501 Forbes Blvd., Suite 200, Lanham, Maryland, 20706.

Once you have established yourself as a competent *VOYA* reviewer, you can elect to begin preparing co-reviews with your teens. The first step is to ask your group if there is interest in participating. If enough members are interested, you can proceed. I have many teens who enjoy doing co-reviews with me, and I try to give a different teen a chance each time. You might find the same situation with your group. Perhaps only a small number of teens want to review, in which case you can have the same teens reviewing more often. There is no reason why a subsection of your group cannot participate; if others see how much they enjoy the partner reviews, they might decide to join in, too. As previously mentioned, one thing teens love is seeing their names and work in print!

You will need to follow some important steps to become part of this process. First, you need to let *VOYA* know that you wish to begin review partnering with your teens. Next, you need to train your teens in the reviewing process for *VOYA*. *VOYA* has made it easy to provide this training; they will send you complete instructions and forms to share with your teen reviewers. It is up to you to prepare for this training and meet with your teens to explain the process.

Now comes the really fun part! Each time you receive a YA book to review (not books from the professional or reference review section), you will receive two copies. One is for you and the other is for your teen reviewer. You will need to appoint a teen reviewer to partner with you each time. *VOYA* sends a form for listing the reading interests of your teens as a helpful tool for finding the right reviewer. Sometimes choosing a teen will be easy if you can tell that the book's subject matter is a good match for a particular person. At other times, you might have a few teens who would like to review the same book. You will need to devise a plan for appointing teen readers so that everyone gets a chance to participate.

When you receive your books to review from *VOYA*, you'll get a deadline when the final review is due. Your teen reading partner also needs a deadline, and you should make it early enough for you to read (and edit with him or her if necessary) the review, attach it to yours, and submit it on time either by regular mail or e-mail attachment.

When a teen reviews for *VOYA* the first time, a minor under age 18 must submit a publication permission form signed by his or her parents. You will need to allow time to mail this permission form to *VOYA* with the required review form and printed review. Once the permission form is on file at *VOYA*, you can partner with the same teen without submitting another form.

The librarian part of the review needs to be about 250 words and concentrates on a brief book description and opinion. The teen reviewer response mainly focuses on the teen's opinion and must be around 75 words. Sometimes you will need to work with your teen to edit his or her review so that it fits the word perimeters, just as you do with your own review.

In addition to the actual review, both you and your teen partner will assign *VOYA*'s Q (for Quality) and P (for Popularity) ratings to the book. It is not unusual for you and your partner to disagree. Whether you love a book while your teen loathes it (or vice versa), *VOYA* prints opposing *or* harmonious opinions because they reveal the real world of differing adult and teen views.

It is exciting for you and for your teens to bring the published reviews from *VOYA* to your teen advisory board meetings and show them to the group. I always make a copy of the review for the teen to keep, a copy for our YAAC Representative, a copy for my files, and copies to give to our administrators, including our Library Director. At each library board meeting, our YAAC Representative proudly shows any recently published *VOYA* reviews as part of his or her monthly report.

Teens' Top Ten/YA Galley Project

We know that teens love to participate, and they love to be asked for their opinions. What better way to focus on these two elements than through books? The Young Adult Library Services Association (YALSA) of the American Library Association experimented with this idea through pilot projects using teenagers who belong to youth advisory boards throughout the country. One ultimate goal was to develop a permanent process through which teens have an opportunity to vote on their current favorite YA books each year.

The first phase of the pilot project began in 1999. Two groups were targeted to participate in the project, our Young Adult Advisory Council at the City of Mesa Library, and Kitty Krahnke's large group of teen readers from Pennsylvania that met in three different schools: Marshall Middle School in Wexford, North Hills Junior High in Pittsburgh, and Carson Middle School in Pittsburgh. Some of the latter group also met in the Northland Public Library in Pittsburgh.

Each group was expected to read books chosen for that year's Best Books for Young Adults List from YALSA. The YAAC group read from a "short" list of about one-third of the titles, deemed by the adults on the YALSA committee to be the "best of the best." The Pennsylvania group read from the full version of the list. In time for Teen Read Week 1999, both groups submitted their final votes, which were combined into one "winners" list. The Teens' Top Ten list was posted on the YALSA Teen Hoopla Web page, now defunct. (Find the results of the pilot project in the December 1999 issue of *VOYA*, pages 303 and 318–19.)

In 2000, the second phase of the project began. This time, publishers and librarian advisors of teen groups joined together in another YALSA pilot program called the YA Galley Project. Publishers sent "hot-off-the-press" copies of books and galley editions to 16 library teen book groups throughout the country. Each group was expected to read the books and complete evaluation forms. For feedback, completed teen evaluation forms were sent to the publishers by the librarian advisors.

Phase three occurred in 2001. The projects from the first two years were merged into one Teens' Top Ten/YA Galley Project. Of the 16 groups involved, 6 groups, including our YAAC, chose to participate in the Teens' Top Ten component. During phase three, all groups once again received galley copies or very newly published YA books and completed evaluation forms. As in previous years, the forms were sent to the publishers so they could gain teen feedback.

Teens also used the forms for a second purpose—to nominate titles for the 2001 Teens' Top Ten (TTT). If a book received at least two teen nominations, it was added to the contender list. Nominations from all participating groups were tallied into one master list. Each group continued reading from the list, and during Teen Read Week (October 14–20, 2001) each group finalized its TTT votes. This list of winning titles was posted on YALSA's Teen Hoopla Web site. (Results also appear in the December 2001 issue of *VOYA*, page 329.)

The really exciting thing about these projects is that YALSA has ultimately decided to make Teens' Top Ten a permanent, ongoing activity! *VOYA* helped to launch the YA Galley/Teens' Top Ten project as the corporate sponsor, its editor serving as project coordinator until 2004. The YA Galley Committee of YALSA began its work at the January 2003 American Library Association Midwinter Meeting in Philadelphia. The information gleaned from the three pilot project years has helped to turn YA Galley/Teens' Top Ten into a forum for *teens themselves* to decide annually what their top YA book choices will be.

It works like this: Every two years, the YALSA YA Galley Committee accepts applications from advisors of teen book discussion/advisory groups in school and public libraries across the United States. Fifteen diverse groups are chosen to serve two-year terms. Only librarians who are YALSA members qualify to apply for consideration. Those selected serve as liaisons for their groups on YALSA's YA Galley listserv, where publishers offer their latest titles and librarians request copies for their groups. YA Galley groups may keep the books to use as they wish, as long as they also keep their commitment to complete and send in the teen evaluation forms to the participating publishers, through their librarian.

Five of the 15 YA Galley groups are designated as TTT voting groups which will choose their top ten favorite new books by Teen Read Week each October. From October through May, teen TTT group members nominate worthy titles, which are posted on YALSA's Teens' Top Ten Web site (www.ala.org/teenstopten) to allow teens throughout the country to participate in an online public vote during Teen Read Week. The winning titles from the Teens' Top Ten groups and individual teens who vote online are reported in two separate, ranked lists of ten.[8]

If your teens decide to apply for membership as an official YA Galley group, check YALSA's Teens' Top Ten Web page for application information. Even if your group does not choose to apply, or if they do and are not among the lucky ones selected, they can still participate by keeping tabs on the posted nominations, reading the books, and voting online during Teen Read Week. In essence, all teens in library advisory groups as well as teens at large become potential participants in this project.

YA Galley/Teens' Top Ten is an exciting opportunity for teens, long in the making but worth the wait. If your teen library advisory board is involved in promoting reading (most of them are), be sure to inform your members about this project and help them get involved if they show interest. Just think: a vote by teens, for teens, of their favorite new books each year!

One teen member of the YA Galley/Teens' Top Ten project at the Allen County Public Library (www.acpl.lib.in.us) in Indiana sums it up best: "Reading all these books in such a short period of time helps me read faster and expand my vocabulary. I've met new and interesting people. . . . I'm involved in the community and it feels so good to make a difference."[9]

Teen Web Advisory Groups

Many libraries have teen sections on their library homepages, but few actually have teens running the show. What better way to get teens interested and involved in your library than by having other teens as part of the process? It works for programming, library promotion, book reviewing, and peer reader advisory. It can also work for the computer connection! Patrick Jones says:

> Most of the pages featuring quality content, the best and most links, and the best designs are those put together by or with YAs. Librarians have long known the value of youth

participation, but it has never been more obvious than on YA Web pages. YAs involved in Web page projects can be the key to making the pages useful, interesting, and attractive—the goals for any Web page. By allowing youth to become involved, not only does the quality of the page increase, the value of the library's overall service to YAs is enhanced.

The YAs in libraries now, and the record numbers emerging, are the first wired generation. Computers are not tools or toys to them; they are everyday artifacts, like television sets. So librarians serving YAs need to work toward the smooth integration of the Internet with our traditional roles. We do this by following the same principles that have always guided YA librarians: access, participation, equality, and advocacy. With these beliefs as a launching pad, our expeditions into cyberspace and virtual YA areas will soar.[10]

Keeping this philosophy in mind, you and your teens need to decide what role they can play in making your teen Web page the best it can be for your particular community. There are various kinds of teen Web advisory groups, and each fills a particular need. Some produce newsletters that appear online, with areas for book, computer, and audiovisual media reviews; original teen writings; entertainment sources; chats; and of course, relevant library information. Some incorporate Weblogs, or blogs, which are Web spaces for reading, research, and especially writing. Others concentrate on connecting teens with helpful and entertaining links. Many more are a combination of these, some with unique slants. As with other kinds of teen library advisory groups, Web group teens need to figure out what they would like to do with their Web page and how they are going to get there.

You can advertise for members in the same fashion that you advertise for regular teen library advisory board members. Sometimes, the regular advisory group members are the same teens who produce the library's teen Web pages. Sometimes they are a separate group.

Kate Brown, the YA Librarian at the Benicia Public Library (www.ci.benicia.ca.us/library.html) in Benicia, California, works with a Teen Volunteers (TV) group and a TAB at her library. However, the Teen Volunteer Web Page, which features information for and about both groups, reflects the contributions of two teenage boys who work in conjunction with the library's Web master. These two teens do not belong to either TV or TAB, but rather work independently as a team on the Web page, gathering contributions by TAB for material to be put on the site. It is a unique method, but it works for them.[11]

As they have done in Benicia, you will need to decide how you and your teens want to proceed with establishing a group and getting your information online. If you are indeed setting up a brand-new group for this purpose, you will need to follow similar start-up procedures to those in chapter 2. Before you do, you will need to provide justification for the existence of your group and to get administrative approval. A previously organized and approved teen library advisory group will need to discuss the implications of developing a Web page as a new group activity.

HENNEPIN COUNTY LIBRARY
Minnetonka, Minnesota, www.hclib.org

Position: TeenLinks Teens Online

Description: This advisory team will support the Hennepin County Library (HCL) TeenLinks Web site. TeenLinks is created and maintained by staff of the Hennepin County Library with the help of Teens Online. TeenLinks offers dynamic and interactive resources specially designed for young adults ages 12–18 to use at home, in the library, or at school. Features include book, music, software, and game reviews, timely homework topics, and links to teen-recommended Web sites. TeenLinks is updated regularly to reflect the needs and interests of teens. Web sites are selected for TeenLinks following HCL collection development guidelines.

Duties:
1. Review TeenLinks Web pages and suggest improvements.
2. Suggest and review Web sites for TeenLinks.
3. Write book, game, software, or music reviews.
4. Develop and maintain Free Time section of TeenLinks.
5. Offer advice on marketing TeenLinks.
6. Other tasks as assigned.

Qualifications:
1. Grades 8–12, resident of suburban Hennepin County.
2. Have current e-mail address.
3. Basic knowledge of Windows and PC environment.
4. Basic knowledge of locating information on the Web.
5. Enthusiastic about providing ideas for TeenLinks.
6. Willingness to participate on a creative team.
7. Web design experience, a plus, but not necessary.

Commitment: Six months (November 2002–April 2003). Participate in monthly meetings and respond promptly to Teens Online e-mail communications.

Training/Supervision: Mentoring and supervision will be provided by eLibrary Youth Services Librarian and TeenLinks staff team.

In most libraries, teens will not be working independently on their Web pages.

Carol McCrossen, Reference/YA Librarian at the Moffat Library (www.rcls.org/moffat/tabmain.html) in Washingtonville, New York, says that their Teen Advisory Board had no teen members with the time or inclination to actually produce and maintain the teen library Web page. However, the teens still wanted input, so they came up with a plan. They would tell McCrossen what they wanted as far as links and text, and she would take care of the technical part of putting the Web pages together for them.[12]

At the Appleton Public Library (http://teen.apl.org/index.html) in Wisconsin, Colleen Rortvedt, Young Adult Assistant, says they have an active TAB that considers the teen Web page one of their main priorities. The Web page includes information about their TAB group, helpful teen-oriented links, details about upcoming programs and activities, and APL's *Teen Voices* writing and artwork showcase for original work by teens. However, the TAB members do not do any of the actual Web page design or posting. The teens submit their work to the library, and staff posts as much as possible. Due to network security issues, nonstaff is not allowed access to the library's Web page files. Consequently, this is a policy issue beyond the teens' and Rortvedt's control.[13]

If you are hoping to have teens involved in direct maneuvering of Web page production, you will want to check on your library's policies and procedures for handling such participation by teen advisory board members to see if it is permitted. Your library's Web master is the person who will know.

No matter what level of participation teens are allowed, it is important for them to coordinate their teen Web page efforts with not only the librarian advisor but also the library's Web master. The first thing any group, whether new or established, needs to do is to contact and set a meeting with their Web master. There is little point in organizing a teen Web advisory group, or extending an existing advisory board's goals to running a Web page, without the Web master's support and expertise. It is important to have the library's homepage contain links to the teen pages, and vice versa, and the Web master can provide guidance in arranging that. The Web master is a vital resource in assuring that the teen Web pages meet the library's Web policies and that procedures for adding, deleting, or changing information are followed.

According to Jen Maney, Web master at the City of Mesa Library in Arizona, here are things for librarians to think about and discuss with their Web masters when setting up a teen library advisory Web page group:

- What kind of page(s) do the teens want for their Web site?
- Will it allow interaction (via Webforms or polling software, for example)?
- Do they want features that require scripting or advanced Web design?
- Will it just be a matter of putting up text and pictures?

Maney also says it is important for the Web master to discuss the technical capabilities with the teens. Some Web sites might not be able to get any fancier than text, static graphics, and an e-mail link, so the teens will need to know what is technically possible before their ideas get too advanced for their Web master. By involving the Web master early, teens can avoid disappointment about not being able to provide advanced features on the site. Alternatively, they might be thinking conservatively (i.e., e-mail link) when the Web master is capable of a much more sophisticated Web design. Teens will need to know if they can use Flash, Webforms, and so on before they start designing their content. By working closely with the Web master, teens can make their Web page an outstanding resource for their peers and their library.

If your library already has an established teen advisory group which is taking on Web page duties, Maney encourages you to invite your Web master to one of their meetings. If you are starting a separate teen advisory group specifically to work on the

WEB SITE REVIEW CODE	
INFORMATIONAL	
5I	*Use this site for an A paper.*
1I	*Expect an F.*
RECREATIONAL	
5R	*Hours of endless fun.*
1R	*You'll fall asleep at the mouse.*
USABILITY	
5U	*Created by an experienced Webmaster.*
1U	*An amateur's page.*
GRADE LEVEL INTEREST	
M	*Middle School (defined as grades 6–8).*
J	*Junior High (defined as grades 7–9).*
S	*Senior High (defined as grades 10–12).*
A/YA	*Adult-marketed site recommended for YAs.*

teen Web page, ask your Web master to participate in the planning and organizing of the group. In the unusual case in which the teens themselves have permission to run their own library Web page with a teen Web master, you will still want to coordinate efforts with your library's adult Web master.[14]

You might be amazed at what a helpful and enthusiastic resource your library's Web master can be. Don't forget this important connection to developing an outstanding teen Web page!

So, now you are ready to start. But where *do* you start? Although there are a number of resources available that give advice on doing book reviews or developing teen programs, how do you approach the evaluation of Web sites with your teens?

Never fear! The Web surfers from the Central Rappahannock Regional Library (www.teenspoint.org) have come to your rescue. For their site reviews in *VOYA*'s "YA Clicks" column, they have devised a code to determine which are the best Web sites for teens, using review criteria that rates sites in informational, recreational, usability, and grade-level interest categories. The evaluation code is loosely based on the *VOYA* book review code, with options to rate a site from 1 to 5, 5 being the best. Web surfers also recommend evaluating a site's appearance, interactivity, and technical aspects in addition to the Web Site Review Code's basic criteria.[15] (Find the Web surfers' reviews in each February, June, and October issue of *VOYA*.)

The Teen Library Council members at the Huron Public Library (www.huron.lib.oh.us) in Ohio were asked to critique various teen pages using a scoring system for each site. The teens were set up in the computer lab with laptops (which they loved) and were asked to randomly visit the sites. Each site was given a score from 1 to 10 in various categories, with 1 equaling a "thumbs down," and 10 equaling a "thumbs up." Totals were based on the following criteria:

- What is your first impression?
- Is the site attractive?
- Rate the site's "coolness."
- Rate the site's use of graphics.
- Rate the site's rollovers.
- Is the site easy to navigate?
- Use one word to describe the site.
- Is the site interesting? Why? (List three reasons.)[16]

It is important to find an evaluation method that your teens enjoy using and that you will find helpful. Ask the teens to work with you in devising a system that will allow them to provide relevant critiques on the Web site content at your library.

You use the Web.
You know the best sites.
We want 'em.

Apply now for Charter Membership in the first Teen Web Group in Mesa's history.
Charter Membership November 2002-April 2003.

What you'll do

- Find and review Web sites that are cool, useful, and interesting to teens.
- Review music, movies, games, software and submit your reviews online.
- Help the library improve its Teen Web site and help us get the word out.
- Name the group and evaluate the first six months of membership.
- Most of the group's work will be done from home and submitted online on the library's Web site.

What you'll need

- Must have access to a computer (either PC or Mac) with Internet and e-mail.
- Must know how to use the Web and e-mail.

What you'll commit to

- Must commit to the first six months of the Charter Membership period, Nov 2002–Apr 2003.
- Must be able to attend meetings at the Main Library, 64 E. First St. in Mesa.
- Must respond promptly to all e-mails.
- Must complete assigned duties on time.
- Time commitment is 1–3 hours per week.

What to do next

- Fill out the application enclosed.
- Call Julie Bassett at 480-644-4638 to set up an interview.
- Bring application to your interview.

City of Mesa Library
64 E. First St.
Mesa, AZ 85201

Application for membership to the coolest Teen Group in town!
City of Mesa Library Teen Web Group

First Name: _____

Last Name: _____

Telephone: _____

E-mail (required): _____

What are your hobbies/interests? (please be as complete as possible)

_____

_____

_____

Tell us a little about your Web habits

1. How often do you use the Web? (check one)

___Every day   ___A few times a week
___Several times a week   ___A few times a month
___Rarely (less than 2 times a month)

2. What kinds of sites do you visit online?

Rate the following list using numbers 1–8 on the frequency of your visits (for example, #1 are the sites you visit most often, #8 the sites you visit least often).

___Online magazines   ___Game/software sites
___Music sites   ___Book sites
___Sports sites   ___Homework sites
___Movie sites   ___Other (please be specific)
_____

3. What else do you do online? (chat, etc.)

_____

_____

_____

Reference
Please give us the name of an adult (a coach, teacher, volunteer advisor, etc.) who we can call about your qualifications.

Name: _____

Phone number: _____

Relationship to you: _____

OTHER EVENTS, PROJECTS, AND ACTIVITIES

In addition to the high-caliber activities already presented, there are myriad ways that teen library advisory groups can sponsor and run interesting and successful programs, activities, and events. For example:

- The Youth Advisory Council members at the Kitchener Public Library (www.kpl.org) in Ontario, Canada, have worked on a special project the last few years. It is called "Celebrity Stacks," which involves the teens writing letters to over 150 Canadian celebrities, such as Sarah McLachlan and Shania Twain, asking them for their favorite book selections. By displaying the choices, YAC hopes to encourage teens to read things of which they might have been unaware. The display is changed regularly to reflect the newest replies from celebrities.[17] In addition to this project, YAC produces an online newsletter called *V.O.I.C.E.S.*, which stands for Views of Interested, Creative, and Enthusiastic Students, and contains book, music, video, and magazine reviews, plus their own poetry. They recently updated *V.O.I.C.E.S.* for their new Web site's "For Teens" section.[18]
- The Teen Advisory Board at the Bloomfield Township Public Library (www.btpl.org/e-teens.html) in Bloomfield Hills, Michigan, not only gets together to talk about good books, they do skits about them which are shown on Bloomfield Cable Television channel 15. Their skits received the Philo T. Farnsworth Award for excellence in community programming, first place in original teleplay.[19]
- Members of the Teen Advisory Board at the Coshocton Public Library (www.cplrmh.com) in Ohio posed for photos for the Teen Read Week display case with conversation balloons that they wrote themselves.[20]
- The Teen Advisory Committee at the Jervis Public Library (www.jervislibrary.org) in Rome, New York, had a float that they designed and built in the Honor America Days parade in July. The parade has been a tradition for over 30 years, but this was the first time that the library was represented. TAC handed out pencils with the library's name and address imprinted on them.[21]
- Many teen library advisors design, plan, and run their library's YA summer reading program. When Teen Advisory Board members at the Grace Dow Memorial Library (www.midland-mi.org/gracedowlibrary/ys/teenspot/html) in Midland, Michigan, took over the teen summer reading program there, they saw a 103 percent increase in participation.[22]
- Teen Advisory Group members at the Fairport Harbor Public Library (www.ncweb.com/org/fhslibrary) in Ohio planned and organized a dance as a fundraiser. They chose the date, made decorations, borrowed lava lamps and other items for a retro look, decided on a menu and prices, designed flyers and posters, set up and cleaned up. The dance was open to sixth to eighth graders, and high school–age TAG members served as chaperones for community service hours.[23]

- As a teen program, the Teen Advisory Board at the Northwest Library (www .worthingtonlibraries.org) in Columbus, Ohio, had a Habitat for Humanity volunteer come to speak about what their organization does, and how they make and sell birdhouses to benefit the families. The teens painted some birdhouses as part of the program. The next year, the teens decided to build doghouses and make dog biscuits for the local Humane Shelter.[24]

- When the Samuel L. Bossard Memorial Library (www.bossard.lib.oh.us/ index.html) of Gallia County in Ohio was having a problem with teens disrupting other library patrons, the StarBoard teen advisory group thought it would be a good idea to have a "peer-shadowing day." Instead of reprimanding a troubled teen, the library would invite that teen to the shadowing day. The idea did wonders for the library environment and involvement in the YA group.[25]

- The Rockingham Library Teen Advisory Council (TAC Team) members in Bellows Falls, Vermont, are big on providing a wide array of programming for their peers. They do a monthly Teen Movie Night & Chat and a Horror Movie Night, during which they sell refreshments. They actively promote books and reading through a Teen Book Club and a Tweens Book Club. In addition, TAC Team offers a variety of Something Cool After School programs on Thursdays, including an Anime/Manga Club, Detective Club, Cool Crafts, and Book Bits. With a grant from the Paul Post Foundation, they held a Cirque du Freak party, which included a Vampire Test, Karaoke Freak Show, Costume Contest, Trivia Bites, and "general dancing and mayhem." Based on the vampire book *Cirque du Freak* by Darren Shan (Little, Brown, 2001), the party's purpose was to reach out to at-risk, lower-level readers, and to have fun with books and reading.[26]

- The Teen Council at the Shaker Heights Public Library (www.shpl.lib.oh.us) in Ohio helped plan the library's new Teen Center, including participation in the process of hiring the Young Adult Librarian. They also helped select homework resource collection materials, magazines, newspapers, board games, and CD-ROMs. For the Teen Center grand opening, the Teen Council organized and hosted a pizza party and served as tour guides.[27]

- The Student Library Advisory Board at Highland High School in Bakersfield, California (www.kernhigh.org/bhs/default2.htm), with representatives from all grades, recommends favorite books, plans ways to promote the library, and raises scholarship money for graduating board members. The board went on graphic novel-buying sprees to build the library's collection. They hosted Expresso Yourself, a full-day celebration of student art, poetry, and music, while sipping espresso in the library. For the Mexican holiday El Día de los Muertos (Day of the Dead), they planned a library event with bilingual students.[28]

- At Johnston High School in Austin, Texas (www.main.org/johnstonhigh), where many students are bilingual and a high percentage are recent immigrants from Mexico, Banned Books Week became a year-long library project. Students created a Teen Advisory Board and book club, met each week to discuss books, posted book reviews, and found additional ways to promote reading. As a result, the library's Spanish-language book collection grew from 20 to more than 600 volumes, and the school was no longer designated as low-performing.[29]

- At the Oakland Public Library in California (http://oaklandlibrary .org), the Youth Leadership Council (YLC) is less "project oriented" than skills focused. They represent the city's youth library users at all the library's public functions and help plan and design new library teen spaces. They also include a unique element in their meeting agendas—interviewing library staff members. The teens learn about staff job responsibilities, and staff gets to know the YLC members as intelligent and respectful youth. The YLC has interviewed everyone from the part-time on-call Sunday librarian to the Foundation Director.[30]

- Galileo Academy of Science and Technology in San Francisco (www.galileosf.net) has two high-tech advisory groups: the School Library Advisory Committee (S.L.A.C.-ers), comprised of juniors and seniors; and Blog, Reading, and Technology Zealots (blogRaTZ), who are freshmen and sophomores. Besides promoting the library as "not uncool" and helping to run it, the S.L.A.C-ers are developing as the school's leadership base for promoting the Web page using Weblog technology. They tutor staff, work with the newspaper to develop blog publishing, host Weblogs for school work, and even produce a Chinese translation of the software user manuals. They have started the "Galileo Crash and Burn Café" series, a monthly event to attract nonlibrary users. Their first event was a teleconferencing link to the commemoration of the Galileo orbiter mission's landing. BlogRaTZ members attend lunch meetings twice monthly to learn everything they can about the library and its technology and domain of Weblogs, with the ultimate goal of defeating the S.L.A.C.-ers in the annual "SLAC-RAT Olympics."[31]

> **IDEAS, IDEAS, IDEAS!**
>
> Share these books with your teen advisory board members to get suggestions and planning details for projects, programs (including teen summer reading), group activities, and special events:
>
> Braun, Linda. *Technically Involved: Technology-Based Youth Participation Activities for Your Library.* Chicago: American Library Association, 2003.
>
> Edwards, Kirsten. *Teen Library Events: A Month-by-Month Guide.* Westport, Conn.: Greenwood Press, 2001.
>
> Honnold, RoseMary. *101+ Teen Programs That Work.* Neal-Schuman, 2002.
>
> Kan, Katherine. *Sizzling Summer Reading for Young Adults.* Chicago: American Library Association, 1998.
>
> King, Kevin A. R. *Give 'Em What They Want: Library Programming for Teens.* VOYA Guides Series. Lanham, Md.: VOYA Books/Scarecrow Press, forthcoming 2006.
>
> Leslie, Roger, and Patricia Potter Wilson. *Igniting the Spark: Library Programs that Inspire High School Patrons.* Englewood, Colo.: Libraries Unlimited, 2001.

There are many other ways that teens can provide helpful, meaningful, and fun programs, events, and activities for their libraries. Brainstorm with them, guide them, support them, and encourage them, and you will be amazed at what they can accomplish.

NOTES

1. Joyce Maltby, e-mail to TAGAD-L mailing list, 18 March 2002.
2. Cathy Norman, e-mail message to author, 7 August 2002.
3. Margaret A. Edwards, *The Fair Garden and the Swarm of Beasts* (New York: Hawthorn, 1969), 48–50.
4. Sarah Cofer, e-mail message to author, 20 September 2002.

5. Ali Turner, e-mail message to author, 2 October 2002.

6. Maureen Hartman, e-mail message to author, 3 October 2002.

7. "Teen Program," Minneapolis Public Library: Library Board Meeting Minutes, August 7, 2002. www.mpls.lib.mn.us/minutes/lb080702.asp (last accessed 13 September 2002).

8. Cathi Dunn MacRae, "YA Galley and Teens' Top Ten Books: Teen-Selected 'Best' Booklist to Debut for Teen Read Week 2003," *Voice of Youth Advocates* 25, no. 5 (December 2002): 334.

9. Rick Farrant, "Peer Review: City Teens Help Decide Top 10 Young Adult Books," *The Journal Gazette*, October 13, 2002, www.fortwayne.com/mld/journalgazette/4276170.htm (last accessed 5 November 2002).

10. Patrick Jones, *Connecting Young Adults and Libraries: A How-To-Do-It-Manual*, 2nd ed. (New York: Neal-Schuman, 1998), 354.

11. Kate Brown, e-mail message to author, 24 September 2002.

12. Carol McCrossen, e-mail message to author, 9 September 2002.

13. Colleen Rortvedt, e-mail message to author, 5 September 2002.

14. Jennifer Maney, e-mail message to author, 10 September 2002.

15. Rebecca Purdy, "YA Clicks: Introducing the Web Surfers' Review Code," *Voice of Youth Advocates* 25, no. 4 (October 2002): 262–63.

16. Carol Barcus, e-mail to TAGAD-L mailing list, 17 November 2003.

17. "For Youth: Youth Advisory Council," *Kitchener Public Library* 2002, www.kpl.org/fy_yac.shtml (last accessed 12 November 2002).

18. Rebecca Hine, e-mail message to author, 12 November 2002.

19. "E-Teens," *Bloomfield Township Public Library 2002*, www.btpl.org/e-teens/e-teens.html (last accessed 6 August 2002.)

20. RoseMary Honnold, e-mail to TAGAD-L mailing list, 2 October 2002.

21. Lisa Matte, e-mail to TAGAD-L mailing list, 1 October 2002.

22. Rebecca Hastings, e-mail message to author, 2 October 2002.

23. Cathy Norman, e-mail to TAGAD-L mailing list, 4 November 2002.

24. Cindy Rider, e-mail message to author, 17 September 2002.

25. Jae Trewartha, e-mail message to author, 15 October 2002.

26. Samantha Maskell, e-mail message to author, 15 October 2003.

27. "Shaker Heights Public Library," in *Excellence in Library Services to Young Adults: The Nation's Top Programs*, ed. Mary K. Chelton (Chicago: American Library Association, 2000), 71–72.

28. Whelan, Debra Lau, "SLJ's People to Watch: Ten Leaders Who Are Making a Difference in School and Public Libraries," *School Library Journal* 49, no. 6 (June 2003): 53.

29. Whelan, "SLJ's People to Watch," 54.

30. Anthony Bernier, "Oakland Public Library: Youth Leadership Council," *YALSA TAGS Spotlights* 2003, www.ala.org/Content/NavigationMenu/YALSA/TAGS/Spotlights/oct03tagspotlight.htm (last accessed 1 December 2003).

31. Patrick Delaney, Weblog message to author, 19 November 2003. www.galileoweb.org/galileoLibrary/SLACerHistory.

5

Teen Representation on Adult Library Boards and Other Community Boards

BREAKING DOWN BARRIERS AND OVERCOMING OBSTACLES

It is rare to find teenagers appointed to serve on adult library advisory boards, or any community advisory boards. There are numerous reasons for this lack of representation. However, many adult advocates for teens and teens themselves are working hard to change this situation. Slowly, change is coming about and more and more teens are being appointed to serve on adult boards.

Why is teen representation to adult boards such a difficult situation to achieve? Some library and city administrators are simply unaware of the concept of having a teen on the board and have not even considered the benefits. Bringing the idea to their attention, using examples of libraries with successful teen representation, and developing a well-planned proposal might help them to envision the positive results. It is worth asking to see if such representation might be an option.

Other library and city administrators might acknowledge that teen representation is important, but they have not taken action to incorporate it. A logical first step would be for the teen services department to establish a library teen advisory board if none yet exists. Establishing such a teen board could be a stepping-stone to attaining teen representation on an adult library board. In communities where a teen library advisory board *does* already exist, the teens themselves, with their librarian advisor's guidance, could be instrumental in taking action and proposing their representation to the adult board. (In a few circumstances, teen representation to the adult library board actually has come first, *before* establishing a group of teen library advisors!)

MESA'S STORY: THE TERM LENGTH STUMBLING BLOCK

A big stumbling block can also be the required term commitment. The situation can get fairly complex, as illustrated by the situation at the City of Mesa Library.

Starting in 1977, YAAC Representatives served on our library board as nonvoting members. Then, 18 years later, our Library Director decided it was time to make that YAAC Rep a voting member. The girl who had been voted YAAC Rep by the YAAC members that summer was in eighth grade, so there was no problem with her accepting the three-year appointment. Each year, the YAAC members approved her reappointment to the library board, and she continued to serve. When she was in eleventh grade, she was again reelected as YAAC Rep and reappointed to the library board. She served the first two years of her reappointment through twelfth grade, and that is where the problem began.

When this YAAC Rep graduated from high school, she was 18 years old and that fall began attending college locally. She still had a year left of her official library board reappointment, and since she was still a teen, our Director expected her to continue as the excellent representative she was for that age group. However, since she had "graduated" from our YAAC group, a new YAAC Rep was elected that summer.

Now there was the former YAAC Rep serving out her term representing teens on the Board, but no longer being the "official" YAAC Rep. The newly elected YAAC Rep began attending the library board meetings as well, to present the YAAC/YA report and participate in discussion, but was now by default once again a nonvoting member.

Recently, we came up with a plan to reinstate voting status for our YAAC Rep. Since the library board term must be three years, we decided that the YAAC Rep must be in tenth grade or younger when he or she is elected and accepts the appointment. This does limit who can run and when, but it is a necessary concession to regain voting status. One good thing is that we have plenty of qualified YAAC members, so nominating competent ones who are in the right age group is not a problem for our council. When a position becomes vacant on the Board, our current tenth grader teen Rep will be recommended to the Mayor for appointment. If the three-year term or other required term length is your stumbling block too, you might want to consider a similar solution.

TEENS AND YOUTH ADVOCATES WORKING TOGETHER FOR MAJOR CHANGE

It is against the law, in some states, to have teens with voting representation on adult nonprofit boards. The reasoning behind these laws is concern that those under 18 could be held liable in potentially complicated legal situations. Another concern involves possible adult manipulation of youth to secure votes. Also, minors with a vote could possibly threaten the validity of contracts or decisions made by the boards.

Forty-three states leave the decision whether or not to allow under-18 representation up to the organizations themselves—the laws in those states are silent on the issue. Also, Michigan and New York recently changed their laws to allow teenage board members to serve and vote under most circumstances. However, a few states retain laws on their books prohibiting younger persons from serving on adult boards: Florida, Georgia, Nevada, New Jersey, and Pennsylvania.

In Pennsylvania, teens themselves are actively working to amend the law so that those 16 or 17 years of age can be permitted to serve as voting members on boards of directors.[1] Because of the political climate in the state, the teens decided to pursue lowering the age incrementally. How teens themselves got involved in pursuing this change in legislation is inspiring and serves to illustrate the dedication and maturity of young adults allowed to work together for a common goal with the support of adult advocates.

In 2000, Teen.TAPS (Teenagers Taking Action to Power Solutions) was started. The group was formed "by teens for teens" to serve as a youth resource center for the Lehigh Valley. They have offered and participated in many trainings, workshops, and conferences for youth and adults to promote teens serving in organizational capacities. Their mission is to advocate for youth empowerment and youth involvement within the world community as well as to develop the youth voice within Lehigh Valley. When they became aware of the hindrance to teens serving on adult nonprofit boards, they took action:

> There is a Pennsylvania state law (15 PA. CONS. STAT. ANN ßß 5722, 5103) that prohibits persons under the age of 18 years from voting on boards of directors of organizations and associations. Teen.TAPS feels that this law fails to take into account the main purpose of many of these organizations, which is to serve youth. Therefore, it is inadequately serving them by not allowing them to play a role in the decision-making effort. This bias against young people only inhibits their empowerment. We work to see more teenagers become active members within their communities and we find that this law directly represses our ability to promote this valuable goal.[2]

Teen.TAPS recognizes the need for *balance on boards*, which includes serious representation from the teen age group. Through meeting with lawyers and legislators, producing a video for their cause, and giving promotional speeches and other presentations, they are effectively working toward amending the law that is an obstacle in their state. Their impressive work can set an example for any community group, including libraries, in seeking and permitting teens to have a voice on adult boards.

You can find out more about Teen.TAPS by contacting Lehigh Valley Asset Builders, 2200 Avenue A, Third Floor, Bethlehem, Pennsylvania 18017-2189.

SUCCESSFUL TEEN REPRESENTATION COMING CLOSE, WITHOUT THE VOTE

As previously noted, a young adult representative on an adult library board is a fairly unique occurrence. When such representation exists, teens have an opportunity to speak up regarding library issues, provide teen perspectives, make proposals to support teen library functions, share information about recent teen library activities, and ideally have an equal vote with other Board members. In Mesa, the Representative attends each monthly board meeting and gives a current report on the Council as well as on programs and events in the Young Adult section. In other libraries, teens serve in similar capacities.

At the Neill Public Library in Pullman, Washington (www.neill-lib.org), the Youth Representative on the library board is chosen through a process of submitting an application reflecting school and community activities and interests, two references (one personal and one from school), and a 50-word statement as to why the applicant wants to serve on the library board. The applicant must be in eighth to tenth grade and be willing to make a two-year commitment.

WANT TO FIND OUT MORE?

Adults and teens working together to advocate for teen representation and participation in their schools and community organizations is becoming an important trend. There are a number of Web sites filled with information about youth involvement, youth activism, youth leadership, and much more! Explore these sites to discover this wealth of resources to justify, support, and build your teen library advisory roles, and to gain meaningful teen representation on your library board. By contributing information to these sites and participating in the discussion groups, you will also help spread the word that school and public libraries are a vital part of the youth participation movement.

At the Table: Youth Voices in Decision-Making: www.atthetable.org

Campaign for Meaningful Student Involvement: www.studentinvolvement.net

The Freechild Project: www.freechild.org

Youth Activism Project: www.youthactivism.com

Youth On Board: www.youthonboard.org

The Youth Representative is not a voting member, but he or she participates in discussions and represents the teen and youth constituency in terms of feedback on and ideas for services.

The Youth Rep is also part of the Youth Services Advisory Board, which is a six- to eight-member constituency-based group (daycare, public schools, private schools, home schoolers, international families, youth, volunteers, etc.) that has met three times a year to review and reflect on services being offered—a tremendous resource for staff in terms of suggestions and ideas.[3]

The first Youth Representative, a long-time patron at Neill Public Library, was appointed in 1991 and served for five years. When he left for college, the Youth Services Librarian developed an invitation for other teens to apply. The Youth Council was formed from the four eligible applicants, with one serving as Youth Representative at the library board meetings. The Youth Council met once a month from September to May with an agenda that included sharing news of interest from the library staff and lots of youth input on what the library should add to collections. The nature of the group changed each year depending on the youths attending, and although it disbanded for a short time and is being reformed, there has continuously been a Youth Representative to the library board since the position's inception. The current Representative is in her second year.[4]

The Stanislaus County Library in California (www.stanislauslibrary.org) has a provision for an at-large member of the library's Youth Advisory Council to be chosen by that group to represent them on the library board, although the position is nonvoting. This situation varies year by year, however, and there is not always a teen representative. Still, the library does provide some opportunity for a teen to serve according to their library board membership rules.[5]

At the Montgomery County Public Library in Maryland (www.mont.lib.md.us), there is a very active Friends of the Library group. Their purpose is to support public library service in Montgomery County, including providing funds for library programs or library publications, matching funds for grants, sponsoring author luncheons, and more. They advise the county government on library services and testify at budget hearings. One position on the Friends of the Library Board is for a teen serving as the nonvoting Student Trustee.

In this capacity, the teen board member has a voice and can make a difference. The student currently serving has goals to work on community service projects with other teens, increase teen awareness of the opportunities provided by public libraries and the Friends group, improve educational opportunities for underprivileged teens, and start a variety of book clubs. She actively seeks input from fellow teens through the library's Web page (www.mont.lib.md.us/cyberteen/teenrep.asp) so she can serve as a link to allow teens to express their ideas and participate in their library, as well as realize the potential the library has in helping them achieve their goals.[6]

This type of representation to a Friends group is another way teens can have a voice through board service. If you have not been successful getting a teen representative on your regular library board, you might want to seek a position on your adult Friends board. Such service may provide an excellent example for your library board to see how well a teen is able to contribute at this level, and perhaps influence them to appoint a teen to their board as well. It might also enable you to attain representation on *both* boards!

A teen advisory group in Bloomington, Indiana, has been active since 1991. The Monroe County Public Library (www.monroe.lib.in.us/home.html) cosponsors this group, called the Bloomington Teen Council (www.monroe.lib.in.us/teens/bloomington_teen.html), which functions as a multipurpose advisory board for the county public library, city parks and recreation department, and the city volunteer network. The Council is also available as a one-time teen focus group or advisory board for any local business, agency, or group seeking teen input.

In addition, each year the Council acts as a grant-making board and awards money to teen-driven community service projects. It is one of the few grant makers that do

You're Invited!

Wednesdays   3:30 pm

The Bloomington Teen Council is an informal group that serves as a community advisory board — Available to let Bloomington know teen's opinions on...just about anything!

Eat, Talk, Have Fun, Give Advice, and Decide how to give away $2000 for community projects. Interested? Bring a drink and get involved.

Teen Council is your chance to talk about issues & voice your opinion.

- Give Advice to local groups
- Sponsor grants for teen-run community projects
- Meet other teens with ideas and opinions.

Call the Library for meeting dates
349-3228

Co-sponsored by Bloomington Volunteer Network, Bloomington Parks & Recreation, and the Monroe County Public Library.

not require projects to be supported by official nonprofits—any three teens with a good idea are eligible!

As with any other teen advisory group, Bloomington Teen Council members find participation affords them an opportunity for positive action in their community, while allowing them a chance to meet with other teens, to eat snacks, and to have fun.

The Bloomington Teen Council is a prime example of how an entire group of teens can serve as representatives together for adult organizations *and* for their peers. In this regard, the Teen Council worked with the local Community Service Council to create and sponsor community discussion focusing upon teens officially serving on adult boards in the future, although this kind of representation has not been achieved yet. However, due to the structure and function of this teen advisory group, their voices are still heard clearly by adult groups, organizations, and government agencies throughout the community.[7]

WHERE VOTING TEEN REPRESENTATION IS WORKING

Glendale Public Library (www.glendaleaz.com/Library) and the City of Glendale in Arizona demonstrate how young adults *can* achieve individual teen representation to adult boards. In 1999, Glendale held a Youth Town Hall meeting. One of the issues on the agenda was respect. The teens at the meeting stated they wanted more say in the boards of the city. A group of people looked at all the official committee boards of Glendale and decided that teens would be most useful working with Parks and Recreation and on the library board. The group took their ideas to the Mayor and City Council, and the Mayor liked them. He started a Mayor's Youth Advisory Council and a Parks and Recreation Youth Advisory Council. An ordinance was then passed to raise the library board membership from seven to nine, designating that the two new board members would be teens.

Currently, two boys serve on the regular Library Board of the Glendale Public Library. They have *full voting privileges* and are fairly vocal at the meetings. They also participate heavily in and attend all of the Teen Advisory Board meetings held in the library.[8]

Likewise in Arizona, the Chandler Public Library's Council of Teen Advisors (www.teenmatrix.org) has a representative on the Friends of the library board. In that capacity, the CTA representative also serves as a *voting* member.[9]

Here are more examples of teen voting representation working. In fall 2001, the Mayor of Waupaca, Wisconsin, appointed a Teen Trustee to their adult library board. Her input from the teen perspective was extremely valuable. In 2002, she graduated from high school in the spring and resigned from the library board in August, expressing how much she had learned through the experience. As a Teen Trustee, she was allowed to vote equally with the other library board members, and she also provided teen representation on the library's Planning and Policy Committee. After her resignation, the Mayor appointed another teen as her replacement, also a senior in high school. Because of the success of the Teen Trustee position on the library board, other boards in the city are considering the addition of youth representatives.[10]

At the Oakland Public Library in California (http://oaklandlibrary.org), a teen member of the Youth Leadership Council (YLC) serves as a voting member on the Library Advisory Commission. In this capacity, the YLC representative has had the opportunity to vote on such pressing issues as the library's public position relative to the USA Patriot Act posture.[11] YLC representation does not stop with participation on the Library Advisory Commission, however. Oakland Public Library's objectives are to offer all YLC members hands-on lessons in participatory civic citizenship and to develop them to serve and represent the library as a junior speakers bureau. For example, YLC makes public appearances at the opening of new library facilities, leads small group discussions during new library teen space design reviews, serves on a panel to select the architects for a future library building, introduces speakers at library programs, and represents Oakland for State Legislative Day.

Director of Teen Services and YLC advisor Anthony Bernier warns that teens need to be allowed to think and speak for themselves when they serve as representatives. He says:

When we say we "prepare" YLC members to represent the library, we aim at a very modest goal. The YLC members learn as much as we can teach about what's going on. But when they represent the library, they do so as individuals, not as handpicked tokens telling adults what they want to hear. Indeed, when we went to the state capitol for State Legislative Day, we briefed and reviewed a few notes on the train. But when they entered officials' offices, they did so with me out in the hall. I watched their book bags. One of the YLC members started passionately advocating for *school libraries*. And we've never talked about school libraries![12]

GAINING SUPPORT AND APPROVAL

As you can see, teen representation that extends beyond the scope of a regular teen library advisory group *can* be accomplished. The avenues to approach such representation are varied, as illustrated by the examples in this chapter. However, the first step must always be support and buy-in from library and other community administrators. Once they observe the positive results of teen input and feedback, they will most likely be convinced of the benefits teen representation affords.

This support and buy-in must be accompanied by respect for the teens on boards and the delegation of equal responsibilities to their adult counterparts. Paralleling the comments of Anthony Bernier, Katie Claussen, cofounder of Teen.TAPS, says:

Whether in a board setting, or any setting involving young people, how do we avoid the tendency to include but not really consider youth input? It's easier said than done, I know. A private high school tried to put youth on their board quite recently, but ended up giving them menial tasks and a limited voice. Moving beyond tokenism means all voices will be heard. Preconceptions aside, it's an issue of democracy and diversity of beliefs. While many organizations, governments, and initiatives have focused on the goal of getting young people into decision-making positions, these positions are only as powerful as the constituencies behind them.[13]

With this philosophy in mind, when you need specific justification to get a teen advisory board member serving in even a nonvoting capacity on your adult library board, you might want consider the following:

- Teens will someday (soon!) be adult library users and supporters. By giving them a voice now, when they are adolescents, they will learn a great deal about their library and continue to use/promote/support it into adulthood.
- Adults can benefit from the candor and fresh opinions of youth. Teens are a large and important part of library clientele, so hearing their viewpoints is important.
- Showing the community that teens have a voice and that the library appreciates and respects them goes a long way in elevating the status of teens.
- By giving teens a real say on their library board, teens are demonstrating firsthand Positive Youth Development in action.
- Through serving on adult library boards, teens can gain support for ideas that will help bring others teens to the library and promote teen reading.

Strive toward the goal of having teens as *voting* library board participants, even if that is not the original role designated. Full representation and a true voice means teen participants not only get to express their *opinions*, they also serve as active *decision makers*— and that means having a vote! Ask questions, provide justification, stand up for your teens, and you might be pleasantly surprised when your administrators and community leaders decide that *voting* teen representation is a good idea for *your* library and community. (See the sample invitation and the position description/application form for a Board of Trustees youth representative at the end of this chapter.[14])

INVITATION TO APPLY
for the Position of

YOUTH REPRESENTATIVE

to the Board of Trustees

NEILL PUBLIC LIBRARY
Pullman, Washington
(www.neill-lib.org)

The Youth Representative to the Board of Trustees of Neill Public Library serves in an advisory capacity on matters brought for discussion and decision by the Board in open sessions. As an ex officio member, the Youth Representative does not have voting power, but is asked to provide the Board with a young person's perspective on issues.

The Youth Representative is appointed by the Board for a two-year term; he or she is expected to attend all regularly scheduled meetings of the Board, which meets at 4 p.m. on the second Wednesday of each month. This person is also encouraged to attend other occasional special functions involving the Board.

Serving as the Youth Representative to the Board provides an opportunity to participate and learn about a policy-making group, the city government of Pullman, and the vision for library service in our community. It provides excellent experience for being an involved citizen, a leader, and a lifelong learner.

Qualities sought in individuals interested in the Youth Representative position include some experience with the public library; the ability to express oneself clearly and directly; a desire to improve public library services to the youth or our community; and an open mind.

Applicants should be in grades 7, 8, 9, or 10; they need to be attending Pullman schools or be residents of Pullman and should be willing to serve the full term if chosen.

Applications for the position will be accepted until Tuesday, October 9.

Application forms are available at the Lincoln Middle School and Pullman High School libraries and at Neill Public Library.

POSITION DESCRIPTION AND APPLICATION FOR
YOUTH REPRESENTATIVE

Board of Trustees
NEILL PUBLIC LIBRARY
Pullman, Washington
(www.neill-lib.org)

The Youth Representative to the Board of Trustees of Neill Public Library serves in an advisory capacity on all matters brought for discussion and decision by the Board. As an ex officio member, the Youth Representative does not have voting power but is asked to provide the Board with a young person's perspective on issues.

The Youth Representative is appointed by the Board for a two-year minimum term; he or she is expected to attend all regularly scheduled meetings of the Board, which meets at 4 p.m. on the second Wednesday of each month, and is encouraged to attend other special functions involving the Board, which are only occasional.

Serving as the Youth Representative to the Board provides an opportunity to participate in and learn about a policy-making group, the city government of Pullman, and the vision for library service in our community. It provides excellent experience for being an involved citizen, a leader, and a lifelong learner.

Qualities being sought in individuals interested in the Youth Representative position include some experience as a young person with a public library; the ability to express oneself clearly and cogently; a desire to improve public services to youth in our community; and an open mind.

APPLICATION FOR YOUTH SERVICES REPRESENTATIVE

Name_____

Address_____

Phone_____ Year in School_____

Activities/Interests_____

References:
Teacher_____

Friend_____

In 50 words or less, please state why you are interested in the Youth Services Representative position on the Board of Trustees for Neill Public Library:

NOTES

1. "Senate Passes Waugh's Teen.TAPS Legislation," *Senator Mike Waugh, Legislative Press Release, April 25, 2002,* http://waugh.pasenategop.com/whatsnew2.htm#teentaps (last accessed 2 December 2002).

2. Katie Claussen, *Teen.TAPS: Teenagers Taking Action to Power Solutions,* promotional video, 2001.

3. Nancy Collins-Warner, e-mail message to author, 15 May 2002.

4. Beverly Poole, e-mail message to author, 16 September 2002.

5. Vanessa Czopek (Director of Stanislaus County Library), in discussion with the author, 2 September 2002.

6. "Friends of the Library," *Montgomery County Public Library,* www.mont.lib.md.us/getinvolved/friends2.asp (last accessed 18 September 2002).

7. Dana Burton, e-mail message to author, 7 August 2002.

8. Kristin Fletcher-Spear, e-mail message to author, 5 September 2002.

9. Phyllis Saunders, e-mail message to author, 9 January 2002.

10. Peg Burington, e-mail message to author, 22 October 2002.

11. Anthony Bernier, e-mail message to author, 3 December 2003.

12. Anthony Bernier, "Oakland Public Library: Youth Leadership Council," *YALSA TAGS Spotlights* 2003, www.ala.org/Content/NavigationMenu/YALSA/TAGS/Spotlights/oct03tagspotlight.htm (last accessed 1 December 2003).

13. Katie Claussen, "Youth Voices, Life Choices" (speech presented at Unleashing the Power of Youth and Community Potential Conference, Allentown, Pennsylvania, October 14, 2002).

14. Nancy Collins-Warner, "Invitation to Apply for the Position of Youth Representative to the Board of Trustees, Neill Public Library" and "Position Description and Application for Youth Representative, Neill Public Library," no date.

6 The Perks of Being a Teen Library Advisory Board Member

Teens who volunteer for library advisory boards are seeking a variety of rewards. The rewards vary from teen to teen. Some join to find friends, especially those, like them, who enjoy books and reading. I have had cheerleaders, football players, band members, drama club fanatics, and more as members through the years—members who shared a common interest in literature but found it hard to hook up with kindred souls. These often make up the core of teen library advisory board members. However, there are other reasons teens join library advisory groups.

Earlier, I addressed the issue of positive youth development and how teen library advisory boards can help to meet that goal. Some teens join library advisory groups to fulfill community service or service-learning requirements. You will find yourself filling out and signing forms for this kind of student participation in your group. Don't ever feel that these members are less sincere than other members because they have a secondary purpose for joining. Welcome them and support them in the work they do for you to attain their special credits. After all, these teens had their choice of places to volunteer for such credit, and they chose your advisory group for it. This is a perk to promote! Encourage teens who need community service or service-learning hours to devote that time to your group. You will be surprised at how dedicated these teens can be, and signing their forms truly takes a minimum of time.

Similarly, some teens are concerned about having the most interesting and well-rounded college application forms possible. Membership in a library teen advisory board looks good and helps an applicant to stand out. You will have many members including their service when they are anticipating college admission. Likewise, you will also have members seeking scholarships and completing special activity applications such as those for foreign exchange programs. You may be asked to fill out forms analyzing your members' worthiness for such programs and activities. Occasionally, you will be asked to be a reference on employment applications and sometimes you will actually be called by phone to assess the qualifications of your board members. These requests take a little more of your time, but members expect you to assist them in return for their service. In a situation where you are unable to recommend a teen wholeheartedly, or when the time you have known him or her is too short to adequately assess abilities, you might want to simply give the teen's dates of advisory board service and mention duties performed. You will need to consider such requests for recommendations or references on a case-by-case basis. In some circumstances, you might need to level with a member whom you do not feel able to serve as a reference.

Speaking of service, all teens on your library council are providing a vital service to your library. Sometimes the service is a reward in itself! Teens who get funding to go on a book-buying trip to build the Young Adult collection, or who march in a parade or write and perform a play for small children, find their roles satisfying. Still, it is important to find ways to say thanks regularly and assure them they are doing something worthwhile and appreciated. The more you do and say, the better!

One way teens appreciate being rewarded is by getting special T-shirts. Teens love T-shirts! You can, of course, use the shirts as a reward for membership, but they also double as a promotional device. If you have a talented artist in your group, encourage him or her to design a shirt for the group. If you are lucky enough to have more than one, hold a contest among your members to design a new T-shirt. Members can vote for the winning design and you can offer a bookstore gift certificate to the artist whose work is selected. If your group lacks artists willing and able to design a T-shirt, as my group did last year, think outside the box. The advisory board could hold a design contest among young adults in your community and choose a winner. You might have a library or community graphics person willing to develop a design for you. However you approach it, be sure the teens themselves have input in the final selection of the design and wording.

Ask your teens about sizes before you order any T-shirts. A few years ago, everyone wanted huge sizes because big and baggy T-shirts were "in." Now, the smaller sizes that fit more snugly are popular. Your teens can advise you on what sizes to get so you don't end up with a stack of shirts no one will wear! Order extras anticipating new members. Also, be sure to get a few plus sizes and some extra smalls, as teens come in all shapes and sizes and you don't want anyone to be left out or embarrassed.

How do you fund all those T-shirts? Perhaps your Friends group would be willing to donate the funds, as ours does. A local business might be willing to help if they can get a small plug on the shirts. You might budget for the shirts through your programming or supply lines. Your teens might also hold a fund-raiser of some sort to get money for shirts. This final idea is a last resort, as the goal is to provide a special perk as a reward. However, if it is the only way to fund T-shirts, you might consider it.

We recently purchased 75 T-shirts, and the total cost with preparing the screen plus tax came to less than $500. The more shirts you have made, the less expensive it is. If your library has branches with individual teen advisory boards, it would be cost-effective to have shirts designed and purchased for the whole system. Another cost-effective idea might be for neighboring teen library advisory boards to work together in designing and funding T-shirts.

Neighboring teen library teen advisory groups can also be perks for one another. Plan joint meetings occasionally, city to city, town to town, or branch to branch. Invite other local boards to come to your programs. Send them flyers and personalized invitations via regular mail or e-mail. E-mail allows you to contact each member of neighboring groups individually, if librarians share their teens' e-mail list.

E-mail can be used for other perks. Use it to send special thank-you messages to your teens or to send an e-card when warranted. Teens love to get e-mail!

Food is always a reward for your teen members. Have food at meetings and special events whenever possible. (See chapter 2.)

Another way to reward your teens is to give them a special membership card. In Mesa, our teens receive a YAAC card that allows them a 45-day book checkout period (compared to 3 weeks for other library users), 3 hours daily of library in-house Internet usage (compared to 1 hour), and no library fines. The last two are the same perks adult library volunteers receive.

YAAC members are included in the roster of all library volunteers and are treated as such. Each year, when the library's Volunteer Luncheon is held, YAAC members are invited to attend and are honored along with adult and other teen volunteers. You might want to provide volunteer perks in similar fashion to your teen library advisory group. Think of unique ways to make your teens feel appreciated.

Another way to honor your advisory board teens is to hold special events just for them. Each year, we provide a volunteer pizza party for our teens at the end of the summer, to thank them for all their hard work on the summer reading program. Our YAAC members meet all summer as well as during the school year, so they are included in the pizza party, its fun activities, and door prizes.

When school starts in the fall, we hold an event just for YAAC and their families. It is called YAAC, Live!, and it is an opportunity for parents and other family members to meet me—the advisor—and the other YAAC teens. It gives me a chance to share information about YAAC, its programs and activities, and to publicly acknowledge the contributions of members. During the program, outgoing YAAC officers are introduced and new ones are installed. The program is turned over to the

YOUNG ADULT ADVISORY COUNCIL 2003 MEMBERSHIP

NAME _____

ADVISOR _____

YOUTH SERVICES DEPT.
CITY OF MESA LIBRARY

Here is the YAAC membership card that teens receive at the City of Mesa Library. The card allows special checkout perks and is renewable each calendar year.

officers and members, who tell about accomplishments. Each member chooses his or her favorite book of the year and presents a three-minute book review. Graduated members are thanked and honored with the presentation of names on the updated "YAAC Plaque," which hangs in the Teen Realm area of the library. The updated scrapbook is also presented, then members and their families have cake (appropriately topped with "Thanks, YAAC!") and punch and a chance to chat. This kind of program is a great way for parents to feel comfortable with and informed about a program in which their teen is involved. (See YAAC, Live! invitation at the end of this chapter.)

Social events beyond the library are perks that develop a cohesive group. Our YAAC goes out to a "meal & movie" two or three times a year. Picnics in parks, trips to zoos, parties at teens' or advisors' houses are also great outside social events. These events usually require some of your own time and money (teens can do Dutch treats or potlucks), but they are worth it! Not only do the teens get to know and enjoy one another better, but they also get closer to you. You will need to find out your city's and library's policy on such outings and if permission forms might be required.

When you go to conferences, review books for journals, or have an opportunity to work with publishers and book distributors, be on the lookout for giveaway books. Teens love to get free books, and your teen library advisory group is a perfect forum to promote and hand out books. Encourage your teens to read the books, share them, and write reviews on them. Let them know that they may keep the books. Our policy on YAAC is that the first reader of a giveaway copy is its owner. Teens are asked to put their names on the inside front page of such books. They are also asked to share them until everyone who wants to read them gets a chance. Then they may take them home for keeps. Also remember that books make great "special service" rewards and door prizes.

You can probably think of additional ways to reward and support your teens. Ask them for ideas. Find out what other groups are doing. (Hint: Chapters 7 and 8 feature a number of active public and school library groups, and each one describes how they reward their teen members.) Then incorporate those ideas into your planning.

Having a teen library advisory group is a two-way street, and providing perks is an important way to thank your teens for their contributions. Everyone likes to hear they have done a good job and that their work is appreciated, teens included. They enjoy having their advisors brag about them. They like being treated as "special." Be sure to reward your teens thoughtfully in both words and actions, and you will see an even more dedicated response from them.

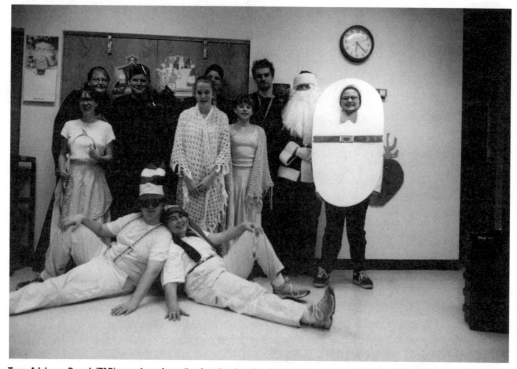

Teen Advisory Board (TAB) members from the Apache Junction Public Library pose following their performance in the play, "Mother Goose's Christmas Surprise," presented at the library in December 2001. (Photo Credit: Liz Burks.)

Youth Advisory Committee (YAC) from the Jervis Public Library stuffs bags for the Books for Babies project. (Photo Credit: Lisa Matte.)

At the Basehor Community Library, the Teen Advisory Group (TAG) was challenged during a meeting to go into the stacks and find a book that says "who they are." They came up with everything from *Winnie the Pooh* to *Webster's Unabridged Dictionary.* (Photo Credit: Jenne Laytham.)

Young Adult Advisory Council (YAAC) members from the City of Mesa Library check out the new book selections for the Teens' Top Ten/YA Galley Project. (Photo Credit: Diane Tuccillo.)

YAAC members from the City of Mesa Library show off their cool T-shirts. (Photo Credit: Diane Tuccillo.)

Please join us to meet and learn about
City of Mesa Library's
Y.A.A.C.
(Young Adult Advisory Council)

Find out what YAAC is all about,
hear reviews of our favorite books of the year,
help us give special honors to our members,
and celebrate the installation of our new officers.

Thursday, August 8, 2002
7–8:30 p.m.
City of Mesa Library
Main Branch
Youth Activity Room
64 East First Street

Refreshments will be served.

7 These Groups Work!

Throughout the country, there are public libraries of all types and sizes that include young adults on advisory boards as an important part of library operations. There are many kinds of teen advisory boards, and each has its own function and purpose. Some include their members among official library volunteers. Some have officers and are run like a club, others decide that leadership will be limited to individuals taking charge of specific projects only. Some groups meet monthly, some twice a month, some on an as-needed basis. Some are literature oriented, some program oriented, some computer oriented, and some a combination of all these things. It is up to each group and librarian advisor to come up with a mission and game plan for their own community.

There are outstanding teen advisory councils that have been active for many years as well as much newer groups that seemed to start off with a bang and never looked back. All these groups have the important feature of a dedicated leader(s) who inspires the teens, and teens who have been encouraged to take their jobs as teen advisors seriously. When teens are respected and given a chance to have a voice in their libraries, it is amazing what can happen!

What follows are some examples of outstanding groups that have taken their jobs to heart and have flourished. You will find wonderful examples from these group descriptions and numerous ideas for starting or developing your own group.

Teen Advisory Board (TAB)

Apache Junction Public Library, Apache Junction, Arizona
www.ajcity.net/libtop1.htm
Advisor: Liz Burks, Youth Services Librarian

The Apache Junction Public Library's Teen Advisory Board started with 13 members in 1992. Currently, the group has 19 members, with a 2-to-1 ratio of girls to boys, and they meet monthly. Apache Junction has a population of 32,524, and the library has no branches. It is significant that TAB attracts such a large group of teens for a community of that size.

Teens who have performed well as Library Team members (specifically, teens who operate the Summer Reading Program) are mailed invitations to join TAB. Teens who volunteer in the library are also asked to join, in addition to other teens recommended by members. All that prospective members need to do once they are invited is to fill out an application form.

After a member has been part of the group for three years, he or she receives a T-shirt. All members receive free food and drinks at meetings, they have the privilege of coming and going from the staff youth workroom as needed, and they get first dibs on new YA books when they are added to the collection.

Every year there is a TAB Recognition Evening. Members for one year receive a certificate, two years a TAB pin, and three years a TAB T-shirt. Teens who remain in TAB longer than three years receive bookstore gift certificates, Sam Goody gift certificates, or movie passes, depending on their interests. TAB members who have made a significant contribution have their names placed on a plaque located in the Young Adult area. TAB members are considered official library volunteers.

A teen Group Leader is appointed by the Youth Services librarian for TAB. Another member is selected by the group to serve as Secretary. One TAB member serves by volunteering as the newsletter Editor, and another serves as Historian. The Group Leader puts together an agenda for each meeting after consulting with the Youth Services librarian, then runs the meeting.

The Group Leader sets the tone for the meeting and keeps it on track. The Secretary keeps notes. The newsletter Editor gathers book reviews and submits them to the librarian for final okay before publication. The Historian keeps a scrapbook of TAB activities. Although there is no representation on the library board by a TAB member, a member makes an annual report to the board.

TAB members plan the Summer Reading Program for teens. They make suggestions for the way the program operates, what prizes should be awarded, and what special programs should be offered. TAB also plans and hosts a party for the Library Team. They sponsor a book discussion group that meets monthly or every other month.

During 2001, at the persistent urging of TAB members, a larger area was set aside in the library for YA materials. TAB representatives, along with other teen volunteers, planned how this room should be arranged and decorated. They then planned a party for the grand opening. The library was open from 6 P.M. to midnight on the Friday night after the first day of school in August. Only middle school and high school students were allowed to be in the facility. A DJ was hired, using Friends of the Library funds, and chips and soft drinks were available. Much to the surprise of TAB members and the library staff, 367 teens came to the event! Teens were asked to give suggestions for naming the new teen area. TAB selected the name Teen Compound.

In addition, TAB plans and puts together special programs for teens. One program they especially enjoy is putting on a coffeehouse that takes place in the library lobby. Round tables are covered with butcher paper, and crayons and markers are put on the tables. Teens draw and write on the tables while music, usually taped but occasionally live, is played. During the program teens read their own writing or read passages from a book they want to share. Coffee, tea, hot cider, hot chocolate, and doughnuts are usually included. Attendance varies, but even if just a few teens come, TAB enjoys the program themselves.

TAB plans and implements a holiday program for children each December. The most recent production was a play called "Mother Goose's Christmas Surprise." Classes from the elementary school next door attend performances, and a public performance is given in the evening.

TAB designs an entry and participates in the annual Lost Dutchman Days parade celebration in Apache Junction, which gives the group and the library even more exposure in the community.[1]

Library Teen Council (LTC)

Burton Barr Central Library, Phoenix Public Library System, Phoenix, Arizona
www.phoenixteencentral.org/tcwebapp/index.jsp
Advisor: Luci Kauffman, Library Assistant at Teen Central

The LTC at Burton Barr Library was formed in September 1995. There are over 160 members, with three-fourths girls and one-fourth boys. The City of Phoenix serves a population of over 1.3 million people and the library has 13 branches. The large LTC group meets on the second Saturday of each month for two hours. Eleven other branches of the Phoenix Public Library system have their own smaller teen advisory boards operating independently from the LTC.

Prospective members are reached in a variety of ways, through flyers, posters, direct mailings to teens, and advertising in the Phoenix Public Library's Calendar of Events. Anyone ages 12–18 from the Phoenix metro area is welcome to join the LTC. Teens can become members by filling out an application and attending a LTC meeting. LTC members are considered teen volunteers of the library.

Five officers are elected to serve as President, Vice-President, Secretary, Treasurer, and Historian. Officers are elected by a majority vote of the LTC and serve a one-year term beginning in October of each year. If an officer relinquishes a position, a two-week notice must be given before an election to replace that officer.

The President is in charge of all aspects of meetings, from setting the agendas to running the meetings. As leader of the group, the President creates committees to facilitate LTC work and works closely with other officers. The President also writes and speaks to other organizations and committees on behalf of the LTC.

The Vice-President keeps records of membership and attendance and contacts members about attendance problems. The Vice-President contacts all members in the event a meeting is cancelled. This teen serves in place of any officer, including the President, as needed. The Vice-President also chairs a committee designed to contact and orient new members.

The Secretary keeps and distributes all meeting minutes, including attendance statistics passed on by the Vice-President. This person organizes and maintains all LTC files and sends out special notices to members as needed. The Secretary maintains an updated mailing and phone list for all LTC members.

The Treasurer keeps an accurate, up-to-date account of all money received and paid out by the LTC. This officer disperses money to the LTC and committees and keeps records of expenditures. He or she also works as a liaison with the Friends of the Library to manage library accounts, reports on the budget as requested, and advises the LTC on the spending of funds.

The Historian is responsible for taking pictures of all major events and projects of the LTC. This officer records pictures and writings in a scrapbook, and eventually on a Web site, and brings the scrapbook to all major events to show others. Additional duties include keeping a file of all old LTC minutes and other important council paperwork.

There is no representative to the library board from the LTC, but the group has had a major voice in developing and promoting teen services at the Phoenix Public Library. The LTC encourages positive relationships between teens and the Phoenix Public Library system. The LTC is the voice of teen issues. It tries to increase the use of the libraries among teens, makes teens aware of library resources, and offers suggestions to library staff on services, materials, and programs. The LTC also works to promote literacy in libraries and the community.

The programs in which the LTC has been involved over the years are varied. The LTC has organized coffeehouses in the library for which more than 30 performers sang, danced, read poetry, and acted out skits. They also compiled booklists for suggested YA summer reading and held successful story and poetry writing contests for teens. Winners of the contests were published in a booklet called *Scribbles 1997* and the Teen Central 'zine titled *Create!* In the past, murals have been made for the library and for the Veteran Administration Hospital in Phoenix.

LTC members have performed community service projects for the library such as rejacketing books for Teen Central, providing storytelling for the Read Across America event, and assisting the Friends of the Library at the Arizona Book Festival and the Día de los Niños celebration.

The LTC has been instrumental in the creation and grand opening of Teen Central in April 2001 at Burton Barr Library. Teen Central is a special room just for teens that has become famous as one of the largest and most well-equipped teen library spaces in the United States. (See Karl Kendall's article, "YA Spaces of Your Dreams: Teen Central: Safe, Structured, and Teen-Friendly," *VOYA* [December 2003]: 380–81.)

The LTC is currently providing input for the programming that is happening at Teen Central and on the Teen Central Web site (www.phoenixteencentral.org/tcwebapp/index.jsp). The LTC sponsors parties in the library to encourage new membership in the teen council.[2]

Teen Advisory Board (TAB)

Schaumburg Township District Library, Schaumburg, Illinois
www.stdl.org
Advisor: Amy Alessio, Teen Coordinator
TAB began in 1998 at the Schaumburg Township District Library and has an average of 23 members, evenly divided between boys and girls. The library system serves a

population of 134,000 and has three branches plus a Central library. TAB meets monthly, although in the summer they have activities such as outings and a lock-in instead of regular meetings.

Information on TAB is given in the monthly library newsletter, the quarterly mailed library guide, and in the Teen Happenings newsletter. There is no application process; if teens show up, they are automatically members! TAB does not have a representative on the library board, but the board is invited to one TAB meeting each year. Likewise, there are no officers for the group, but Amy Alessio sometimes appoints a teen to be in charge of a specific event or promotion. Members are not considered official library volunteers as the library system does not have a volunteer program, but TAB does volunteer at many author functions.

There are special perks for TAB members. Members have lots of speakers and activities just for them, including a Halloween party, a holiday party, outings, and the lock-in. TAB members also get free books when they volunteer at programs plus occasional gifts such as journals.

During the summer TAB toured the police station, had their lock-in where they made a movie for the Drug Abuse Resistance Education (DARE) program, went to a baseball game, and ran Monday game programs. They also helped with other teen programs, such as a barbecue, scavenger hunt, and a nighttime storytelling event. The group helped with a book drive for a school with no library and made cards for kids with cancer. They do lots of craft projects and contests at meetings to keep them fun.

The teen TAB members occasionally confide in Alessio that they are involved in some questionable activities, so the librarian has developed a relationship with a wonderful police officer who comes and does a role-playing party with them. The teens adore her and she is invited to their outings and other activities. At their last holiday party, TAB made gingerbread houses, had a charity gift drive, and had a K-9 officer do a sample drug search. The teens loved it and Alessio was happy to see that they got the message about how easy it can be to get caught with illegal substances.

Every year, TAB has a pre-prom discussion about drinking. Alessio has a friend who is an assistant state attorney who came to see the group in April to explain the legal costs for teens who get caught with a DUI, even without hurting anyone else. Then he divided the costs by what they earn at their jobs. It was quite a revelation.

TAB worked with a designer to remodel the Teen Center. Alessio was able to convince the library board to support the idea by describing the features that the teens wanted. As a result, the new area is designed in a sports theme and includes lots of new features just for teens! There are books, magazines, CDs, games, and comfortable chairs for reading, studying, or meeting with friends, plus game tables and a listening center. Check it out on their Web page (www.stdl.org/teenpage/teencent/teencent.htm) and in *VOYA*'s "YA Spaces of Your Dreams" column, June 2002, pp. 160–61.[3]

Teen Library Council (TLC)

Carmel Clay Public Library, Carmel, Indiana
www.carmel.lib.in.us/default.htm
Advisor: Hope Baugh, Young Adult Services Manager

Carmel, Indiana, is part of the Clay Township area in Hamilton County, which has a population of more than 65,000. The Teen Library Council at its Carmel Clay Public Library has been active since 1994. There are 30 members, two-thirds female and one-third male. The group meets at least once a month. The general business meeting is the first Tuesday of every month but special committees might meet more frequently.

TLC solicits new members by word of mouth, press releases, and advertising in library publications and through posters. Prospective members must submit an application and then have an interview. Selection for membership is based on the interview. Teen members of TLC choose the new members. Hope Baugh writes acceptance and rejection letters after the interviews.

Members have the privilege of participating in an annual book-buying spree at Barnes & Noble or Borders to get books for the YA department. They can purchase a variety of books, from popular paperbacks to high-interest nonfiction to comics.

The teens had input when a new building was being planned as well as in the Long Range Plan process. The Library Board President and the Director met with the TLC to get input for the latter. TLC officers had the opportunity to present at a program on teen advisory boards at the Indiana Library Federation Annual Conference.

TLC members are considered official library volunteers. The hours they spend at meetings and programs are sent to the state library for statistics along with the adult volunteer hours. Carmel Clay Public Library also has a separate Teen Volunteer Corps (TVC), for which more than 100 teens are registered and which does not hold meetings. It is open to anyone, while TLC is a closed group. TLC members can join TVC and do other volunteer activities if they wish. TLC is limited to 30 because it would be difficult to keep meetings on track with a larger group. TLC members also appreciate that they have to apply and be selected, which makes it more prestigious.

The teens from TLC elect a president and vice-president. These officers' only official duty is to call fellow members to remind them of meetings. They serve as the "elders" of the group by being the ones to do such things as the library conference presentation and passing on TLC lore to new members via oral history. There is no TLC representative on the library board, but they find that an interesting idea!

At monthly meetings, members meet and discuss books as part of the Choice Picks process. There is a nomination sheet that gets passed around. One person nominates a title. If two others decide to read the book and deem it worthy of a vote, and it gets three total votes, then it becomes a Choice Pick and gets displayed in a special face-out aisle in the YA department. The Choice Picks have a special sticker and a note in the catalog.

Members have also been participating in the Teens' Top Ten/YA Galley Project for teens sponsored by the Young Adult Library Services Association (YALSA). For this project, the teens read and review galleys of new young adult books, send their reviews to the publishers, and nominate and vote for their favorite titles in this annual, nationwide Teens' Top Ten booklist. (See detailed description of the project in chapter 4.)

At each meeting, members may discuss not only books but also movies and music. Members can write annotations of movies or CDs they like which are posted to the teen Web page as AV Picks. Titles do not have to get three votes and the works are not shelved together like books, as AV is a separate department. Also, the teens figured that it was pointless to put the materials on a special shelf because they circulate so heavily that they are rarely there. It is better just to post their picks on the Web.

From 1994 through 1999, TLC produced a mystery play for Halloween weekend. The first was an adaptation of a box kit but the others were all original plays. In fall 2001, the teens did not do a play but instead began an experiment of videotaping a comic mystery short film. Newer members do not seem as interested in drama, so the direction of programming might change as time goes by.

For the past four years, TLC has hosted a sleepover in the library for fourth and fifth graders. The teens pick the games and activities for the event and they act as "camp counselors" for the younger ones. There are two teens assigned to every group of about four children. The teens name their team and each team gets different colored bandanas. It is a lot of work for staff and the teens, but also a lot of fun!

Other programs include Open Mic Nights for local teen bands and sponsoring an award festival for films made by local teens. (See TLC brochure, information sheet, application form, and interview questions at the end of this section.)[4]

Carmel Clay Public Library

Teen
Library
Council

President—
Joel Street

Vice-President aka
"Duchess"—
Jamie Burnett

▲ Mari Hardacre
TLC Advisor
Young Adult
Services Department

Tel: 317-814-3983

Carmel Clay Public Library

Carmel Clay Public Library
Young Adult Services Dept.
55 4th Avenue SE
Carmel, IN 46032

Phone: 317-814-3983
Email: ya@carmel.lib.in.us

Advisory Activities

Another TLC specialty is giving advice. TLC members had input into the plan for the new library (which opened in 1999). More recently, TLC served as a Focus Group for the library's long range planning activity. TLC also gives advice on such topics as prizes for summer reading. A big challenge for the group is coming up with a fresh summer reading slogan each year.

Mysteries

Traditionally, TLC has produced an original mystery play each year. This year, students are working on making the first ever TLC mystery movie. Later this year, the group will sponsor a Teen Film Fest of original short films by local teens.

Open Mics

In the past TLC sponsored a couple of very popular open mics for local teen bands. This year, we hope to present an end-of-summer music fest for Carmel teens.

Volunteering

Many TLC members also help out at the library with other programs such as the Friends of the Library Book sales, reading to children at the Read Aloud Roundups, and helping set up Anime Saturdays.

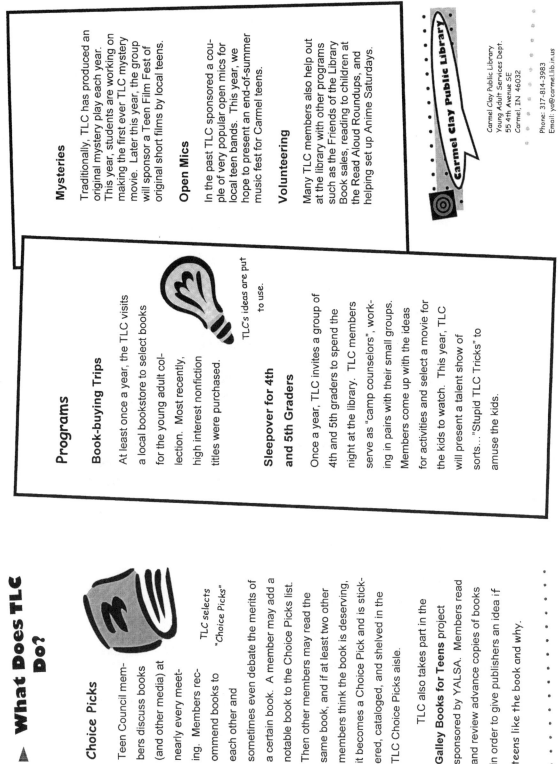

Programs

Book-buying Trips

At least once a year, the TLC visits a local bookstore to select books for the young adult collection. Most recently, high interest nonfiction titles were purchased.

TLC selects "Choice Picks"

TLC's ideas are put to use.

Sleepover for 4th and 5th Graders

Once a year, TLC invites a group of 4th and 5th graders to spend the night at the library. TLC members serve as "camp counselors", working in pairs with their small groups. Members come up with the ideas for activities and select a movie for the kids to watch. This year, TLC will present a talent show of sorts…"Stupid TLC Tricks" to amuse the kids.

▲ What Does TLC Do?

Choice Picks

Teen Council members discuss books (and other media) at nearly every meeting. Members recommend books to each other and sometimes even debate the merits of a certain book. A member may add a notable book to the Choice Picks list. Then other members may read the same book, and if at least two other members think the book is deserving, it becomes a Choice Pick and is stickered, cataloged, and shelved in the TLC Choice Picks aisle.

TLC also takes part in the **Galley Books for Teens** project sponsored by YALSA. Members read and review advance copies of books in order to give publishers an idea if teens like the book and why.

Carmel Clay Public Library
Young Adult Services Dept.
55 4th Avenue SE
Carmel, IN 46032

Phone: 317-814-3983
Email: ya@carmel.lib.in.us

Carmel Clay Public Library
Teen Library Council

Information Sheet

The Teen Library Council (TLC) is an advisory board of thirty students in grades 7 to 12 who meet regularly with the Manager of the Young Adult (YA) Services Department to discuss books, to help plan library programs for teenagers, to give input on library issues related to teens, and to assist in selecting books to purchase for the library's High School Area.

New members are accepted each year in August based on the results of an interview conducted by TLC members and the Manager of the YA Services Department. Criteria for selection include:
- A desire to promote reading;
- The ability to work cooperatively with people of various ages and backgrounds;
- A commitment to attend meetings on a regular basis.

Students who are frequent library users, who are former library volunteers, or who are recommended by a teacher or librarian are given special consideration. We strive to maintain an age, gender, and school balance on the council and to select members with different personalities and interests.

The TLC meets from 7:00–8:30 PM on the first Tuesday evening of every month (unless that Tuesday is a holiday or spring break, in which case the meeting is moved to the following week). Members who miss more than one meeting are put on probation. Members who miss more than three meetings in one year forfeit membership on the Council.

Part of each meeting is devoted to getting TLC feedback and input on library programs and issues. For example, the TLC creates the theme for the Young Adult Summer Reading program every year, and helps select the prizes. Another part of every meeting is devoted to discussing books and voting on titles to go into the "Choice Picks" area of the collection. Of course, another part of each meeting is devoted to just socializing and enjoying each other's company while eating snacks.

In addition, the TLC sponsors several special events such as:
- Fall Orientation
- Fall Project (in the past, this has been a mystery play, but it could be just about anything, based on TLC members' interests)
- Winter Book Buying Trip
- Spring Sleepover for fourth and fifth graders

Members should plan to participate in at least one of these special events, including attending planning meetings separate from the regular TLC meetings.

Membership is renewable for the duration of a student's junior high and high school years, and nearly all members remain on the council until graduation. This provides consistency and continuity and allows the council to develop as a team. As old members graduate, spaces open up for new members, providing a fresh perspective each year.

Carmel Clay Public Library
Teen Library Council Application for 2002–2003

(Please print! Please feel free to write on the back and to attach extra paper. Return this application to the Young Adult Services Department desk by Saturday, June 15.)

Name:

Age: **Grade Level (fall of 2002):**

Address (include ZIP code):

Phone: **E-mail Address:**

School:

1. How did you find out about the TLC?

2. Have you read the "TLC Information Sheet"? Would you be able to meet the attendance requirements?

3. What skills and/or experiences would you bring to the TLC? For example, what are your favorite hobbies and/or extracurricular activities?

4. Discussing books and promoting reading is a big part of the TLC's mission. What was the last book you read? What did you think of it?

5. What is your favorite book or author, and why?

6. Promoting the library is a big part of the TLC's mission, too. Describe your use of the Carmel Clay Public Library. (For example, how often do you come? How do you use the library? What do you like about it? What would you like to change, if you could? What would you like younger people to know about it?)

7. Have you ever participated in the library's summer reading program for teens? If so, please describe your experience.

8. Have you ever volunteered at the library? If so, please describe your experience.

9. Have you attended programs or workshops at the library? If so, please describe your experiences.

10. Is there a teacher, librarian, or job supervisor who would be willing to recommend you for TLC? If so, give their name(s) and position title (such as "teacher at Carmel HS").

11. Is there anything else you would like us to know as we consider your application?

**Carmel Clay Public Library
Teen Library Council**

Interview Questions

Applicant's name:

Interview date and time:

Interviewer's name:

1. Why would you like to become a member of the Teen Library Council?

2. How do you think you would be an asset to the group?

3. Why do you think the public library is important?

4. Have you ever done any volunteer work for the library (or other volunteer work)? Please tell us about it.

5. How do you think the public library can better serve teenagers?

6. What kind of books do you enjoy reading?

7. What do you like best about your favorite book or author?

8. What are your hobbies, interests, and extracurricular activities other than reading?

9. How would you describe yourself to someone who didn't know you?

10. If you could have dinner with anyone in the world, past or present, real or fictional, who would it be, and why?

11. Is there anything else that you'd like us to know about you?

12. Do you have any questions about the TLC?

NOTES:

Teen Advisory Group (TAG)

Basehor Community Library, Basehor, Kansas
www.basehorlibrary.org
Advisor: Jenne Laytham, Assistant Director

The Basehor Community Library serves 7,000, the smallest population of all the featured groups. There are no branch libraries. Still, they started a Teen Advisory Group (TAG) in the summer of 1999, and they have 15 to 20 members, with a ratio 2-to-1 of girls to boys. The group meets once a month.

There are a variety of ways that the group seeks new members. In the summer, during the sign up for the YA Summer Reading Program, each teen registrant is asked if they would like to join. TAG reports they got several new members this way. They also advertise online on the library calendar and have flyers in the YA area. When teens are checking out library materials, staff asks if they might be interested in TAG membership. They say the best way to gain new members, by far, is by word of mouth from current members.

Prospective members provide Jenne Laytham with their name, phone number, and address. It is that simple. Postcard reminders are mailed to members about meetings, or a TAG volunteer calls.

TAG members get advance notice of library events, invitations to special events such as the yearly Literature Festival at Kansas University, volunteer opportunities, a voice in matters concerning the YA area and collection, and the opportunity of socializing with a different crowd than at school. Only members who sign up to volunteer on a regular schedule are considered official library volunteers.

There are no officers for the group, although they have thought about having them at some point. They have also considered a teen representative to the library board, but do not have such a position yet.

TAG is in charge of planning all teen programs such as the YA Summer Reading Program and Teen Read Week activities, which include Book Buddies and the Teen Coffeehouse. They have given a performance during a Mystery Night for grade schoolers and run an intergenerational project where teens interviewed a senior citizen from their community and featured stories and pictures (of teens and seniors!) in the library. Booktalking sessions are held at meetings and written reviews are done on the books. During the holiday season the teens go to the Senior Housing Center and either deliver fruit baskets while caroling at each apartment or put on a holiday performance in their community room. Of course, TAG members also volunteer as needed for the library as scheduled or for special projects. For example, there was a fire next to the library necessitating many volunteers coming in and wiping down each book and shelf to prevent soot and smoke damage. Several TAG members worked all day on this task!

Some comments from Laytham: "When I jumped in to this, I had no idea how it would go or what we would do, but it took on a life of its own because of the teens. They are all so different and come to the library for different reasons, but belonging to this group has brought them together and has given them a different view of our library. Mainly, they see that we want them here and they are important to us. I have learned so much from them—and they are just lots of fun."[5]

YOUNG ADULT ADVISORY BOARD (YAAB)

Salina Public Library, Salina, Kansas
www.salpublib.org
Advisor: Kristi Hansen, Youth Services Coordinator

The mission of the Salina Public Library is to provide for the diverse needs of the community with staff, resources, and services for lifelong learning, information and technological literacy, entertainment, and cultural awareness. With the materials, programming, and the newest technology for patrons, the library continues to strive toward meeting this goal.

The Salina Public Library serves Salina, which has a population of around 47,000 and is located in Salina County, population 53,000. They also serve other surrounding counties. There are no branch libraries.

The Youth Services Department of the Salina Public Library, located on the lower level, covers approximately 10,000 square feet and offers a wide variety of materials for youth of all ages. There are more than 85,000 items in their collection of books, magazines, read-alongs, recorded books, CDs, DVDs, and videos. They also have Christian Fiction, Parent/Teacher collections, and a growing Spanish collection.

YAAB was formed in May 2001 and meets monthly. The board consists of 36 young adults ranging in age from 12 to 17 with the average age being 14.5. After some discussion, it was unanimously decided that their first priority was to define a space for teens. YAAB had so many cool ideas that it didn't take too long to figure out what they wanted. As a relatively new group, YAAB is truly a "work in progress."

For their Teen Village, a section of the Youth Services Department, the teens selected a "hand chair" and *tried* bubble furniture. It looked extremely cool but it lasted about a week. They now have "cool and sturdy" furniture. Black lights were installed in half the fixtures and library staff can always tell when the teens arrive because the regular lights go off and the black lights go on. There is popular music piped into the Teen Village. YAAB would eventually like to add graffiti boards and possibly a Nintendo 64 and/or PlayStation.

Another future idea is starting a homework help center where older students would be available to work with younger ones after school. YAAB is considering using the Reference area, which would be a great location because of the resources and the large study table there.

There are 29 girls and 7 boys in YAAB. Actually, the boys seem to be even more involved and regular in their attendance than the girls. Kristi Hansen appreciates having so many boys in the group; they bring a whole different perspective.

An application form is sent out to the schools to recruit new members. The teens also invite friends to join. There are posters promoting YAAB in-house, at the schools, and around town in different businesses. They also advertise in the local *Buyers Guide* paper that is delivered to every home in Salina once a week at no charge. In addition, the teens try to get information into the school newspapers and during morning announcements. YAAB members especially enjoy making public service announcements for the local access television station and radio stations to advertise membership in their group.

In order to be on YAAB, teens must complete and turn in an application. They are then scheduled for an interview. The interview process gives YAAB a chance to get to know prospective members better and likewise, it is a good experience for the applicants. At the interview, YAAB members explain expectations and ask the teens some questions. In return, candidates are given an opportunity to ask YAAB what they want to know.

As far as perks, members receive T-shirts that they helped design, funded by the Friends of the Library. T-shirts are given after eight hours of service, which includes meetings, volunteering in the library, and helping with programs. YAAB members consider receiving the T-shirts a prestigious step, as do the Teen Volunteers who receive a shirt with a different design, also funded by the Friends, to identify them to patrons and library staff.

Several young adults on YAAB also serve as Teen Volunteers. The Teen Volunteer Program was started 11 years ago and has grown every year, currently averaging 50 teens. Teens who apply are interviewed, during which they learn the job responsibilities while the librarians learn about them. At the interview, they and a parent or guardian sign a contract saying that they agree to follow program rules. The Teen Volunteers work three-hour shifts once or twice a week during June and/or July, with three or four teens scheduled per shift. They are responsible for registering 2,000 children for the Summer Reading Program, overseeing weekly games, checking the heavily used drive-through book drop, and assisting with a party at summer's end. Teen Volunteers are rewarded with a volunteer appreciation celebration in August. (For complete information and samples of the forms used, see the description of Salina Public Library's Teen Volunteer Program in the book *Teen Volunteer Services in Libraries* by Kellie M. Gillespie, VOYA Guide 1 [Lanham, Md.: VOYA Books/ Scarecrow Press, 2004], 108–13.)

The library considers YAAB members as volunteers in a separate program. Members can keep track of the hours they spend at meetings and doing projects and can count them as service hours. The Friends of the Library now offers three $1,000 Teen Volunteer Scholarship awards to high school seniors who have volunteered at least 30 hours in the library. YAAB hours count toward this scholarship.

There are no officers on YAAB. Meetings are fairly informal, which seems to make the teens more comfortable and willing to share. There is no problem getting them to volunteer for committees and other tasks.

COMMENTS FROM YAAB MEMBERS AT SALINA PUBLIC LIBRARY

The Young Adult Advisory Board is an outstanding opportunity for teens to have an enormous impact on the local community through the use of library resources.

—Travis

I think it's a valuable opportunity to help the library and the community as a whole. It's fun and I'm glad I joined. I look forward to our meetings.

—Steven

It's pretty neat coming up with new ideas for the library and I like spending time with my friends at the library. And one of the best parts of our last meeting was the cheese. I like cheese!

—Justan

I think it's cool to help the library get new stuff for the teens and other people. I have a lot of fun at the meetings.

—Brandon

At the time of this writing, teens plan to have YAAB representation at library board meetings beginning in 2004. Scheduling is a consideration since the teens start school at 7:30 A.M. and the Library Board meets at 7:00 A.M. one Monday a month. Hansen feels that it is worth arranging, as teen representation is a good experience for teens as well as a learning experience for the library board. Library board and Friends of the Library Board members have been extremely supportive of the goal to reach young adults and get them into the library. Teen representation at Board meetings reinforces that support.

YAAB enjoys projects that allow them to perform and work with younger children. The teens have written and produced puppet shows, helped with jewelry making activities, and would like to start a tutoring program. Their first big project for peers was designing the Teen Village. They also have talked about doing bake sale or car wash fund-raisers at some point. One of their favorite projects is to do public service announcements in the local media to let people know what they're doing and what's going on at the library.

The YAAB Universe Web page is a work in progress. As of this writing, it is awaiting migration to a new server. The Web page includes book reviews done by teens, homework help, YAAB news, teen-recommended links, and a "Get Involved" bulletin board. Advertising in the school papers and library for ideas and help from all teens, not just YAAB members, is an ongoing goal. YAAB might find other teens who are extremely creative and could help improve their Web page, even if they don't have the time or inclination to be YAAB members.

Since the teens have such busy schedules, getting YAAB members who are working on the Web page to the library at the same time is difficult. A computer specialist who enjoys working with young adults has been a great help with the technology as well as getting the members excited about Web site possibilities.

Hansen says it is wonderful to work with these young adults who bring a lot of new ideas and a youthful spirit to the library. They have earned respect through their dedication and willingness to be a part of making the library a better place for others. Hansen and her co-advisor have learned so much by seeing things through the eyes of YAAB members. They look forward to the meetings because they're actually fun for them, too! They can laugh and joke and learn (and eat!) with their advisory board and can't imagine how they got along without them. An additional benefit that library staff hadn't expected is that those who are not such "young" adults feel younger when they are around teens![6]

Teen Advisory Council

Elizabeth Public Library, Elizabeth, New Jersey
www.njpublib.org
Advisor: Kimberly Paone, Teen Services Librarian

The Teen Advisory Council at Elizabeth Public Library began in 2000, and even though they are one of the newer groups, they are very active. The group is comprised of about 25 members, two-thirds girls to one-third boys. They meet once a month for regular meetings, then for other activities depending on what they have planned.

Elizabeth, New Jersey, is a city of approximately 120,000 residents. The city has 33 middle and high schools (public, private, and parochial), including the largest high school in the state of New Jersey, with more than 5,000 students. The library consists of a main library and three small branches. Each branch has a YA collection, but no YA staff. All teen programs currently take place at the main library, but hopes are to expand them to the branches eventually.

The Teen Advisory Council gets new members through school visits, word of mouth and "bring a friend" incentives, and flyers posted at school and in the library. Teens ages 12 to18 or in sixth to twelfth grades are welcome. There is no application necessary.

Members get a number of perks. They have first dibs on new books and get the first chance at signing up for teen programs. They also receive Teen Advisory Council T-shirts and pencils.

Although the Teen Advisory Council is not considered an official volunteer group, they still help out quite a bit in the Teen Department with shelving, weeding, photocopying, and other tasks. There are no officers and there is no teen representative on the library board.

The Teen Advisory Council helps to plan teen programs, does book reviews, and gives input on new materials that they feel should or should not be added to the teen collection. As a group, the Teen Advisory Council also works on programs for the Children's Department, such as a Winnie-the-Pooh Reader's Theater, face painting, and Book Buddies.

A subgroup of the Teen Advisory Council meets regularly as the Best Books for Young Adults Teen Task Force for YALSA. The teens read and review galleys and hot-off-the-press books from publishers and their comments are passed on to the Best Books for Young Adults Committee by Kimberly Paone.

The Council has also participated in various community service activities including the American Heart Association's Heart Walk. They raised $1,100 and are signed up to do it again. They helped at a local mall's nonprofit night called Magical Night of Giving. The Teen Advisory Council also makes crafts to donate to a senior citizen center and they write letters to terminally ill children through the Love Letters organization.[7]

Youth Advisory Committee (YAC)

Jervis Public Library, Rome, New York
www.jervislibrary.org
Advisor: Lisa Matte, Adult Services Librarian

Jervis Public Library is situated in Rome, New York, a small city with 35,000 residents. There are other small libraries in neighboring communities, but Jervis Public Library draws from their communities for patronage because of their sizes and limited hours. There are no branches, and the library is part of the Mid-York Library System, which allows for resource and service sharing for 43 libraries in 3 counties.

The Youth Advisory Committee (YAC) was started in 1999. There are eight core members, five girls and three boys. The group meets once per month during the school year and at least twice per month in the summer, with additional drop-in sessions for preparing props for their summer plays. Other teens belong to offshoot groups of YAC, the Book Buddies Committee and Computer Camp Volunteers.

YAC advertises for membership through posters in the library, personal contact with teens who are browsing the YA section (which is especially successful), plus invitations to those who sign up for the summer reading club and who volunteer for summer Book Buddies or Computer Camp programs. The group also has information about YAC on the YA Web page for the library. They send press releases to local newspapers. Notices are also sent to home schooling and other teen-serving organizations such as Boy Scouts, Girl Scouts, YMCA, Salvation Army, church youth groups, Boys and Girls Clubs, and school drama clubs. Some parents of members recommend other teens or see performances by YAC and ask about the group. Members sometimes bring their friends as prospective members to meetings. Initially, teachers and principals nominated members to get the group started. YAC has used many additional techniques to promote membership from that point onward.

There are no officers in YAC, and the group does not have a representative on the library board.

YAC is very involved in special library projects. One is stuffing bags for the Books for Babies program. Every baby born in Rome Memorial Hospital receives a bag to promote reading. The bags contain booklists, a library card application, and a board book. Initially supported by a grant, this program is now funded by the library itself. YAC members play a big part by having two or three meetings center around stuffing and checking 500 bags.

Some YAC members belong to a separate group, the Book Buddies Committee, which is comprised of seven additional members. These volunteers go to sites around the area to read to children who might not be able to come to the library otherwise. Readers promote the library and provide a craft activity after story time.

YAC has another program called Teens for Tots. Each holiday season, YAC makes holiday ornaments to sell in the library in exchange for a donation to the year's adopted charity. Previously, they adopted Head Start. Now they have adopted the children at Lucy's House, a domestic violence shelter. They purchase food, personal needs items, and small gifts for the children and give them one of the handmade ornaments. Each year they make a different kind.

One of the newest YAC endeavors is participating in the Erie Canal Haunted Festival at Halloween. Members of YAC and the Book Buddies Committee read spooky stories and sing scary songs. They give out booklists, bookmarks, and library card applications. The event runs for six nights in October, so scheduling can be flexible with volunteers only having to read for one night. Each night, a member of the library staff is on hand to supervise and participate. Each teen receives a coupon for free admission to the Festival in exchange for participation. This is an exciting partnership for YAC. The turnout is large and YAC's participation helps by adding another greatly needed attraction to the crowded festival, and getting the library in the public eye at the same time.

Some YAC members also participate as a special committee of YAC called Computer Camp. Four additional members run this program. The teens guide children, ages 5 and up, through four stations of computer discovery in this four-week program. Stations include making M & M abacuses, reading stories related to computers, looking at the insides of a computer, and doing a human Turing Test to decide if the teen is a person—or a computer!

Each summer, YAC writes an original play or dramatizes popular children's books. They perform as part of the children's Summer Reading Program. They have performed "Who Stole Seuss" (original), "Wolf Theatre," and "How the Grinch Stole Summer Vacation" (original). It takes almost a year to prepare for this program, and they begin early to brainstorm for the next year's performance.

YAC helps the young adult cause at the Jervis Public Library in many other ways. They suggest materials for purchase and suggest display themes. They choose posters for teens and help put them up. They keep Lisa Matte up to date on teen trends by completing a survey each fall on current teen interests. "Readalike" bibliographies are produced with YAC input, as are special library programs for teens.

Some of the special program ideas, for which YAC assists with prop making and other preparations that will not ultimately spoil the fun for them, are Survivor Quiz Show (Matte doesn't let them see the questions) and Teen Mystery Night (likewise, Matte doesn't let them know whodunit).

YAC assisted in developing a term paper topic list so that Matte could create a Browser's Guide and a Surfer's Guide to Term Paper Topics to distribute in-house and at the junior and senior high schools.

In addition, YAC helps make name tags for Book Buddies and participates in any "making" project that leads to assembly-line work. These kinds of activities are great conversation boosters for the teens, even the self-conscious ones.

This busy group does even more! They suggest movies for the summer program, Don't Judge a Book by Its Movie, and assist children's librarians with craft times and the Summer Reading Program.

Matte says, "I never anticipated the contribution these teens would make to the library when I dove into the teen advisory group waters. I was so happy to find there are no sharks, but many starfish."[8]

Teen Advisory Board (TAB)

Coshocton Public Library, Coshocton, Ohio
www.coshocton.lib.oh.us
Advisor: RoseMary Honnold, Young Adult Coordinator
The Teen Advisory Board (TAB) at Coshocton Public Library was started in 1995. There are 20 members, and the group varies year to year, gender-wise. TAB meets once a month, on the last Monday at 4:00 P.M.

The library is located in Coshocton, the county seat for rural Coshocton County, which has a population of about 37,000.

New members are sought by word of mouth, putting up a poster in the YA room, and through posters displayed in the school libraries. Prospective members fill out application forms, which are then reviewed by RoseMary Honnold. They receive an acceptance letter that includes the next meeting date and an item or two from the agenda, so they know what to expect.

TAB members are treated to a Christmas dinner party, first dibs on new books, special treat bags on holidays that include items such as stickers, pencils, ornaments, lip balm, bookmarks, and collector cards, and shopping trips to Borders.

The trips to Borders allow TAB to select books for the YA collection. They get a 20 percent discount. Going to Borders takes the group one and a half hours away, so it is a day trip and a great bonding activity. The teens look forward to it and are proud of their selections, especially since bookplates are added to the books to show which members chose them. (See the parent permission slip for the Borders trips at the end of this section.)

TAB publishes a newsletter called *YA Today*. The teens choose the content, layout, and title, and they write most of the articles. Two members have been learning how to edit the newsletter in MS Publisher and they also run copies.

Members are considered official library volunteers. With no set officers, the positions of meeting leader, minute recorder, and booktalkers change each month, so everyone gets a chance. There is no TAB representative on the library board.

TAB members plan YA programs, assist with Children's programming, wrap homebound patrons' Christmas gifts, help set up the Friends of the Library book sale, perform reader's theater, and register participants for summer reading. They also decorate for holidays and programs, set up displays, decorate a Christmas tree for a community festival, do booktalks, choose music CDs, select books for the YA collection, assemble summer reading materials, do cutting and folding for staff members, and various other activities as they arise.[9]

Borders Book-Buying Trip Permission Form

The Teen Advisory Board will be shopping Saturday, August 23, at the Borders book store in North Canton, Ohio (330-494-4776) to make additions to the YA Room collection. We will leave the library at 10 a.m. We will have brunch at the Cracker Barrel (330-966-1144) when we arrive in North Canton and then go to the bookstore. After we finish shopping, we will take a picture and head home. We plan to be home by around 3:00 p.m.

The Friends of the Library Book Sales fund the lunch and some of the book purchases.

I need this permission slip signed by a parent for anyone under 18 who is planning to go. Those over 18 just let me know you are coming. Everyone planning to go let me know as soon as possible!

RoseMary Honnold

Permission Slip for a Shopping Trip to Borders in North Canton
on August 23, 2003, 10:00 a.m. to 3:00 p.m.

I give permission for my son/daughter

_____

to go on the Borders shopping trip.

Signature of parent or guardian:

_____   Date_____

Teen Advisory Board (TAB)

Lester Public Library, Two Rivers, Wisconsin
www.tworivers.lib.wi.us
Advisor: Terry Ehle, Youth Services Coordinator

Two Rivers is a small community of 13,000 and the Lester Public Library is their only library. However, their Teen Advisory Board (TAB) is as large as groups in bigger communities, and as active. There are 36 members, three-fourths girls and one-fourth boys. They meet every other week, about two times per month, with more meetings during the summer.

Advertising for the group is mainly by word of mouth. They also advertise in the library's newsletter and at every event they hold. Applications are kept in the Young Adult area at all times.

The application is just a formality. If someone fills one out and comes to the meetings, he or she becomes a member. If a teen comes to two meetings in a row, he or she receives a binder to hold his or her meeting notes and other information. Members are also allowed to use staff computers to type minutes and other projects.

Since the library does not have any kind of official volunteer program, TAB members are not actually considered official library volunteers, although they do help with some programs in the Children's section. Terry Ehle tries to save their energies for teen programs and TAB responsibilities. Occasionally, they do assist with Friends of the Library activities if they are asked.

TAB has two officers. The President is responsible for each meeting agenda, tie-breaking votes, and overall running of meetings. The President meets with Ehle before each meeting to go over what needs to be done. The Co-President fills in when the President is absent, keeps minutes of each meeting, and is responsible for e-mailing or calling with meeting reminders to each member.

A recent addition is a TAB Selection Committee. This group of eight TAB members reads book reviews for each meeting and helps to choose books, magazines, and other materials. Once the selections have been made they are brought to the whole group for final decisions.

At this point, there is no TAB representative on the library board. The group is just for fun and programming. A future evolution might bring a representative, but for now the teens are more interested in the social aspects of TAB than anything else.

TAB does all programming for young adults in sixth to twelfth grades, including planning, publicity, set up, clean up, and everything. They also make bulletin boards in their area to publicize events. They have done magazine selection and some book reviewing, and also have set up a music CD suggestion box that they check at each meeting. Occasionally they assist at other library events.

Last summer, TAB hosted a "Name That Tune" game show, a Karaoke party, a Murder Mystery night, and a Library Survivor Hunt. They also have had a YA Open House, several coffeehouses, and a CD Exchange.

Each year, the library hosts a lock-in activity just for TAB members, to thank them for all they do.[10]

Teen Advisory Board End-of-the-Year Lock-In Permission Form
Friday, December 14 7:30 PM – 8:00 AM

The end-of-the-year lock-in is the library's way of thanking the Teen Advisory Board (TAB) for all of their hard work during the year. TAB members will enjoy an evening of board games, computer games, Internet, movies, music, pizza, and friendship. The following is a list of information about the evening. TAB members will not be allowed to attend the program unless this form has been read and signed by themselves and a parent. TAB members may bring the completed form the night of the program. If you have any questions regarding the evening, please feel free to call the TAB advisor at 793-7116 before December 14.

- 2 Adult chaperones (names, positions) will be present at all times.
- Both girls and boys will be present and sleeping in the same area.
- Access to the Internet including chat & email will be allowed.
- Viewing of movies with a PG rating or lower will be allowed.

- Doors will be locked at 7:45 PM and no one will be allowed in or out after this time until the scheduled pick-up time of 8:00 AM. TAB members who will not be spending the night must make arrangements with Terry in advance and must be picked up no later than midnight.

- TAB members may participate in a $5.00 gift exchange. Names will be picked at our December 3 meeting.

- TAB members should wear what they will be sleeping in to the library. They may also bring sleeping bags, blankets, pillows, cd's, radios, and whatever toiletries they may need—all other items must be approved in advance by the TAB advisor.

- The library will provide pizza, soda, donuts, and juice. TAB members may bring additional treats if they bring enough for everyone.

Any inappropriate behavior will result in immediate pickup by a parent or guardian. Rules of behavior were discussed at the December 3 TAB meeting.

I, _____, hereby understand and agree that in many recreational activities, or the use of unfamiliar recreational facilities, accidents can and do occasionally occur. I am aware of these inherent risks. Being aware of these inherent risks, I take full responsibility for any injuries that I may sustain as a result of my involvement in any Lester Public Library ("municipality") activities. I further release and hold harmless the municipality, its agents and employees from any and all claims, for any responsibility, liability, penalty, forfeiture, suit, cost, and expenses (including attorney fees), with respect to any and all injuries and claims resulting from any and all Library activities even if the same should arise from the negligence of the municipality.

As the parent or guardian of the above named minor, I hereby agree to all the above terms on behalf of the above minor.

_____   _____   _____
(Parent Signature)   (Date)   (Emergency Phone Number)

I, _____, agree to follow all rules as discussed by the Teen Advisory Board.

_____   _____
(TAB Member Signature)   (Date)

NOTES

1. Liz Burks, Youth Services Librarian, Apache Junction Public Library, interviewed by the author, e-mails 28 November 2001 and 6 February 2002.
2. Luci Kauffman, Library Assistant, Phoenix Public Library, interviewed by the author, letter and enclosures 9 July 2001 and e-mail 18 August 2002.
3. Amy Alessio, Teen Coordinator, Schaumburg Township District Library, interviewed by the author, e-mails 27 September 2001 and 28 January 2002.
4. Mari Hardacre, former Young Adult Services Manager, Carmel Clay Public Library, interviewed by the author, e-mail 13 July 2001; Hope Baugh, Young Adult Services Manager, Carmel Clay Public Library, interviewed by the author, e-mails 25 and 26 July 2002 and 30 August 2002.
5. Jenne Laytham, Assistant Director, Basehor Community Library, interviewed by the author, e-mails 10 September 2001, 17 January 2002, and 24 July 2002.
6. Kristi Hansen, Youth Services Coordinator, Salina Public Library, interviewed by the author, e-mails 25 September 2002 and 14 November 2003.
7. Kimberly Paone, Teen Services Librarian, Elizabeth Public Library, interviewed by the author, e-mails August 15, 2002 and September 3, 2002.
8. Lisa Matte, Adult Services Librarian, Jervis Public Library, interviewed by the author, e-mails 27 August 2001 and 20 January 2002.
9. RoseMary Honnold, Young Adult Coordinator, Coshocton Public Library, interviewed by the author, e-mails 16 July 2001 and 13 November 2003.
10. Terry Ehle, Youth Services Coordinator, Lester Public Library, interviewed by the author, e-mails 17 July 2001, 21 January 2002, and 24 July 2002.

8

Schools Can Have Advisory Groups, Too!

STUDENTS AS LIBRARY ADVOCATES

Public libraries are not the only places where teens can take part in advisory groups. Some school libraries have discovered the joys and benefits of having a core group of teens to promote their libraries, assist in their operations, provide programs to fellow students, and encourage peers to enjoy reading. Although there are not many, middle school, junior high, and high school groups do exist and all have different missions and goals, just like their public library counterparts. Some school libraries partner with their local public libraries and the results can be quite impressive.

Secondary school librarians might feel that there is little time to plan, run, and serve as advisor for such groups. Consider this: What better way to give exposure to the library and foster its primary activities than by getting students involved? As Mike Eisenberg outlined in a recent *School Library Journal* article, school libraries have three basic functions that include information literacy instruction, reading advocacy, and information management.[1] Students can participate in many ways in promoting these functions.

Margaret Edwards's vision for school libraries advocated planning with student advisors to do just that. Her suggestions were as workable in the 1960s as they can be today. Her recommendations said:

The plan might include:

- A library club where books are discussed and aides are taught to give book talks. From this training, qualified student speakers could go through the school, visiting classes to introduce books and selling the idea of reading for pleasure
- A regular column in the school paper advertising new books in the library
- Designing, reproducing, and keeping on hand a supply of bookmarks that would advertise the library and correlate reading and the school's activities
- Planning and putting on a school assembly
- A book-reviewing periodical by and for teenagers
- A P.T.A. program
- Keeping a paperback bookrack stocked with up-to-date titles approved for young adults, from which books will circulate to all
- (Arranging) for the sale of books which could be handled by the student aides

- A poll of the student body to determine the ten most popular books
- A faculty meeting in the library early in the year where the aides and the librarian would "model" the new books (like a fashion show)

If such a program were presented to teenagers with personality and creativity, it is quite likely they would want to have a part in it. These young people could make the library the dynamo of the school, and think what it would do for the students themselves.[2]

As you can imagine, student participation at this level would definitely put any school library in the limelight. Further, to promote school libraries and make them a truly active and viable part of the school at large, librarians need to become politically savvy. Eisenberg suggests creating a formal library advisory committee composed of a key administrator and two or three classroom teachers who are "movers and shakers." Others, such as parents, technology or curriculum coordinators, and students may be added. He explains: "A library advisory committee reinforces the view that the library isn't the personal domain of the school librarian—it belongs to everyone in the school community. A library advisory committee also provides a support base for the library program and librarian. Not only do its members lend clout but it also creates a mechanism for setting priorities, troubleshooting, and long-term planning."[3]

Notice that *students* are part of the mix that Eisenberg recommends in developing a well-rounded library advisory board. Not only can students help plan for and manage their school library, they can support its reading guidance role through their efforts to reach peers through programming and promotional activities. The ultimate effect of such young adult participation, as it is in public libraries, is a feeling of "ownership" by the students toward their library and a willingness to help it flourish as an important element of the school. Principals and other administrators cannot help but notice!

In 1995, Edgewood Middle School in Warsaw, Indiana, located in rural Kosciuski County, started a student library advisory group by order of the principal. At first, school library media specialist Susan Eberhardt was daunted, but soon she realized that she could not only manage such a group, but also do it well. The students responded positively to the call, and she developed an active and involved advisory group. They helped run the school library, and also took part in book selection and organization. They used dramatic presentations to give booktalks to fellow students via morning announcements and original videotapes. Bookmarks were designed to inspire other students to read, and book sales and swaps were planned. Eberhardt said, "These experiences have been exciting and worthwhile for both librarian and student. Reading in our building has become more prominent and acceptable as more and more students get involved. There are, of course, many more possibilities leading to the promotion of reading within the advisory group context and I would encourage you to start such activities soon."[4]

PROFILES OF OUTSTANDING GROUPS IN SCHOOL SETTINGS

The following featured groups serve as additional prime examples of how teen advisors can be active and supportive players in school library settings. If you have yet to try running such a group, they will give you even more ideas and plenty of inspiration for how a student advisory group can become an important and visible part of your school library.

TEEN LIBRARY ADVISORS

John O'Connell High School, San Francisco, California,
www.sfusd.edu/schwww/sch651
Librarian: Kay Hones

The O'Connell Teen Library Advisors have been active since 1998. The high school where the group operates is 1 of 21 in the San Francisco Unified School District, with a student population of about 750. It is located in a new building as of fall 2000. The original building was destroyed in the Loma Prieta Earthquake of 1989 and it took 11 years to rebuild.

Most students come from the historic Mission neighborhood and over 70 percent are Latino, mostly recent immigrants or first generation from many Latin American countries. There is also a population of special education students of over 20 percent.

This state-of-the-art technology high school provides its students with a project-based/work-based learning curriculum. The idea is to prepare the students for the careers of the future. Teen Library Advisors is one of many Service Learning clubs and organizations at the high school that can help lead them to this goal.

Membership varies from 15 to 25, with the larger number showing up on the days food is available during meetings. There are about one-third boys to two-thirds girls. The group meets weekly on Fridays at lunchtime. New members just need to show up to join. They find out about the group by word of mouth.

Teen Library Advisors have one or two representatives from the group on the Student Council. Representatives attend on a voluntary basis, and if other students are interested, they can take a turn during another semester.

Perks for members include being first to get and read new books, being able to eat in the library for the weekly meetings, and field trips, which include presenting at conferences. Most eleventh-grade continuing members are assigned four days a week "advisory" time in the library. Teen Library Advisors take the lead in setting up special projects and programs. Since they are usually involved in the planning, they get to attend author programs and other special activities.

For Teen Read Week, Teen Library Advisors planned several events. On Monday, they held a classroom door-decorating contest. Tuesday was "Read a T-Shirt Day." Wednesday through Friday they held a paperback book exchange.

Booktalking to fellow students is a major focus of the Teen Library Advisors. In January, they presented booktalks on the theme of peace, and in February they did

READ-IN booktalks using picture books appropriate for teens, written and illustrated by African Americans. The group also created literacy displays featuring books for each month's theme. They booktalked selections from the Spring Book Fair, and Kay Hones reports that titles they recommended sold out quickly and needed to be re-ordered! Titles suggested included such notable works as David Almond's *Kit's Wilderness* (Delacorte, 2000), winner of the Printz Award from the Young Adult Library Services Association (YALSA).

Teen Library Advisors sponsored an O'Connell Read 2002 Challenge. All students were encouraged to read books and write the titles on strips of paper available in the library. Each time a hundredth strip was reached, that person received a gift certificate to Cover-to-Cover Bookstore. The Teen Library Advisors asked the O'Connell Site Council for $450 to pay for the gift certificates, with a goal of 2,002 books!

Members of Teen Library Advisors have presented at a number of youth conferences. At the "Youth Peace, Youth Power" Service-Learning Conference, they gave a workshop that included booktalks, a teen pregnancy prevention survey, and related peace activities. After joining O'Connell's Health Team (which Hones chaired), the group helped with a local Water Grant and presented at an Environmental Summit. Their presentations included booktalks plus a display. Soon the O'Connell library made additions to its collection reflecting environmental issues and emphasizing Bay Area resources. Ten Teen Library Advisors attended a Youth for Environmental Justice conference as well.

Another project involved examining a controversial part of U.S. history. Student members prepared and planned an in-depth study of Japanese Internment during World War II, including film clips, newspaper articles, books, historical photos, and documents.

Author visits are an equally important focal point for the group. Teen Library Advisors helped to organize a visit with Chizu Omori, author/researcher of the film *Rabbit in the Moon*. Then, at the recommendation of the San Francisco Public Library, the group hosted a Blue Ribbon author visit by Andrew Solomon, who won the 2001 non-fiction National Book Award for his *Noonday Demon, an Atlas of Depression* (Simon & Schuster, 2001). Teen Library Advisors planned and organized the whole program. They read selected quotes from Solomon's book *A Stone Boat* (Faber and Faber, 1996) and sent questions via e-mail prior to his arrival. Each student got an autographed copy of *A Stone Boat* at the conclusion of the visit.

Betsy Levine, the Teen Librarian at the San Francisco Public Library, who serves on the Best Books for Young Adults Committee for YALSA, donated several new titles to the Teen Library Advisors at O'Connell. The teens eagerly read the books and Levine plans to bring them more next year.

At the end of each school year, the group does a "year reflection" to figure out its direction. One thing they decided is that they want more field trips! They also hold a retreat at the end of September to plan the coming year's activities.

Hones has been given a Golden Apple Award from the San Francisco Education Fund for the Teen Library Advisors' grant projects. She does presentations on the group at local conferences such as the California School Library Association. The teens love to accompany her to award presentations and conferences (when funds are available) so they can share their perspectives on being part of this active and inspiring group.[5]

Writers and Readers Advisory Panel (WRAP)

Carmel High School, Carmel, Indiana
www.ccs.k12.in.us/chs
Media Specialist: Connie Mitchell

The purpose of WRAP is to encourage fellow students in their large Indiana high school to write and read for personal pleasure. Students are selected to serve on the WRAP Council and to plan and implement activities. Most activities are open to all students.

WRAP began in 1998, preceded by Readers' Advisor Panel (RAP) for a few years. Students join WRAP by participating in its activities. There is not a set roster of members. More than 70 students participated in WRAP the last few years, with twice as many girls as boys.

The WRAP Council meets as needed to plan. There are no set group WRAP meetings. Students participate in the activities that interest them and that can fit into their schedules.

To recruit new members, WRAP has a booth at the eighth grade Academic and Activities Fair in January and they take the names of those interested. When high school starts the following fall, letters are sent to those teens about the group.

Early in September, WRAP Council members go to each freshman Student Resource Time, which is similar to a homeroom, to promote WRAP. They have callouts before school one morning and after school in combination with the first coffeehouse event of the year. At these, Council members describe WRAP activities. They also advertise each activity through announcements, signage, and word of mouth (friends bringing friends).

Coffeehouses are held monthly with about 25 teens attending each one, and with several teens coming to every coffeehouse. WRAP also sponsors monthly book discussions, which attract students who have read the featured book and want to discuss it. Different students attend each discussion. Sometimes they hold a book/film discussion as a variation.

Students who are active in WRAP may apply to be on the Student Council. Connie Mitchell and her co-advisor select the Student Council members. WRAP does not have officers, but students volunteer to cochair various projects and activities.

Some additional projects and activities are Book Buddies, a Writing Marathon, Read-Aloud Contests, a Poetry WRAP-Up, and storytelling events. WRAP members get to hear visiting authors speak and participate in a Barnes & Noble shopping trip. The group also promotes Banned Books Week and Teen Read Week.[6]

BEMIDJI MIDDLE SCHOOL MEDIA CLUB (BMS CLUB)

Bemidji Middle School, Bemidji, Minnesota
www.audubon-center.com/School_Pages/Bemidji_Middle.htm
Media Specialist: Edee Lund

The BMS Media Club was started in Bemidji, Minnesota (population 11,200) in 1991. The group averages 40 to 50 members per year, with a surprising number of seventh- and eighth-grade boys. Many students join and remain in the club all three years of middle school, from grades 6 to 8.

The group meets about five to seven times during the school year. Meetings are irregular since the school needed to abandon a structured advisor program.

The BMS Media Club is listed in the school's handbook. They put publicity blurbs in the school bulletin and they also get lots of word-of-mouth advertising.

Members plan and run such programs as two book fairs each year, Teen Read Week festivities, occasionally an evening Reading Festival with local authors, and a school dance to raise funds. BMS Media Club designs and puts up bulletin boards and book displays in the library.

Members work behind the library desk during their scheduled hour and use the computer to check books in and out. They receive "candy" wages for shelving and other tasks and earn a day-long field trip in May to one of the state parks.

The BMS Media Club members are considered official library volunteers. They do not have officers. Members must sign a Media Club Contract at the beginning of each school year to become enrolled. (See contract on the page following this section.) Their assignment to the Media Club is considered the same as any employment contract and they are required to keep schoolwork current.[7]

Bemidji Middle School Media Club Contract

Name_____ Grade____ Pod_____

Please tell why you would like to be in Media Club.

_____

_____

_____

(You may use the back of the sheet if you want.)

****

Commitment

I am willing to help in the media center one hour per week during the school year. I will miss a class one time every 7 weeks. I agree to make sure my schoolwork is caught up before I leave for my media center duty.

      If I have a conflict (test, new material, or unfinished assignments), I will be excused from my scheduled duty time by Ms. Edee or Ms. Barb. If there is a conflict with my schoolwork and media club, I agree to a conference with my teacher(s) and Ms. Edee to work it out.

Duties

During my assigned time, I will check books in and out and help patrons behind the desk. I also agree to shelve books each week and read 2 sections of shelves each week to make sure the books are in order.

      Privileges include earning points for extra shelving, learning computer skills, getting first chance at new books, and our annual field trip. Besides that, I will be trained in library and computer skills that will help me in high school and beyond.

I understand and agree to these conditions.

Signed_____ Date_____

****

Note to Parent/Guardian: We have a very active Media Club where students learn about media/technology, books, and "people skills." Our overall goal is self-discipline for each student. Please discuss this "contract" with your student. If you have any questions (or would like to visit our Media Center), please call (333-3311) or just drop in.

Thank you,

Ms. Edee (Edee Lund)

Each student must have written permission from 1 parent/guardian and 3 teachers.

Parent/Guardian_____

Teacher_____

Teacher_____

Teacher_____

Young Adults Reading Young Adult Books ("YaYas"), Bibliomaniacs, Sequoyah's Ultimate Fanatical Exceptional Readers (SURFERs), Lunch Bunch, Book Groupies (BGs)

Sequoyah Middle School, Edmond, Oklahoma
www.edmond.k12.ok.us/sequoyah
Library Media Specialist: Michelle Hasenfratz

Books, books, and more books. That is the focus of the many student book clubs at Sequoyah Middle School.

The student population of Sequoyah is around 900, serving grades 6 to 8. The population of Edmond is 68,000, and it is located right next to Oklahoma City.

One of the strongest assets of this middle school is its principal, Jeff Edwards, the founder of the after-school book club movement at Sequoyah. Schools that want to get young teens motivated to read, involved in their schools and libraries, and hear their reactions and recommendations about books will find some exciting ideas in Sequoyah's story.

Edwards is a former English teacher who loves reading and young adult books. He started the YaYa group and recruited his friend, Joe Fine, a principal at nearby Cimmarron Middle School, to join in the project. The principals read and discussed the books, then set up the reading list for the school year. The list was publicized, then the students checked out or bought the books, and read them before each meeting. The principals would have discussion questions, which got the students actively thinking and critically reviewing the books, and there was a lot of participation.

For the first seven years, the principals hosted the groups monthly in each school's media center, with each principal driving a bus to the other's school on alternate months. When the total group became too large, they decided it was time to have separate groups at the respective schools. The groups currently operate in the same fashion, independently at each school.

The YaYas meet once a month after school during the school year in the media center, and once a week during the summer in a local bookstore. Group sizes vary depending on the book being discussed. The smallest groups are 15 to 20, but *Holes* by Louis Sachar (Farrar Straus & Giroux, 1998) attracted 174 students! The gender breakdown is evenly split. There is always food available at meetings, usually popcorn, pretzels, goldfish, and soda. Michelle Hasenfratz and some teachers usually help with the meetings.

Now that an extensive list of books has been developed, the group has turned its name into a verb! When a book has been the group's focus, it is added to the list as one that has been YaYaed. Student members talk up the group and foster peer readers' advisory by recommending the books being read to other students.

Other ways that the YaYa books are promoted is through school book displays and reviews. Many of the Reading and Language Arts teachers have bulletin boards or areas in their classrooms where they display the year's YaYa books. Hasenfratz scans the book covers so the teachers can use those, too, if there is space. There is also a bulletin board case display on the wall in the school building's front foyer where the students in the "I Teach" elective classes fix a YaYa display featuring the current month's book.

In the media center, a big bulletin board faces out to a ramp going past windows. This YaYa Book Group board shows scanned covers of all the books and a blurb about each one. Hasenfratz has a long table in front of her desk to display the YaYa and other books.

The current YaYa book is also included in the book reviews that Hasenfratz e-mails to teachers biweekly. Many teachers who have 32-inch classroom television monitors display the reviews when the students are coming into classes. Some read the reviews aloud. A few of the reading teachers do booktalks for their students, including YaYa books.

Mr. Edwards puts information about the current YaYa book on the daily bulletin's calendar and includes the book on the monthly faculty agenda so it can be reviewed during meetings. Teacher and administrative support plays a big part in promoting reading to the students, and consequently from student to student through the reading clubs.

Hasenfratz says it is wonderful to see principals who love reading, and even better to see them modeling reading for the students. An additional benefit is that two principals from other schools have become interested and have started their own versions of book clubs in their schools.

Another group run by Mr. Edwards, in its third year, is called the Bibliomaniacs. They meet once a month on Saturday evenings. It is a small group of 12 to 15 regular members who are strongly opinionated about the books. When they meet, they have pizza and soft drinks, and also enjoy a game designed around the title selected.

The SURFERs meet once a month, usually on Fridays, for pizza and a book discussion. This group is in its second year. There are plans to start an additional group of students new to Sequoyah. Again, Mr. Edwards runs these groups.

The Lunch Bunch groups have been active for about seven years in the media center. The groups were started informally to promote books by visiting authors, but then became established. Membership varies from 25 to 40, about two-thirds girls and one-third boys. There are six different Lunch Bunch groups, and they each meet four times per year, twice per semester with each group.

Membership is gained by word of mouth, flyers posted in classrooms and around the school, intercom announcements, and through Reading/Writing Workshop teachers promoting the groups in classes. All students need to do is to sign up when there is an open time slot and start attending.

Lunch Bunch groups meet (when else?) at lunchtime during the school day. Membership space is limited to 8 to 10 students, and lunch is 30 minutes. Students bring their lunch and a drink, and Hasenfratz provides dessert. The students spend the time discussing the book for that session, which is sometimes tied to author visits. The students discuss the book, then spend the last five to seven minutes book sharing—discussing other books they have read, want to read, or have heard about. If an author visit is imminent, the librarian gives some brief biographical information about the author and tells about a book the group will read by that person. The emphasis is on reading for fun, and the meetings are relaxed and low-key.

Hasenfratz says, "This is a great way to get to know students one-on-one and see what they like to read and what they are reading. It is good for me, too, because sometimes they have found books that I haven't seen or read about. Their comments are always interesting and for the most part, they aren't shy about sharing their opinions, so that is fun, too."

Who are the members of the Book Groupies, or BGs? They are the teachers—it's a teachers' book group! This group has been together for about eight years, meeting monthly to discuss an adult title or two young adult titles. They meet at a local restaurant for dinner and discussion with the group size at 20 to 24 for most meetings.

When educators get involved in promoting reading among themselves, what better way to show teens how enjoyable and important books are?[8]

Teen Advisory Board (TAB)

Wilson Middle School, Plano, Texas
http://k-12.pisd.edu/Schools/Wilson
Teacher-Librarian: Mary Long
The Teen Advisory Board (TAB) started at the Wilson Middle School in Plano, Texas (population 234,000), in 1998. There were 43 members from 2001 to 2002, 7 boys and 35 girls.

Wilson Middle School's philosophy statement says: "Each student will be recognized as a contributing member of the school community and provided an appropriate educational program with the support needed for social and academic growth." TAB is a way that students are able to meet that philosophical goal.

TAB meets every other week during the school year. They advertise for membership via schoolwide broadcast announcements and through signage. All interested students are welcome to join.

Offices in TAB are Chair, Vice-Chair, and Secretary. To run for an office, students must have attended 80 percent of scheduled meetings or more. The Chair runs TAB meetings, the Vice-Chair assists and runs meetings in the absence of the Chair, and the Secretary keeps and reads minutes from each meeting.

Members of TAB get refreshments at every meeting, plus advance opportunities to sign up for special events hosted by the library. Members are prestiously classified in the volunteer capacity of "library board members."

TAB plans all the activities and programs hosted in the library, ranging from author visits to lunch programs, book and writing clubs, contests, book fair promotions, and philanthropic activities. The latter includes raising money for the public library's adult literacy program and hosting book drives to collect books for Plano's sister cities in Mexico.

A subgroup of TAB is Readers R Us, which is a designated Teens' Top Ten voting group for the 2003–2004 YA Galley Project of the YALSA. Readers R Us developed out of Mary Long's two book clubs and TAB. Long says it was a natural evolution for such a subgroup to form. Members are students who love to read and who are active library supporters, and they enjoyed the idea of being one of five groups in the nation to work on the Teens' Top Ten list of books selected entirely by teens. (See chapter 4 for full details about the Teens' Top Ten/YA Galley Project.)

TAB is a valuable group to the Wilson Middle School Library and all their programs. However, Long sees their role as having multiple purposes: to support the library in all its programs, but also give the students learning opportunities about such things as Roberts Rules of Order and how to run a meeting. In addition, the students learn to work successfully with adults in the community.[9]

Teen Advisory Board (TAB)

Arlington County Public Library, Arlington Public Schools, Virginia
www.co.arlington.va.us/lib; www.arlington.k12.va.us
Librarian Advisor: Margaret Brown

In a cooperative effort with Arlington Public Schools (APS), Arlington County Public Library (ACPL) Teen Advisory Board (TAB) members are middle and high school students who meet to review and evaluate books and make recommendations regarding their quality and appeal.

Currently, ACPL has TAB groups in six middle schools, one of which offers a second group for HILT (High Intensity Language Training), and one high school group meeting at the Central Library. TAB was selected as 1 of 50 outstanding programs nationwide for the second round of Excellence in Library Services for Young Adults awards from YALSA in 1997, and 1 of 6 library programs recognized by the American Library Association (ALA) in 2000 as outstanding examples of after-school programs for teens.

TAB began in 1990 as a pilot program at one Arlington County middle school. It was designed and planned to be an after-school reading and reviewing group with books supplied by the Arlington County Public Library. The ACPL staff felt that for TAB to be successful, the group had to meet at the schools to eliminate transportation problems for the students. Having TAB meet at the schools also allowed the public library to partner with school library media specialists who were an important link in promoting and facilitating the group meetings, as well as providing assistance to members between meetings.[10]

Built-in flexibility makes TAB work in many locations with a variety of participants. TAB has been offered before school, at lunch, after school, and from 5 to 6:30 P.M. The frequency of meetings varies from every other week, to twice a month, to monthly. Although emphasis has traditionally been on reading Best Books for Young Adults committee nominations, groups and individuals can read and report on any book. (For several years one group read science fiction exclusively and called itself SPHERE.)

Students read books provided by the public library, complete a review index card, and give a brief oral summary, answering the question, "Would you recommend this book to a friend?" At the end of the year, groups vote on favorites, lists are published, and books are marked with a "TAB Recommends" seal. Food, such as pizza or make-your-own-sundaes, is a definite enhancement to the program. Special events include trips to regional book discussions (such as Books for the Beast in Baltimore; ALA Midwinter Best Books meetings in Washington, Philadelphia, and New Orleans; and local Shakespeare Theater productions), visits by authors (such as Suzanne Staples, Walter Dean Myers, Chris Myers, and Jacqueline Woodson), and countywide All-TAB meetings.

There were a number of primary objectives in initiating TAB. These include creating a forum where teens could share their opinions about books, magazines, music, and current fads, locating these groups at sites where teens could easily participate without transportation as a barrier; connecting with schools to foster a love of reading for pleasure; using teen advice to improve the appeal of and to promote YA collections; increasing staff contact with and knowledge of YA clientele; and empowering teens to make recommendations to the library and their peers while honing their critical thinking skills and broadening their exposure to literature.

TAB has successfully accomplished these objectives. In addition, TAB provides teen advocates for the library who testify at county budget hearings, give advice to the AV department on music, and to the YA staff on a new Web-based directory of services and activities for teens. They work at Friends of the Library book sales and serve as volunteers for special projects, including being the basis for strong summer and school-year YA volunteer programs. TAB members also give insights into selecting materials for English as a second language (ESL) students.

There are even more benefits to the TAB program. Library staff has been able to translate their broad experiences working with TAB teens into other programs, such as working with youth at risk. TAB provides a venue for a very special group of teens to come together and share their interest in books. It is an adaptable model that can be used in working with many types of teen groups.

As a school/public library cooperative venture, the public library provides books, refreshments, and a YA librarian for each group, and the schools provide the meeting site and a teacher or librarian liaison to co-lead the activity and provide support between meetings.

Although the program was initiated by ACPL, which at first provided most of the materials and financial support, participation by schools and particularly individual English and ESL teachers and librarians has been critical to TAB's success. The enthusiasm of school staff in promoting the program, motivating students, and chaperoning trips has been invaluable. In addition, APS now matches ACPL funds for materials to ensure that all middle school groups have the option of reading the Best Books for Young Adults (BBYA) nominations. In spring 1999, APS paid half the cost of bringing Jacqueline Woodson to speak and participated in a first annual joint planning meeting of all TAB public library and school liaisons that was just the beginning of increased joint ownership and responsibility for this program.

Borders Books has provided some copies of *Benet's Readers Encyclopedia* to all graduating seniors who have participated in TAB since sixth grade, as well as gift certificates for special events.

An ACPL YA librarian and a like-minded middle school English teacher initiated TAB when it began in 1990. The pilot group of 25 students met and discussed books furnished by the library, traveled to Maryland to weigh in with confidence at a regional BBYA discussion, took a field trip to TCBY for frozen yogurts after six books were read, and designed a bookmark to promote their favorite books of the year.

The following year, TAB groups were started at all public middle schools. Soon after, groups were started at a parochial school and a new middle school, and a special HILT program was offered at the school that inaugurated TAB. Upon graduating from middle school TAB, some students lobbied for a high school group, and in 1996 four students graduated who had been in TAB since its inception. By the 2002–2003 school year, a consistent 25 to 35 high school students attend TAB from many of the local high schools, public and private, including 13 seniors, the largest number yet, many of whom have participated since sixth grade.

With money from a state Library Services and Technology Act (LSTA) grant, the TAB concept was adapted in 1999 to a group of 17- to 19-year-old ESL and other at-risk students at the APS Career Center. Called SOAR (Selections of Arlington Readers) (www.co.arlington.va.us/cbo/meetings/2002/jan/6N1c.PDF), members read and recommend books of high interest and low reading level for students learning English and other nonreading high school students. Students vote on their favorites at the end of the year and the library prints a list and marks the books with a SOAR Recommends seal, similar to its TAB seal. A Web site has also been created to promote their selections. With a follow-up grant in 2002, a five-minute video was produced to share the program with other school staff.

The first year that TAB was offered, there was no budget, just staff time. Library or unaccessioned review books were used. Food was provided by Pizza Hut, which gave individual pan pizzas to nonprofit groups working with teens. Transportation to a regional BBYA discussion was in individual cars. A bookmark of favorites was printed by the county within the library's printing budget.

Many permutations have been tried since then to provide books to an expanding TAB population: letters to publishers of YA books for free review copies, which has been successful, rental books, and most recently an allocation from the Friends of the Library, now with a match from schools, to purchase the books outright.

The costs of the current program include:

- Materials (books nominated for BBYA, four copies each for middle schools and one for the high school); $3,000 from Friends of the Library and $3,000 match from APS.

- Public library staff time (eight staff, meeting an average of twice a month, for seven months, an average $19 an hour) is approximately $4,000, plus school staff time.
- Food, programming (including authors), and printing come from $2,000 allocation for TAB activities from the Friends of the Library.

The TAB program represents a major investment in a teen participation program that reaps substantial benefits to the libraries, the students, and to other library clientele. Expenditures are more than justified. It is important to note, however, that this kind of program can also be done simply, on a very small scale, and for a minimal cost.

TAB has been overwhelmingly successful in reaching stated goals. Every year at least 200 students read and review books for the library. Monthly attendance is about 215 students, and monthly circulation is 250 to 300 books.

Observable outcomes include:

- Circulation of TAB favorites from a display that constantly needs refilling and continual reprinting of TAB lists. Of note: YA circulation has continued to increase over previous years, in contrast to a drop in adult and children's.
- The number of requests for information/handouts come from as far as Alaska and as close as Washington, D.C.
- Successful modeling of local groups after TAB in Falls Church, Fairfax County, and an elementary school group that calls itself "Books 'R Us." Although several additional Arlington schools have asked for TAB groups, the program is currently stretched to capacity.
- Periodic student evaluations that say TAB is "great" and complain mostly about "not enough" trips or meetings. One recent evaluation called TAB "one of the highlights of high school."
- Longevity of appeal that keeps many active through high school.
- Adaptability to students learning English, many of whom "graduate" to regular and high school TAB. (Two HILT students were hired as shelvers by the library.)
- Increased comfort of staff with groups of teens and current literature.
- Students who attend and finally speak, or who read only Nancy Drew and discover other authors.
- Student comments to BBYA Committees and their reception at those gatherings.
- The national notoriety of a "reviewer extraordinaire," Adam Balutis, who started in TAB in sixth grade, became a library volunteer, then a paid staff member, and was sought after by publishers and librarians all over the country for his colorful opinions.
- The obvious excitement of teens over books. At one point a teacher at Jefferson Middle School was stunned by the fact that the cart her students were pushing to get to contained not food, but books!

ACPL is committed to continuing the TAB programs in some format and for those audiences that can benefit from the program and/or provide benefits to library staff and patrons. They will continue to adapt the program to meet the needs of new groups, as they did with SOAR, and to look for ways to extend the range of its effectiveness. Most recently, because the regular TAB groups practically run themselves, they are trying to focus on reaching HILT and other non-English-speaking or non-reading groups. Their work with an APS program, New Directions (ND), for high school students removed from the schools for behavior reasons, contains a literature component that they could probably not have offered without many years' experience with TAB. One year, ND students read almost all of Jacqueline Woodson's books. Each was given a copy of *If You Come Softly* (Putnam, 2002) to have autographed in their one-hour meeting with her after she spoke to an All-TAB group. They were also given copies of *Monster* by Walter Dean Myers (HarperCollins, 1999), which they discussed with teachers and library staff, including one who served on the Printz Committee that gave Myers the award. Since that time, they have read books by Chris Myers and met with him, and have been given copies of *Bad Boy: A Memoir* (HarperCollins, 2001), also by Walter Dean Myers, which they have read and discussed.

In addition, ACPL's YA summer reading program, Cool Reflections, a read-review-and-win-a-prize event from June to August, is a spin-off of TAB, with feedback but no meetings. Teens can write minireviews or enter virtually by e-mailing them. Perhaps in the not-too-distant future there will also be "Virtual TAB." One step in that direction launched during Teen Read Week 2002 is a new online form for teens to submit reviews and recommendations throughout the year.

ACPL has developed Tips for a Successful Teen Advisory Board. Some of the points they feel important to consider include:

- Go to where teens are (schools, community centers) so that transportation is not an issue, and pick a time when most can come.
- Partner with enthusiastic advisors at your location.
- Find opportunities to bring TAB groups to the library, expose them to authors and other readers.
- Make the groups teen centered, and ensure that they see the results of their work with books you buy and lists of their recommendations, have opportunities for them to share their opinions with the larger or library community, share a spot on your Web page, and give them a choice in the end-of-year celebration.
- Let the teens talk about any book, whether or not it is or ever will be a library book, or let them attend and have the option to listen and not talk at all.
- Be flexible and let the needs of the group dictate the structure and process.
- Be aware of the political climate of your community and consider sending a letter to parents explaining the nature of the reviewing that their students will be

doing. Choose books to review that are appropriate for your audience. We find that teens self-select what they can handle, but parents may be more concerned about content.

- Learn the names of your teens and have fun! This could be the best thing that you have ever done. It is for them![11]

NOTES

1. Michael B. Eisenberg with Danielle H. Miller, "This Man Wants to Change Your Job," *School Library Journal* 48, no. 9 (September 2002): 49.
2. Margaret A. Edwards, *The Fair Garden and the Swarm of Beasts* (New York: Hawthorn, 1969), 148–49.
3. Eisenberg, "This Man Wants to Change Your Job," 48.
4. Susan Eberhardt, "Middle School Reading Promotion with Student Advisory Groups," *Indiana Media Journal* 18, no. 3 (Spring 1996): 78–80.
5. Kay Hones, Librarian, John O'Connell High School, interviewed by the author, e-mails 9 and 20 September 2002.
6. Connie Mitchell, Media Specialist, Carmel High School, interviewed by the author, e-mails 23 August 2001, 18 January 2002, and 20 February 2002.
7. Edee Lund, Media Specialist, Bemidji Middle School, interviewed by the author, e-mail 11 January 2002.
8. Michelle Hasenfratz, Library Media Specialist, Sequoyah Middle School, interviewed by the author, e-mails 6, 20, 23, and 26 September 2002.
9. Mary Long, Teacher-Librarian, Wilson Middle School, interviewed by the author, e-mails 7 and 27 August 2002 and 1 December 2003.
10. Mary K. Chelton, ed. *Excellence in Library Services to Young Adults: The Nation's Top Programs*, 2nd ed. (Chicago: American Library Association, 1997), 49.
11. Margaret Brown, Librarian, Arlington County Public Library, interviewed by the author, e-mails 26 September 2002 and 2, 11, and 12 October 2002.

Appendix A

Libraries as Safe Havens for Teens

YA 101
What Every YA Librarian
Needs to Know

The Young Adult Advisory Board:
How to Make It Work

Evie Wilson

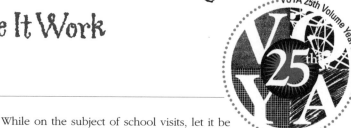

VOYA 25th Volume Year 2002-2003

*Editor's Note: When this article appeared in the April 1979 VOYA (pages 11-14), it was the first explanation ever about how to run a library YA Advisory Board. Adapting for librarians the concept of youth participation (YP) introduced by the National Commission on Resources for Youth when it was founded in 1967, this article preceded the 1981 creation of the Youth Participation Committee by the Young Adult Services Division (YASD, now YALSA) of the American Library Association, and the 1983 publication of YASD's first YP handbook, **Youth Participation in School and Public Libraries**. For more than a decade, Wilson's VOYA article was the only resource available for help in creating a YAAB; your VOYA editor was one of many YA librarians who considered it a bible. This classic article preserves a rare slice of YP history—and its bibliography reveals the roots of today's exploding movement to give teens a voice in their own library services. Wilson's guidelines remain as inspiring and useful as they were nearly a quarter century ago. Accompanying this pioneer piece is VOYA's latest take on the topic, Jan Chapman's* The Care and Feeding of a Teen Advisory Board *on page 449.]*

Let's face it. Genuine (as opposed to "token") youth participation is not popular among adults these days. Two major causes of this attitude are the lack of experience youth have in responsible decision-making, and a lack of commitment (time, patience, and experience) to youth learning these skills from adults who have become caught up in the fast pace and "future shock" of our present culture. The issues of "why youth participation" and "why the public library" have been reiterated elsewhere (see the last item in Additional Readings). Here you will find some practical suggestions (based on experiences at the Finkelstein Library, New York, and the Tampa Public Library in Florida) for making legitimate youth participation a reality.

The principles involved apply to all youth advisory boards, regardless of agency, but the examples have come from the public library field because that is where I have had my experiences.

How and Where to Get the Kids

The answer seems obvious: anywhere young people come together. This means game rooms, handy shops, pizza parlors, skating rinks, shopping centers, and hopefully, the public library. A proven successful way to have a record of the names and addresses of those who are interested is to use a survey flyer handout. This flyer would be in bold colors and design; it might request name, address, phone number, age, school, as well as preference for time and day for meetings and programs, preference for types of programs (book discussion, films, self-defense, crafts), and indication of favorite types of reading subjects (SF, romance, mystery, teen novels, etc.). In addition to being the basis for developing a YA Advisory Board, this type of questionnaire can be used for planning programs based on expressed interests, formulating a bulk mailing list for programs, and even purchase of titles for YA collections.

The questionnaire can be distributed within the community as well as the library system and in classes being visited for booktalks.

While on the subject of school visits, let it be said that students who fill out questionnaires in a captive audience classroom situation often do so to impress a teacher or even under the pressure of a teacher. You must decide whether you want to develop your advisory board under the auspices of repressive public school practices where student participation in school administration is rarely encouraged. Those YAs who express interest by filling out questionnaires voluntarily in locations of their own choosing (library branch or rec areas) are likely to be far more committed to their YA Advisory Board. They're also likely to associate the public library with a more positive image. Your search for new Board members should never cease, even when you have a good working core group. As YAs move into the upper teens, they often assume increased responsibilities—jobs, school plays, clubs, or school newspapers, for example. The questionnaires should be on continuous display in the YA areas of libraries and in key community locations.

A page from the original 1979 VOYA article

IF YOUR ADMINISTRATION DOES NOT SUPPORT THE CONCEPT OF GENUINE YOUTH PARTICIPATION ...DO NOT BEGIN THIS PROJECT AT ALL

At left and below, Leo Weinose, Director of the Tampa-Hillsborough County Public Library System, talks with members of the Young Adult Advisory Board.

****

likely you'll have a core group of about fifteen. The easiest way to reduce initial drop-out rate is to be very clear in expectations and taks. Have a clear delineation of responsibility. Make assignments based on indicated YA interest; their priorities, not yours. If possible, start with a small activity which will be immediately rewarding. The Commission states:

Move to action as fast as possible. Nothing can put off youth more than interminable planning sessions which do not result in concrete action of any kind. Many adults tend to want to teach everything about a problem before allowing youth to have any experience with it. Young people do not come into the program to be lectured.

Keep close personal contact with your YAs. If they miss a meeting or haven't been by the library for a while, call and find out why. Be available when they come in with their concerns whether they be personal or school related.

Transportation is always a problem for the young as well as the old. Today's parents aren't happy with the role of chauffer. "Thumbing" isn't safe for anyone, old or young. So schedule meetings carefully—never two in one week or even a meeting the same week as a library program. Also be aware of the secondary academic calendar—no meetings during finals or Regents. The best months for programs and meetings seem to vary in different parts of the country. In

(1) How can we make library services more meaningful to YAs?

(2) What changes do you feel should be made?

(3) How can the smaller advisory boards get more YAs interested?

(4) Does the book collection at your branch satisfy your needs?

(5) Do you think YAs should have a greater role in book selection for the YA collection?

(6) What kind of library programming would you like to see and be a planning part of?

(7) How would you feel about creating a YA newsletter, literary magazine type publication?

(8) How do you feel about youth advocacy? Would you like to be involved in advocacy in your community?

(9) Would you like to see more library programs concerning youth problem areas such as alcoholism and runaways? If so, name the most serious problem areas for your community.

FOLLOW-UP: HOW TO KEEP THEM COMING BACK

Consider these five key elements which should be present for successful operations. They are part of the definition of Youth Participation as set forth by The National Commission on Resources for Youth. The five elements are:

(1) Responsible, challenging action which is meaningful, valued activity and requires reaching beyond the previous range of one's knowledge or performance;

(2). Meeting genuine needs that both youth and community value;

(3) Opportunities for planning and/or decision-making;

(4) Provision for critical reflection, and

(5) Group effort toward a common goal.

If you start with thirty young people, it's

VOICE OF YOUTH ADVOCATES   12   April 1979

The First YA Advisory Board Meeting

Members of the group might be strangers to each other; playing a get-acquainted game breaks the ice. The game used initially at all branch meetings in Tampa was for each person in the group to interview the person next to them for five minutes, taking down the important items (school, age, interests and hobbies, siblings, pets). Each person then reported to the entire group. It was a resounding success at easing tension, and one group at the West Gate Branch was in hysterics over stories of unmanageable siblings and large pet dogs who ate gerbils! You will find other such games in **Awareness Games: Personal Growth Through Group Interaction** by Claus-Jergen Hoper (St. Martin's, 1975).

Be well-organized. Have your agenda carefully worked out. At the same time encourage discussion and avoid lecturing. The National Commission on Resources for Youth says:

One of the dangers of presenting your ideas unequivocally and clearly in the beginning stages is that first impressions are lasting, and youth could accept this as a pattern for collaborative planning. On the other hand, deliberate bumbling or equivocation on your part will often be construed as manipulation or conning of youth and be interpreted by them as a lack of respect for them as individuals. In addition, you will run the risk of discouraging a lot of young people if there is too much fumbling around in the initial stages.

Tell the group who you are, something about the nature of your job, what you're trying to accomplish, the purpose of the YA Advisory Board(s), and why they're being formed, along with some possible programs and activities. Show publicity flyers from other libraries so they can see what kinds of things have been done elsewhere. The fact that they've come to this meeting indicates an interest upon which you can build. The group should be told some of the things they will be expected to contribute to the total effort if they continue, such as their time, their talents, and their ideas. This might sometimes mean their giving up a Saturday afternoon and reorganizing homework for a weeknight meeting. Solicit artists from the group for artwork for the program flyers. These are some of the questions you might wish to put to the group at this or subsequent meetings:

(1) How can we make library services more meaningful to YAs?
(2) What changes do you feel should be made?
(3) How can the smaller advisory boards get more YAs interested?
(4) Does the book collection at your branch satisfy your needs?
(5) Do you think YAs should have a greater role in book selection for the YA collection?
(6) What kind of library programming would you like to see and be a part of planning?
(7) How would you feel about creating a YA newsletter or literary magazine publication?
(8) How do you feel about youth advocacy? Would you like to be involved in advocacy in your community?
(9) Would you like to see more library programs concerning youth problem areas such as alcoholism and runaways? If so, name the most serious problem in your community.

Follow-Up: How to Keep Them Coming Back

Consider these five key elements which should be present for successful operations. They are part of the definition of Youth Participation as set forth by the National Commission on Resources for Youth. The five elements are:

(1) Responsible, challenging action which is meaningful, valued activity and requires reaching beyond the previous range of one's knowledge or performance.
(2) Meeting genuine needs that both youth and community value.

(3) Opportunities for planning and/or decision-making.
(4) Provision for critical reflection.
(5) Group effort toward a common goal.

If you start with thirty young people, it's likely you'll have a core group of about fifteen. The easiest way to reduce the initial dropout rate is to be very clear in expectations and tasks. Have a clear delineation of responsibility. Make assignments based on indicated YA interest—their priorities, not yours. If possible, start with a small activity that will be immediately rewarding. The Commission states:

Move to action as fast as possible. Nothing can put off youth more than interminable planning sessions that do not result in concrete action of any kind. Many adults tend to want to teach everything about a problem before allowing youth to have any experience with it. Young people do not come into the program to be lectured.

Keep close personal contact with your YAs. If they miss a meeting or haven't been by the library for a while, call and find out why. Be available when they come in with their concerns, whether they be personal or school-related. Transportation is always a problem for the young as well as the old. Today's parents aren't happy with the role of chauffeur. "Thumbing" isn't safe for anyone, old or young. So schedule meetings carefully—never two in one week or even a meeting the same week as a library program. Also be aware of the secondary academic calendar—no meetings during finals or Regents. The best months for programs and meetings seem to vary in different parts of the country. In Spring Valley, New York, September, November, December, June, and July were good months. In Tampa, September through November and January through April were best. YAs should assume some of the administrative responsibility for keeping the group together, such as making calls or sending cards for meetings. If there are members of the group who shirk assigned tasks, the group should decide what should be done about this. Allow time at each meeting to do some discussion and evaluation of how projects and programs have measured up to the group's expectations.

Some Possible Activities

If you are working in a large system with several branches, a system-wide YA Advisory Board can be formed with representatives from each branch. This system-wide board could meet with the system director to discuss YA needs, interests, and recommendations. A director might even be receptive enough to advocate for a YA member of the library board. The system-wide advisory group might want to consider formulating by-laws, electing officers, and planning overall system activities, such as a YA newsletter and a get-together for all branch groups at the end of the school year. Most libraries have some days set aside for in-service training for staff. It's proven very good for bridging the generation gap between library staff and YA patrons to have a panel of representatives from the YA Advisory Board to answer questions about their needs and interests from the entire library staff. After conducting such a program for the staff at the Tampa-Hillsborough County Public Library System (and it's being repeated for the county library association), one staff member stated, "It's the best in-service program I've been to here—really helped me to better understand young people and their problems."

Young adults have expressed interest in becoming involved in the selection process for materials which are to be made available to them and their peers. This seems to be a reasonable request, especially if the library is on a purchase plan such as Greenaway, which supplies new books quickly upon publication. Otherwise new YA titles purchased from professional reviews could still be given to members of the Advisory Board on a regular basis to test the books' appeal and validity to YAs. A simple review card can be devised which could be posted for other YAs to read when browsing through the YA collection.

Youth participation within the community with outside groups is another viable possibility. Members of the YA Advisory Board have attended meetings in Hillsborough County on youth suicide, alcohol abuse, and adolescent pregnancy. Other youth workers often call the office of the YA Services Specialist; they are anxious for youth reactions to task force recommendations for services and have encouraged youth involvement in peer counseling on alcohol abuse. It seems reasonable that a 17-year-old mother (also a member of the library's YA Advisory Board) could give valuable input to a community group seeking better sex education in the public schools. Other community projects which have been successfully executed and recorded in **New Roles for Youth** are youth radio programs, youth recording oral history, youth tutoring youth, youth in business at the Soul Gate Shopping Center (Cleveland, OH), and youth beautification with original wall murals in the inner city. This involvement in the total community as well as the library is received with enthusiasm by youth who can't find jobs and are bored to the point of considering much more negative alternatives such as vandalism and substance abuse. YAs are anxious to contribute, and indeed, they have much originality and creativity to give when the opportunity is available.

Further Considerations for Success

It has been assumed here that you have full administrative support toward forming a Young Adult Advisory Board. If your administration does not support the concept of genuine youth participation and does not back that up with good faith (making your time free to develop this group and in turn taking action on at least some of the YA recommendations), DO NOT begin this project at all. YAs are already accustomed to being low on everyone's priority list, and furthermore, institutional credibility is "at the pits" with youth as it is. Don't alienate your future patrons (and taxpayers) by promising something you can't deliver!

Some training or at least outside reading in the areas of values clarification, role-playing, problem-solving, adolescent psychology, small-group facilitation, and crisis intervention would be extremely useful. The question of the YA librarian as counselor is another issue (see Fine article on reading list), but if you are empathetic and you work with youth, you are going to hear about their problems, some very serious. You must be able to deal with them right then and there, even if you do a referral to a community agency. And honoring confidentiality has as much to do with your credibility and the library's image as delivery of library services.

Familiarize yourself with youth in the total community. Check census tracts for areas of high youth population percentages. Know the statistics on youth problems in your community—such as adolescent pregnancy, VD, youth crime, and substance abuse (new collective word of alcohol, cigarette, and drug use). Know the organizations (and staff in them) that provide help to youth in these problem areas. All these things can provide that all-important statistical justification to reluctant administrators who question youth participation as well as to patrons who might question certain titles in your collection.

Here are some personality characteristics that young adults have expressed as necessary in an adult facilitator: liberal, open-minded, assertive (bordering on aggressive), warm, sensitive, caring, creative, organized, CRAZY, and comfortable in dealing with youth.

Finally, before undertaking any Advisory Board project, remind yourself again of the five points necessary for genuine youth participation. In a library situation, this means more than shelving books or stamping date due slips. Good example: planning a library program from beginning to end, including PR, calling speakers, room set-up, the whole gambit. This type of activity provides youth

with the responsibility and confidence that comes from being needed by society, as well as the achievement of self-determined goals. And important investment in the future!

Further Reading

ACTION. **Student Volunteers: A Manual for Communities**. 1971. 69p. paper.

Fine, Sara. "The Librarian As Youth Counselor." **Drexel Library Quarterly**, v. 14, no. 1, January 1978, p. 29-44.

Gordon, James S. "Youth Helping Youth." **Social Policy**, Sept./Oct. 1976, p. 48+.

National Commission on Resources for Youth, 36 W. 44th Street, New York, NY 10036. **New Roles for Youth** (and other materials on youth participation). Citation Press, 1974. 245p. $4.95.

Pearl, Arthur, et al. **The Value of Youth**. Responsible Action (P.O. Box 924, Davis, CA 95616), 1978. 320p. paper. $5.75.

Pollock, Shirley E. **Youth Worker's Success Manual**. Abingdon, 1978. 80p. $3.95.

Teen Age Health Consultants (TAHC), St. Paul, MN. **TAHC Program Guide**. 143p. $5 pb.

U.S. Department of Health, Education, and Welfare, Office of Human Development, Office of Youth Development, Division of Youth Activities. **An Introductory Manual on Youth Participation**. (Prepared by the National Commission on Resources for Youth). GPO, 1976. 48p.

Wilson, Evie. "The Young Adult Advisory Board: Decision-Making As Recreation and Responsibility." **The Bookmark** (New York State Library). Winter 1978, p. 55-59.

Evie then.

Evie now.

Evie Wilson-Lingbloom is Managing Librarian at Edmonds Library in the Sno-Isle Regional Library System in Marysville, Washington. Back in the '70s during her "hippie days," as Evie Wilson describes them, young adult services were revolutionary. It was no accident that this first article about YA Advisory Boards was published in **VOYA**; *Evie credits* **VOYA**'s *co-founder for its basic premise. "Remembering back to those early days, I have Mary K. Chelton to thank for the direction I took, for when I asked her once about something in my teen area, she said simply, 'Why don't you ask the kids?' Just like so many librarians in those days (and now, too, sadly), I just hadn't thought of doing that. It certainly has been my way ever since."*

Appendix B

YA 101
What Every YA Librarian Needs to Know

Ten Tips for Starting a Teen Advisory Group

AMY A. CANADEE

Starting a Teen Advisory Group (TAG) in a public library can be a daunting prospect. So many factors need to be present and in sync. Administrative support for young adult services is crucial. Your library's mission statement or strategic plan should mention the importance of service to young adults. There must be a staff member with the time and talent to work with teens—and there must be interested teens. Then, if Jupiter aligns with Mars, all will fall into place.

Actually, all these important factors were present when OH YA! (pronounced like the expression "oh, ya") was born at Wadsworth Public Library in Ohio. A community survey indicated that some patrons were upset by disruptive middle school students in the library after school. This feedback was incorporated into the library's Strategic Plan. One of my tasks as Young Adult Librarian was to develop strategies to meet the challenge of the teens' sometimes problematic behavior. The discipline problems have been handled with effective use and enforcement of the library's Patron Behavior Policy, as well as improved communication with the library staff, schools, and local police department. Another task of mine was to meet the needs of underserved teens.

OH YA! started in the fall of 1997. Since then, active group members have conceived, planned, and produced many excellent library programs. There are eleven group members from the ages of thirteen to seventeen. We meet weekly during the school year and less regularly in the summer. The most popular programs were a **Magic: The Gathering**™ Team Tournament, a Spring Art Contest, and a summer sleepover program. Along with the successes have been the growing pains of an evolving group: personality conflicts, dropouts, and misbehavior. These challenges helped me achieve my goal: kick kids into, not out of, the library.

Everyone has their fifteen minutes of fame, and OH YA! had theirs when they hit the front page of the local newspaper. Rumors spread that I was an expert on teens! I was invited to speak to children's librarians at Columbus Metropolitan Library about starting a TAG. A field trip was born. Three members of OH YA! traveled with me to Columbus to spread the word. It was a fun and exciting sojourn, with the added adolescent thrill of being dismissed from school for the day.

The ten tips below are offered as possible ways to avoid some of the pitfalls, or at least be prepared for them. This type of youth participation will reap many rewards for the teens, the library, and you. Benefits far outweigh the trials and tribulations—which are par for the course when working with young adults.

Amy Canadee is presently working for Americorps as a Child Advocate in a homeless shelter in Akron, Ohio. She can be reached by e-mail at: amityz@hotmail.com.

The Ten Tips

1. Know your community's teens.
Is there a group that hangs out at the library? Do you have a rapport with them? What community activities do the teens participate in—sports, band, church, and so forth? Do they have time for another activity? Has there been a survey of the teens in the community at large or of the teens who use the library? What services does the library offer teens?

2. Recruit members or select members?
Teen Advisory Group demographics may be very different depending on whether you are selective about members or send out open invitations. How inclusive do you want the TAG to be? Do you want only mature, serious teens? Or younger, less mature ones? A mixture? Do you want members to represent the ethnic, racial, and economic make-up of your community? Do you want to be the final arbiter of who is accepted, or leave it up to the teens to vote?

When recruiting members, use these possible sources for contacts: YA summer reading club name lists, honor society, Boy/Girl Scouts, library "regulars," library pages or teen volunteers, teachers, media specialists, and home school associations.

3. Be ready for surprises.
Throw out all of your preconceived notions about teens, if you still have any. Realize that running a TAG will *not* be a time saver.

4. Start small.
Tiny, perhaps minuscule. Build relationships and rapport before tackling larger projects.

5. Go with the flow.
Each group will have an energy of its own depending on the mix of teens and the librarian's style. At the first meeting consider an icebreaker exercise, have teens fill out membership applications, and do a brainstorming session on project ideas.

6. Channel the flow.
With group input, set up fair rules to provide structure. Give feedback, guidance, and direction to keep them on task. Consider using a talking stick. Encourage attendance by keeping track of absences. Phone or e-mail members with meeting reminders. Think about electing officers. Prepare an agenda for each meeting, or designate a teen secretary to do so.

7. Allow for social time.
Before and after the formal meeting, provide snacks and time for socializing.

8. Reward them.
Every so often, show them how much you appreciate their volunteer work. Ideas: pizza, group T-shirts, field trips, first in line for new books they suggest to order, framed group photo, overnight at the library, recognition at annual library volunteer function, celebrating birthdays.

9. Think to the future.
How can the group keep going? Will it be self-sustaining or is there a need to recruit new members annually? Will it meet over the summer? Review the TAG's progress periodically.

10. HAVE FUN.
Laugh often (but not too loud).

Appendix C

the Care and Feeding of a teen Advisory Board

jan Chapman

Libraries as Safe Havens for Teens

A toast to the king and queen at Medieval Madness.
PHOTO CREDIT: jan Chapman

[Editor's Note: For guidelines on the initial process, see Amy A. Canadee's Ten Tips for Starting a Teen Advisory Group on page 102 of VOYA's June 1999 issue. Proceed to the next step with this article. And don't miss Evie Wilson's classic overview of the process in this article's 1979 partner on page 446, The Young Adult Advisory Board: How to Make It Work.]

You've done it! Your Teen Advisory Board is up and running. Your group is loudly enthusiastic, committed to action, and brimming over with ideas. Your meetings are often chaotic, occasionally frustrating, but always lively. How do you keep the momentum, especially when your teens are juggling so many other activities?

Once your group formed, your first question was probably "What do we do now?" At our first meeting, our TAB decided to focus its energies on planning and implementing new programs, helping with displays and community relations, publishing a peer newsletter, and recommending new materials for the library to purchase. These tasks might seem daunting to many adults, but this group of energetic and idealistic teens didn't give them a second thought.

Teens enjoy new challenges and usually don't let obstacles or objections from more cautious adults dissuade them from attempting ambitious projects. But once the novelty wears off, it can be a challenge to keep them interested and coming back for what are basically planning meetings. What keeps them coming? More importantly, what developmental needs are nourished by this group's interaction?

What Brings them together

Socializing

Teen Advisory Boards are like any other group that meets regularly. Bonds develop, friendships (and even the occasional romance) form, and sometimes it is difficult to keep the group focused on the task at hand. As leaders/facilitators, we would do well to remember that socializing is an important aspect of this group. It is easier to allow for structured socializing than attempt to ban it altogether. If the socializing becomes overwhelming, I warn the group that we will conclude the meeting immediately if it continues to be disruptive. I had to act upon this threat once; the teens were so appalled at the consequences that they made a real effort to police themselves at meetings thereafter. Our solution is to get the work part of the meeting out of the way first and then chat over refreshments.

"Did they actually wear these things in medieval times?"
PHOTO CREDIT: jan Chapman

Community Service

Chances are that teens attracted to this type of group already have a strong public service ethic. Teens also are motivated to participate because of schools or organizations (church, National Honor Society) that require community service hours. You will undoubtedly be asked to document hours for your teens. When I recruit for this group, I like to point out that volunteer hours are a great asset on a job application, particularly a first job application when the teen has no previous work experience.

Empowerment and Achievement

One of the most powerful motivators for TAB members is the sense of accomplishment and empowerment that they feel when a program that began as an idea tossed out in a brainstorming session becomes a reality. One of our most successful programs, a Teen Art Show, was the brainchild of one extremely determined TAB member, who overcame my initial qualms, lobbied hard at the high school to coax teens into entering their artwork, and transformed our plain meeting room into an art gallery, complete with lighting effects and artfully placed display stands. She was absolutely glowing with a sense of achievement on the day of the show.

Encouragement

Teens also need to have interested, objective, and friendly adults in their lives who enjoy their company and encourage their dreams. Parents are committed to raising strong, healthy adults; teachers are committed to educating future citizens. Teens still need other interested adults who can nurture their growth as unique individuals.

All the above factors are important to ensure the continuity of your TAB. But even the most active, successful group can fall prey to boredom. How do you keep things lively?

Jazz up your Meetings

I try to keep meetings lively by introducing new elements in every meeting. Icebreakers and games are a great way to make your meetings fun, and they also help newcomers acclimate to your group. Booktalk new books at every meeting. Bring in other new materials of interest to your teens, such as new CDs, DVDs, and videos. Teens enjoy getting a first look at brand new materials that

tie-dying socks at the TAB Appreciation Party.
Photo credit: jacqui Huskey

have just come into the library. You can also add variety by bringing different refreshments to the meeting. My teens are always impressed when I bring homemade brownies or order pizza for a change of pace. Occasionally, to break the routine, I will have a meeting that is simply a fun get-together, when we don't do any planning, but instead enjoy a game, such as a library scavenger hunt.

Problems and Solutions

Conflict

All small groups develop an occasional dysfunctional tic. The most common problem is conflict between individual members. Personalities will clash. A domineering member can irritate other members who resent being bossed around; two members who become close friends might develop a problem in their relationship, which is then brought into the meeting. These tics often resolve amicably and without intervention, but sometimes you will need to speak to members privately about behavior concerns. It is wise to have a behavior guidelines policy for the group established at the outset—encourage your members to assist you in creating such guidelines. I have never had to ask a misbehaving member to leave the group; often peer pressure encourages them to amend their behavior.

Clique Behavior

It is possible to have too much of a good thing when it comes to peer bonding. Your members can become so "tight" that they will be dismissive, even hostile, towards new members. Sibling rivalry can emerge when teens from the same family join your group.

It is important to squelch clique behavior the moment it surfaces. I am constantly reminding our older TAB members that they were once "newbies" and needed guidance to be part of the group. It is a good idea to enlist experienced TAB members to mentor newer members, which gives the older members a sense of importance and helps the new member to fit in quickly.

Stagnation

Small groups run out of steam from time to time, when they just need to re-evaluate their goals

Return of the Mummy to the TAB Halloween Party.
Photo credit: Jacqui Huskey

or their mission. Flexibility is paramount in keeping a group viable and active. I might ask our group to take another look at our organizational structure, for example, to see if they wish to make changes. Our group has never elected officers, but that does not mean that we have dismissed this idea as unworkable. Group dynamics change constantly; an awareness of this tendency will help you sense when change might be just the ticket.

Dropouts

With all the activities competing for the attention of teens these days, it is inevitable that some TAB members will drop out because of hectic schedules. Your teens also will be graduating from high school someday. It is important to cultivate new potential members to save your group from an untimely demise. Most of the time, new members will be recruited by your current TAB members. Also keep in mind those teens who like to haunt your teen area (if you're lucky enough to have one) or teens who volunteer at the library over the summer. An interested teacher can be a wonderful recruiter; I have had several teens join because a teacher thought the group was a great idea and encouraged her students to try it.

Conclusion

Starting a TAB has been one of the most rewarding experiences of my career. Teens can have a profound impact on your library; they are instrumental in helping librarians make savvy programming and collection development decisions. A TAB can increase your program attendance, boost your circulation, and help your library and community recognize the value of its teen citizens.

What are you waiting for? Start your own TAB today—and then nurture it for many satisfying and exciting years to come.

Clockwise from top: "Yeah we rule!" the TAB at Akron-Summit County Public Library; Breaking the Ice—the Lifesaver Game; "Let them eat cake"—TAB International Dessert Night program.
Photo credit: Jan Chapman

Jan Chapman is a young adult librarian at the Norton branch of the Akron-Summit County Public Library in Norton, Ohio. The TAB that she has advised for the past three years has been one of the joys of her career. She is passionate about the importance of this type of group, both to the library and the community.

SELECTED BIBLIOGRAPHY

Alessio, Amy. "Meet VOYA's Teen Reviewers! Adults and Teens Share 'Monkey Books' and More." *Voice of Youth Advocates* 27, no. 3 (August 2004): 202–06

Braun, Linda W. *Teens.library: Developing Internet Services for Young Adults.* Chicago: American Library Association, 2002.

———. "Tag Team Tech: Surfing for TAGs." *Voice of Youth Advocates* 26, no. 5 (December 2003): 377.

———. *Technically Involved: Technology-Based Youth Participation Activities for Your Library.* Chicago: American Library Association, 2003.

Brown, Margaret, and Pat Muller. "TAB: A Middle School/Public Library Success Story." *Voice of Youth Advocates* 17, no. 5 (December 1994): 255–58.

Canadee, A. A. "Ten Tips for Starting a Teen Advisory Group." *Voice of Youth Advocates* 22, no. 2 (June 1999): 102.

Carton, Debbie. "Cover to Cover at Berkeley PL." *School Library Journal* 38, no. 7 (July 1992): 34.

Caywood, Carolyn. "What's a Teen?" *School Library Journal* 39, no. 2 (February 1993): 42.

———. "Advocates-in-Training." *School Library Journal* 43, no. 11 (November 1997): 51.

Chapman, Jan. "The Care and Feeding of a Teen Advisory Board." *Voice of Youth Advocates* 25, no. 6 (February 2003): 449–50.

Chelton, Mary K. *Excellence in Library Services to Young Adults.* Chicago: American Library Association, 1994.

———. *Excellence in Library Services to Young Adults,* 2nd ed. Chicago: American Library Association, 1997.

———. *Excellence in Library Services to Young Adults,* 3rd ed. Chicago: American Library Association, 2000.

Chelton, Mary K., and Dorothy M. Broderick, eds. *VOYA Reader Two.* Lanham, Md.: Scarecrow Press, 1998.

Dunn, Susan. "Birth of 'Teen Scene.'" *School Library Journal* 39, no. 2 (February 1993): 42.

Duwel, Lucretia, Diane Stackpole, and Barbara Blosveren. "So That You May Know: Teen Reading Group Meets Holocaust Survivors." *Voice of Youth Advocates* 25, no. 4 (October 2002): 249.

Eberhardt, Susan. "Middle School Reading Promotion with Student Advisory Groups." *Indiana Media Journal* 18 (Spring 1996): 78–80.

Edwards, Kirsten. *Teen Library Events: A Month-by-Month Guide.* Westport, Conn.: Greenwood Press, 2001.

Edwards, Margaret A. *The Fair Garden and the Swarm of Beasts: The Library and the Young Adult,* centennial ed. Foreword by Betty Carter. Chicago: ALA Editions, 2002.

Eisenberg, Michael B. "This Man Wants to Change Your Job." *School Library Journal* 48, no. 9 (September 2002): 46–50.

Falck, Kara. "VOYA's Most Valuable Program 2002: Munching on Books." *Voice of Youth Advocates* 25, no. 4 (October 2002): 238–39.

Gillespie, Kellie M. *Teen Volunteer Services in Libraries.* VOYA Guides, no. 1. Lanham, Md.: VOYA Books/Scarecrow Press, 2004.

Gorman, Michelle. "Wiring Teens to the Library." *School Library Journal Net Connect* 48, no. 8 (Summer 2002): 18–20.

Herald, Diana Tixier. "Buy More Books! & Other Bright Ideas from a Teen Advisory Board." *School Library Journal* 42, no. 7 (July 1996): 26–27.

Hillyard, Blaine. "Assets and Outcomes: New Directions in Young Adult Services in Public Libraries." *Public Libraries* 41, no. 4 (July/August 2002): 195–99.

Honnold, RoseMary. *101+ Teen Programs That Work.* New York: Neal-Schuman, 2002.

———. "The Who, What, When, Where, Why and How of Managing a Teen Advisory Board." *YAttitudes* 1, no. 2 (Winter 2002). www.ala.org/yalsa.

Jones, Patrick, Michelle Gorman, and Tricia Suellentrop. *Connecting Young Adults and Libraries,* 3rd ed. New York: Neal-Schuman, 2004.

———. *New Directions for Library Service to Young Adults.* Chicago: American Library Association, 2002.

Jones, Patrick, and Joel Shoemaker. *Do It Right!: Best Practices for Serving Young Adults in School and Public Libraries.* New York: Neal-Schuman, 2001.

Lesko, Wendy Schaetzel. *Maximum Youth Involvement: The Complete Gameplan for Community Action,* rev. ed. Kensington, Md.: Youth Activism Project, 2003.

MacRae, Cathi Dunn. "Watch Out for 'Don't Read This!': How a Library Youth Participation Group Was Silenced by Schools Yet Made Its Voice Heard." *Voice of Youth Advocates* 18, no. 2 (June 1995): 80–87.

Meyers, Elaine, "The Coolness Factor: Ten Libraries Listen to Youth." *American Libraries* 30, no. 10 (November 1999): 42–45.

———. "The Road to the Coolness: Youth Rock the Public Library." *American Libraries* 32, no. 2 (February 2001): 46–48.

Minkel, Walter. "Reaching (and Teaching) Teens." *School Library Journal Net Connect* 48, no. 2 (Winter 2002): 28–29.

Munson, Amelia H. *An Ample Field.* Chicago: American Library Association, 1950.

Purdy, Rebecca. "YA Clicks: Introducing the Web Surfers' Review Code." *Voice of Youth Advocates* 25, no. 4 (October 2002): 262–63.

Razzano, Barbara Will, "Creating the Library Habit." *Library Journal* 110, no. 4 (February 15, 1985): 111–14.

Reed, Sally G. "Norfolk Architect Becomes Volunteer Extraordinaire." *American Libraries* 33, no. 4 (April 2002): 74–75.

Rutherford, Deana. "My Life as a Rodenite." *Young Adult Library Services* 1, no. 1 (Fall 2002): 8–10.

Sprince, Leila J. "Whose Teen Advisory Board Is This Anyway?" *Journal of Youth Services in Libraries* 9 (Spring 1996): 247–50.

Squicciarini, Stephanie A. "Teen Advisory Groups/Teen Friends Survey, Submitted to YALSA-BK & YA-YAAC Listservs." *YSS Spring Conference*, April 2002. www.nyla.org/yss/springconf02/ADVISORYGROUPSurvey.doc (last accessed 14 September 2002).

Stevens, Terry. "Young Adult Advisory Committee or the Saga of YAAC and Me." *Voice of Youth Advocates* 6, no. 2 (June 1983): 81–84, 118–19.

Tuccillo, Diane. "A Young Adult Advisory Council Can Work for You, Too." *Emergency Librarian* 13, no. 5 (May–June 1986): 15–16.

———. "Happily Ever After? Teens and Fairy Tales." *ALAN Review* 28, no. 2 (Winter 2001): 66–68.

Vaillancourt, Renée J. "Couch Central." *School Library Journal* 44, no. 7 (July 1998): 41.

———. *Bare Bones Young Adult Services: Tips for Public Library Generalists.* Chicago: American Library Association, 2000.

———. *Managing Young Adult Services: A Self-Help Manual.* New York: Neal-Schuman, 2002.

Walter, Virginia A. *Output Measures and More: Planning and Evaluating Library Services for Young Adults.* Chicago: American Library Association, 1995.

Walter, Virginia A., and Elaine Meyers. *Teens & Libraries: Getting It Right.* Chicago: American Library Association, 2003.

Wilson-Lingbloom, Evie. *Hangin' Out at Rocky Creek: A Melodrama in Basic Young Adult Services in Public Libraries.* Metuchen, NJ: Scarecrow Press, 1994.

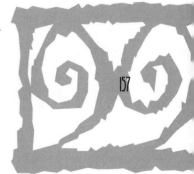

———. "The Young Adult Advisory Board: How to Make It Work." *Voice of Youth Advocates* 25, no. 6 (February 2003): 446–48. (Reprint from April 1979.)

Youth Participation Committee of the Young Adult Library Services Association, Carolyn A. Caywood, comp. and ed. *Youth Participation in School and Public Libraries: It Works!* Chicago: American Library Association, 1995.

Youth Participation for Public and School Libraries: A Training Video. Michael Cart, host and writer. Videocassette. Manual. North State Cooperative Library System, 2002 (48 minutes).

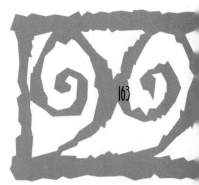

ABOUT THE AUTHOR

After starting out as an English teacher, **Diane P. Tuccillo** earned her MLS degree from Rutgers University and has been Young Adult Coordinator at the City of Mesa Library in Mesa, Arizona, since 1980. In this capacity, she is the advisor for the Young Adult Advisory Council (YAAC), one of the longest-standing library teen advisory groups in the United States.

Tuccillo is active in the Arizona Library Association (AzLA), the Adolescent Literature Assembly of the National Council of Teachers of English (ALAN), and the Young Adult Library Services Association (YALSA). She has been a presenter at ALAN Workshops, AzLA and American Library Association conferences, Literature for Adolescents classes at Arizona State University, and other forums.

Her numerous articles and book reviews have been published in *The ALAN Review*, *School Library Journal*, *VOYA*, *Emergency Librarian*, *Kliatt*, and other journals. She has also been a contributor to professional resources such as *Literature for Today's Young Adults* by Nilsen and Donelson, and the *Booktalk!* series by Joni Bodart. She serves by appointment on the editorial board of *VOYA* magazine and was elected to the 2005 Michael L. Printz Award Committee for YALSA.

Tuccillo is the recipient of the first Rising Moon Outstanding Youth Services Librarian Award from AzLA in 1998 and YALSA's 2004 Sagebrush Award for an outstanding teen library program that promotes reading, the *Open Shelf* newsletter from City of Mesa Library. She authors the monthly "YA Korner" column for the AzLA newsletter and serves as the Library Connection Editor for *The ALAN Review*. In the fall of 2004, she fulfilled a dream by teaching Literature for Adolescents at Arizona State University part time.